H50 247 776 0

COUNTDOWN TO CASSINO

By the same author:

The Recollections of Rifleman Bowlby (Leo Cooper, 1968)

COUNTDOWN TO CASSINO

THE BATTLE OF MIGNANO GAP, 1943

by

Alex Bowlby

LEO COOPER

LONDON

First published in Great Britain in 1995 by
LEO COOPER
190 Shaftesbury Avenue, London WC2H 8JL
an imprint of
Pen & Sword Books Ltd,
47, Church Street, Barnsley, South Yorks, S70 2AS

Copyright © Alex Bowlby, 1995

ISBN 0 85052 410 5

A CIP record for this book is available from the British Library

Typeset by CentraCet Limited, Cambridge
Printed by
Redwood Books Ltd.
Trowbridge, Wilts

DEDICATION

TO THE INFANTRY ON BOTH SIDES, AND TO
THE INHABITANTS OF SAN PIETRO
1943–1993

Contents

Maps

Glossary: Military terms, ranks, and abbreviations

G2   Intelligence section of division, army corps, or army. Also refers to officer in charge of section.

G3   Operations section of division, army corps, or army. Also refers to officer in charge of section.

US	*British*	
Commanding Officer	Commanding Officer	(Battalion level)
Executive Office	Second-in-command	
Operations Officer	Adjutant	
S.2 (II)	Intelligence Officer	
Communications Officer	Signals Officer	
Master Sergeant	Regimental Sergeant Major	
1st Sergeant	Company Sergeant Major	
Staff Sergeant	Platoon Sergeant	
Squad Sergeant	Lance Sergeant	
Corporal	Corporal	
Private First Class	Lance Corporal	
Private	Private	
Assault guns	Self-propelled guns – Usually 105mm mounted on tank chassis.	
Shoes	Boots	
Overshoes	Galoshes	
Wiring section	Signals section	
Railway ties	Railway sleepers	
Trail	Path	
Mortar shells	Mortar bombs	
	Sangar: Stone breastwork built by infantrymen when ground too rocky to dig slit-trenches.	

Advance H.Q.	Tac H.Q. (Tactical) – H.Q. in advance of main battalion H.Q.
Aid Post	R.A.P. (Regimental Aid Post)
D.F.	D.F. – Defensive fire
O.P.	O.P. – Observation Point
C.P.	C.P. – Command Post
L.O.D.	Start Line – Line from which an attack starts.
To zero in on	To zero in on – To get the range of.
O.C.	O.C. – Officer command (company).
I.C.	I.C. – In charge of.

Preface

I wrote this book with one object in mind: to ensure that the Battle of Mignano Gap, which opened the way to Cassino, is finally given full recognition for its particular importance in the Italian Campaign. After a lapse of nearly fifty years I did not expect to make contact with officers who had held key positions at divisional or battalion level during the battle but a number of them turned out to be very much alive and, like all junior officers and other ranks who wrote in, were anxious that someone should tell things as they were. Their eyewitness accounts underpin the tactical drift of the actions listed below.

1. San Pietro. Colonel Fred Walker, Jun, who, as G3, US 36th Infantry Division, helped plan the attacks on the village; Major-General Charles Denholm, DSC, and Colonel Milton Landry, Silver Star, whose battalions helped carry out the attacks; Colonel Helmut Meitzel, Knight's Cross, whose battalion defended the village; Colonel George Fowler, who led the tank attack on it; Colonel Harold Owens, Captain James Skinner, and Lt Nick Bosic, Silver Star, Forward Observers; Major-General Wendell Phillippi, Silver Star; former non-coms Sammie Petty, William Gallagher and Ray Wells; Lee Fletcher; Antonio Zambardi, a boy of 15 in December, 1943, who lived in the great cave shared by 800 San Pietrans.

2. Monte Camino. The After Action report of F Company, 2nd Battalion, Scots Guards, written by Major Richard Coke, DSO, MC, immediately after the battle, and which also covers 2 and 3 Companies, 6th Grenadiers, is supplemented by letters from Major Coke to the author; a manuscript written by former Grenadier Len Sarginson in 1992; information about the death of Grenadier George Beale given to the author by Mike Sterling which made clear how important the 2" mortar was to the Guards. The author is also grateful to the Grenadier and Scots Guards for permission to research their Regimental archives. Lieutenant Michael Wheatley wrote an account of the action in 1945, and Captain Ralph Howard, DSO, OC 2 Company, 6th Grenadiers, who was in overall command of F Company, Scots Guards as well as the Grenadiers, made notes of the early part of the action. The

author has discussed 2/5th Queen's assault on Monte Camino with Major-General Fergus Ling, CB, CBE, DSO, the battalion's second-in-command during the action, and with Colonel Toby Sewell, 2/6th Queen's whose platoon portered ammunition to the top of Monastery Hill. Major Alan 'Sandy' Sanders, DSO, whose company went up Monastery Hill to accept the enemy's surrender, describes the turn of events in a letter. A tape made by Major-General John Douglas-Withers, CBE, MC, a Forward Observer with 113 Field Regiment, Royal Artillery, facing Monte Camino, describes the difficulties the Regiment had in stockpiling ammunition.

3. Monte La Difensa. Conversations between the author and Brigadier Edward Thomas, Executive Officer, 1st Battalion, 2nd Regiment, at the time of the assault. Unpublished manuscript by Brigadier Thomas. Tape made for the author by Bob Davis. Manuscript written by Donald Mackinnon. Letters from Colonel Robert Moore, CO, 2nd Battalion, 2nd Regiment, and Bill Story.

4. Monte Sammucro.

A. Pt 1205. Brigadier Richard Burrage, Adjutant 1/143rd Regiment during its action on the mountain and now Colonel of the Regiment, and Lt-Colonel Fred Young, Silver Star, who commanded the Battalion's pioneer platoon, have between them sent in over 100 letters. Brigadier Burrage's letters deal mainly with the background history of 143rd Regiment and US 36th Infantry Division. Lt-Colonel Young's not only supplied a wealth of information about US infantry companies and their weapons but passed on the author from one veteran to another. The letters of Joe Gallagher and Leonard Rice pinpoint conditions on the peak.

B. Pt 957. 3rd Rangers. Colonel James Larkin's unpublished memoirs of the action – 'I only wrote them because the doctors said I was losing my memory' – are outstanding, as are the letters of former 1st Sergeant Anders Arnbal and Squad Sergeant Carl Lehmann, who invited the author to the Rangers' 'Last Hooray' in London.

The author is particularly grateful to Colonel Gerhard Muhm, formerly 71st Regiment, 29th Panzer Grenadier Division, and now lecturing at the Italian School of War, Civitavecchia, for sending him a detailed Order of Battle of 29th P.G. Division, 1943–44, a copy of the divisional history which gives a vivid description of the 'other side of the hill', and for putting him in touch with the Divisional Old Comrades Association; to Rechtsanwalt und Notar Jürgen Wöbbeking for letters showing how his outnumbered batteries managed to hold their own against US ones, and how the development of an old technique enabled German guns to zero in on Allied wireless sets; to Colonel Toby Sewell, who read a draft of this book and suggested alterations and revisions; to Martin Blumenson for his pathfinding *Salerno to Cassino*, and his remarks on why this book was written. The kindness of Lt-Colonel

Clayton Newall, late Chief Historian, Center of Military History, Washington D.C. in sending documents from the Center's library, of Herr Meyer who found documents at the Militarchiv Freiburg in addition to those ordered, and of Peter de Lotz, who lent many books on the Italian campaign, was much appreciated. Curtis Utz, who completed the author's researches in the States, did a fine job.

Finally I am indebted to the following for permission to reproduce the photographs used in this book:

National Archives, Washington, D.C.: 1, 4, 12, 13, 16, 17, 18, 19, 22, 32, 33, 34, 35, 36, 37, 38.

Imperial War Museum, London: 6, 7, 8, 10, 11, 14, 15, 24, 26, 31.

Angelo Fasci: 2, 3, 23, 25, 27, 28.

The Queen's Royal Regiment archives: 30.

U.S. 36th Infantry Division achives: 20.

Nos 5 and 9 are taken from *The Scots Guards, 1939–1955*, by David Erskine; no 29 from *The First Special Service Force* by Robert D. Burhans and no 21 from *Neither Fear nor Hope* by General Von Senger und Etterlin.

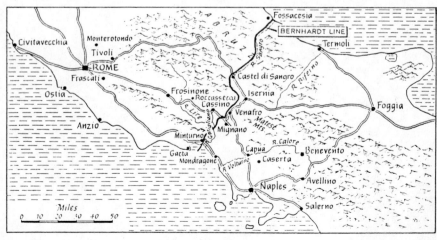

CHAPTER I

PART I

Kesselring and the Raising of the German 10th Army

In November, 1941, Field-Marshal Albert Kesselring was made Supreme Commander of Axis operations in the Mediterranean sector. His headquarters was at Frascati near Rome. He got on well with the Italian General Staff, understood the problems of the Italian Army in North Africa and believed the Italians were reliable allies. His experience as a Luftwaffe general – he had been its Chief of Staff and had later directed Airfleets in France, the Battle of Britain, and Russia – and as an army staff officer in the First World War gave him considerable insight into the strategic problems facing the Axis. He directed the air offensive against the vital British base of Malta and planned to capture the island with airborne troops. This was potentially a much easier target than Crete, but Hitler vetoed the plan because he believed the Italian navy would fail to protect the island once it was captured.

Kesselring made frequent visits to North Africa. Although he admired Rommel as a fighting general and played a decisive part in persuading Hitler to let the Afrika Korps retreat after El Alamein, Rommel's refusal to obey orders during the retreat would have resulted in his being relieved of his command if Kesselring had had his way.[1]

In May, 1943, the Axis forces in North Africa capitulated. Rommel, out of a job, decided to go for Kesselring's. He had a conference with Hitler where they discussed the likelihood of the Italian Armed Forces defecting from the Axis and how to deal with them if they did. Hitler gave Rommel a secret command called Army Group B, which would be made up of sixteen divisions. It would assemble close to the Italian borders and, at the first sign of Italian treachery, cross into Italy and disarm the Italian Army. Although Kesselring would retain the title of Supreme Commander South for the time being, Rommel could give him any order he saw fit. A crisis on the Eastern Front resulted in Army Group B being cut to eight divisions. Rommel pointed out that this force would not be sufficient to secure the whole of Italy from the Italian Army and Hitler decided that, in the event of the Axis breaking up, the southern and central parts of Italy would be abandoned.

1

Army Group B would move into Northern Italy and defend a mountain line running from Pisa to Rimini.[2] In the meantime Kesselring submitted his own plans for defending Italy, based on his belief that the Italian Armed Forces would remain loyal. All Allied landings would be vigorously opposed wherever they took place. Kesselring was sure that the Allies' first objective would be Sicily.

By late June Kesselring was no longer so sure about Italian loyalty. When he tried to persuade General Ambrosio, Chief of Staff of the Italian Armed Forces, to let him reinforce the two German divisions – the Hermann Göring Panzer and the 15th Panzer Grenadier – already in Sicily, with the 29th Panzer Grenadier Division, stationed near Bari, Ambrosio refused his request, pointing out that the Italian 6th Army was defending Sicily as well as the two German divisions. The 6th Army wasn't up to much, even on paper. Its regular divisions were supported by coastguard divisions. Ambrosio, who intended to co-operate with the Allies, had good reason for not wanting the Axis forces in Sicily reinforced. Kesselring tried another tack, pointing out that there were only two German divisions on the mainland – the 3rd Panzer Grenadier Division was stationed near Orvieto – and asked for another to be sent to Italy. Ambrosio agreed to the request and the 26th Panzer Division came south. Kesselring stationed its Panzer regiment at Rome airfields near Ostia and sent its two Panzer Grenadier regiments* to Calabria. He was suspicious of Ambrosio, but took comfort from the fact that General Roatta, the Chief of Staff of the Italian Army, was apparently doing his best to circumvent Ambrosio and get more German divisions into Italy. In reality Roatta was helping Ambrosio plan an Italian Army coup. Both generals believed that the Axis was close to breaking up and were ready to co-operate with the Allies when they landed on the mainland of Italy.

On 10 July the Allies invaded Sicily. Hitler ordered General Student to fly in his 1st Parachute Division from France to Rome airfields, authorized Kesselring to drop two of the Division's regiments in Sicily and to put the 29th Panzer Grenadier Division on stand-by to move to the island. At Rommel's request[3] OKW† authorized the dispatch to Sicily of a most formidable battle formation – Lt-General Hube and his XIV Panzer Korps HQ. General Hube had commanded the XIV Panzer Korps at Stalingrad and the way he handled it impressed Hitler. When the German 6th Army was surrounded by the Russians Hitler ordered Hube and his Korps HQ to

* Panzer Grenadiers were motorized infantry. At full strength a Panzer Division had two regiments of tanks and one/two Panzer Grenadier regiments. A Panzer Grenadier Division had one regiment of tanks and two/three Panzer Grenadier regiments. German and US regiments were the equivalent of British brigades.

† Oberkommando der Wehrmacht was the Armed Forces High Command and served Hitler in his capacity as Head of the Armed Forces. For the Alice in Wonderland chain of the German High Command in Italy see Appendix A.

be flown out.[4] The rest of the 6th Army's Korps commanders were left at Stalingrad. OKW gave Hube and his Korps HQ the job of training divisions to take the place of those lost at Stalingrad and in Tunisia. The two divisions that Hube trained in Italy, the 16th Panzer Division and the 15th Panzer Grenadier Division, were outstanding.

The fall of Mussolini on 25 July accelerated the German take-over of Italy. Army Group B moved into northern Italy. Hitler ordered General Student to fly in his 2nd Parachute Division to Rome airfields and establish an independent force there. It would be known as Fliegerkorps XI and consist of the 3rd Panzer Grenadier Division and 2nd Parachute Division. Kesselring, who would be in overall command of the force, told Ambrosio that the 2nd Parachute Division would reinforce the 1st Parachute Division's regiments in Sicily. An emergency plan, code-named Axis, to deal with the Italian Armed Forces should Italy defect to the Allies, was put in hand. Hitler also authorized the dispatch of the 29th Panzer Grenadier Division to Sicily – the Italian 6th Army was disintegrating – and the raising of the 10th German Army. It would come under Kesselring's overall command and would consist of the German divisions in Sicily and Southern Italy. If necessary, Kesselring could call on part of the Fliegerkorps XI as back-up troops.

The Allies now had twelve divisions in Sicily and almost total air superiority. There was no longer any question of the Axis forces holding the island. They were retreating towards Messina, where they would cross the straits to the mainland. Hube made the most of the mountainous terrain, retreating at his own speed and keeping his line intact. But if the evacuation to the mainland was prevented by Allied air and sea power or Hube's German divisions were badly cut up as they crossed the straits the 10th Army would no longer be a viable force. Its remaining divisions would be pulled back to join Army Group B. Hitler would make Rommel Supreme Commander in place of Kesselring.

The job of preventing a successful evacuation rested with the British High Command. On 3 August General the Hon Sir Harold Alexander, Commander-in-Chief Allied Land Forces – 15th Army Group – had sent signals to Air Chief Marshal Sir Arthur Tedder, Deputy Commander Mediterranean sector, and Admiral Sir Andrew Cunningham, Commander-in-Chief Allied naval forces, warning them that the Axis forces were probably planning an evacuation across the straits of Messina. 'You have no doubt coordinated plans to meet this contingency,' he remarked. Admiral Cunningham believed that, once the Italian coastal batteries had been knocked out by aerial bombardment, the navy could patrol the straits and stop the evacuation. Air Marshal Tedder at first agreed, but then decided it would be easier and more effective to bomb the enemy ferry ports. The bombing would be carried out by Wellington night bombers belonging to the North-West Tactical Airforce. Its commanding officer, Air Vice-Marshal Sir Arthur Coningham, would be responsible for stopping the evacuation. In Sicily the enemy had always retreated by night to avoid being harried by Coningham's fighter bombers. He was confident that they would try and evacuate by night but knew that if they risked a daylight crossing they would have the protection of anti-aircraft guns firing from both sides of the straits.*. The guns' arcs of fire would make things very difficult for Coningham's fighter bombers and mediums. Tedder resolved this potential problem by putting Flying Fortresses from the US XII Air Support Command on standby. The 'Forts' could bomb from a height beyond the range of anti-aircraft guns.

The enemy made their first crossing on the night of 11/12 August. The bombing of the ferry ports was so accurate that the German naval team organizing the evacuation only got away half the men and equipment they intended to. Coningham, certain that the evacuation would continue by night, told Tedder he no longer needed the Flying Fortresses on standby, so Tedder directed them on to other targets. The enemy's second crossing took place on the night of 12/13 August. It fared no better than the first. On the morning of 13 August the officer in charge of the German† forces' evacuation, Captain von Liebenstein, decided to risk a daylight crossing. Baade's batteries saw off Coningham's fighter-bombers and the enemy landed twice the amount of men and equipment as on the previous run. The enemy continued to cross by day, with one more night crossing thrown in for good measure, and only on 16 August, when Coningham sent in 47 mediums and 247 fighter-bombers, did his force inflict serious damage. By 17 August the evacuation was successfully completed. The Germans had landed 39,569 men, 9,605 vehicles, 47 tanks, 94 guns and 17,000 tons of stores and ammunition. The Italians landed 62,000 men. The Axis casualties in the ferry ports and on the crossings totalled around 2,000.[6]

Kesselring called it 'The Miracle of Messina'. General Heinrich von Vietinghoff gennant Scheel, who commanded the 10th Army, noted, 'The evacuation was of decisive importance to the whole future course of the Italian Campaign.'[7] Hitler sent Kesselring his warmest congratulations and

---

* Colonel Ernst Baade, German Commandant Messina Straits, had assembled 235 anti-aircraft guns on both sides of the straits. Colonel Baade was already well known to elements of the British 8th Army. As commander 115th Regiment, 15th Light Division, he had led a series of raids and patrols into the British lines in North Africa. When he got shot up on a reconnaissance he shouted over the wireless: 'Baade here! No need to shoot! I'm retiring!' British artillery observers, amused by his cheek, called off their shoot. Baade, who admired the fighting qualities of the British, always wore a kilt, carrying a Lüger instead of a sporran. On New Year's Eve, 1943, he broadcast greetings to 'all my old friends in the 8th Army'. The broadcast infuriated Nazi staff officers in XIV Panzer Korps, but by then Baade was a major-general and too outstanding a solider to be called to account.[5]

† The Italian 6th Army had made its own evacuation plans.

earmarked Hube for the command of a Panzer Army in Russia. The Italian government awarded Hube the Order of Savoia. This must have amused him. Towards the end of the retreat Marshal Guzzoni, commander of the Italian 6th Army, had suggested a 'last man, last ditch' stand in north-west Sicily. Hube had told him if he wanted such a stand he could make it with the 6th Army.[8]

Ultra decrypts had enabled Alexander's 15th Army Group Intelligence to identify and monitor the movements of all German divisions in Sicily.[9] In spite of this they had 'wildly overestimated' the number of German troops on the island – 100,000 they said – and their losses: 27,000 dead.[10] Actual figure 4,325[11] (someone walked round the German military cemeteries in Sicily to settle the matter). 15th Army Group Intelligence never realized the importance of the evacuations to Kesselring and the 10th Army.

Marshal Badoglio, who had replaced Mussolini as Head of State, had been negotiating with the Allies. He wanted an armistice and promised that a substantial part of the Italian Army would attack German divisions as soon as the Allies landed on the mainland. As proof of his sincerity he told the Allies the location of all the German divisions in Italy. Although Ultra decrypts confirmed their whereabouts, the best the Allies could offer in return was an armistice after Badoglio had surrendered unconditionally. The armistice would be announced simultaneously by Badoglio and Eisenhower six hours before the main Allied landings took place. The Allies refused to give the date or location of the landings but promised to drop an airborne division on Rome airfields the same day as the landings took place. Badoglio reluctantly accepted the terms. The secret unconditional surrender took place in Sicily on 3 September, the same day as the British 8th Army landed two divisions at Reggio Calabria. General Castellano, who signed the armistice on behalf of Badoglio, informed him that Major-General Walter Bedell-Smith, Eisenhower's Chief of Staff, had said that the main Allied landings would take place between September 10th-15th, the 12th being the most likely date.[12] It seems unlikely that General Castellano would have invented the conversation. General Bedell Smith could well have been under orders to give disinformation so as to ensure that the actual date of the Salerno landings – 9 September – remained secret. General Roatta and General Carboni, who commanded five pro-Allied divisions around Rome, planned their coup to take place on 12 September. Carboni already had two divisions close to the Rome airfields and planned to use them as a blocking force against Fliegerkorps XI whilst his three motorized divisions south of Rome advanced on the city. Badoglio did not tell Roatta or Carboni about the promised airborne drop on the Rome airfields.

Von Vietinghoff opposed the two British divisions in Calabria with massive road demolitions and a minimum of troops. Both he and Kesselring expected the Allies' main landings elsewhere. Kesselring thought they might be in Sardinia, at Civitavecchia, near Rome, north of Naples, or at Salerno. Von Vietinghoff believed the landings would take place in the Naples-Salerno sector. He stationed the Hermann Göring Division at Gaeta and the 16th Panzer Division, which had joined XIV Panzer Korps in August, at Salerno. The division spent three weeks digging themselves in behind the bay's beaches.

The eighth of September was a hard day for Italy. Major-General Maxwell Taylor and another officer from US 2nd Airborne Division, scheduled to land on the Rome airfields later that day, arrived in the city on a secret mission to make sure the drop was feasible. Carboni told them that his two divisions would not be able to secure the airfields from Fliegerkorps XI. General Taylor sent a signal aborting the operation to his divisional head-quarters in Sicily. The US 82nd Airborne Division's planes had already begun taking off when the signal was received. Carboni took the two US officers to Badoglio's house in Rome. Taylor told Badoglio that the Allies main landings were imminent. They would take place later that night or early on 9 September. Carboni warned Badoglio that his three motorized divisions south of Rome did not yet have enough petrol or ammunition to move on Rome and that a premature armistice broadcast would ruin his chances of taking the city.[13]

Badoglio, acutely aware that any armistice broadcast not backed up by Carboni's motorized divisions would result in retaliation against himself, the government and King Umberto, as well as wrecking the coup, sent a signal to Eisenhower asking for a postponement of the simultaneous armistice broadcasts on the grounds that the pro-Allied divisions around Rome had been geared to attack the German divisions on 12 September and were not yet ready to carry out the operation. He also asked permission for General Rossi, Carboni's Chief of Staff, to fly to Algiers so as he could explain the situation to Eisenhower. Permission was granted, so General Rossi flew to Algiers and told Eisenhower what the consequences would be if the broadcasts went ahead. Eisenhower was sympathetic but told General Rossi that the Allied invasion fleet was already nearing Italian waters. There was no question of the invasion being postponed. Simultaneous broadcasts would have to be made.

At 5.30 pm Badoglio received a telegram from Eisenhower insisting that simultaneous broadcasts of the Armistice were to go ahead as planned. At 6 pm Eisehower made his broadcast. The BBC re-broadcast the news of the Armistice. Badoglio was in conference with the King, senior ministers of the government, Ambrosio and Carboni. (Roatta was at the Italian Army's GHQ at Monterotondo near Rome, planning a joint Italian-German offensive with Lt-General Siegfried Westphal, Kesselring's Chief of Staff.) Carboni and the

Minister of Defence were against making the broadcast. The remainder believed it would have to be made. Badoglio eventually made it at 7.45. Not surprisingly he did not urge the Italian Armed Forces to rise up against the Germans.[14]

Shortly after the broadcast a German staff officer rang General Westphal at Monterotondo and told him its content. Roatta assured Westphal that the Italian Armed Forces would remain loyal to the German Armed Forces. He then rang Kesselring and told him the same thing.[15] Kesselring still trusted Roatta, and delayed activating Operation Axis, but Hitler himself operated it at 8 pm. General Student's units advanced on the two Italian divisions near Rome airfields. When they refused to surrender the Germans attacked them. Leaving rearguards to hold up the new enemy the Italian divisions retreated towards Tivoli. (Carboni had ordered all his divisions to take up defensive positions in the hills behind the town.) Whilst the US 5th Army was building up its bridgehead at Salerno early on 9 September a battalion from Student's 2nd Parachute Division dropped on the Italian Army's headquarters at Monterotondo. Although they captured thirty generals some parts of the headquarters held out against them, and Ambrosio and Roatta had left shortly before the drop. The two generals were on their way to Pescara with Badoglio and the King. The party escaped by sea to Sicily. In northern Italy it was the civilians* who fought the Germans. The Italian Army† remained docile. Rommel ordered all ranks to be rounded up and sent to Germany. The news reached the Italian troops before the Germans. Many officers and senior NCOs took to the hills and formed the nucleus of the Italian resistance movement. Rommel also ordered Kesselring to send all prisoners to Germany, but Kesselring ignored the order. (He also ignored one from Hitler ordering all Italian officers who had fought the Germans to be shot.‡) Although Carboni's five divisions at Tivoli no longer posed a threat to Rome or its airfields other pro-Allied Italian troops had established roadblocks on the main road to Naples and were holding up reinforcements and supplies for Salerno.[16] Kesselring had no forces available to deal with the units manning the road blocks. Fliegerkorps XI had their hands full guarding Rome airfields and containing Carboni's divisions at Tivoli. Kesselring realized he would have to offer Carboni attractive terms to persuade

---

* In Ferrara they killed so many of them that the German town commandant forbade the Italians to bury their own dead on pain of death. The women of Ferrara covered the bodies with poppies.

† The whole of the Italian Navy defected to the Allies.

‡ Not all German commanders were so humane. On the Greek island of Cephalonia the Italian Acqui Division fought a German Division from 15 to 22 September, losing 1,250 killed and several thousand wounded. When the Division surrendered its Commanding Officer, General Antonio Gandini, was immediately shot. Later that day the Germans massacred 401 officers and 4,750 ranks. Many of them had already been seriously wounded in the fighting and were dragged out of their hospital beds to be shot.[17]

7

him to surrender and lift the roadblocks. On the evening of 9 September Carboni sent emissaries to Kesselring's headquarters. Kesselring told them that once Carboni had surrendered all his troops could return to their homes and that he would declare Rome an Open City, making it out of bounds to the German Army and saving it from destruction from Allied bombing. He left Westphal to settle the final negotiations. Carboni accepted the terms on 18 September. The roadblocks on the Rome-Naples road were lifted and Kesselring sent Hitler a telegram explaining why he had refused to carry out Rommel's order and why he had negotiated with Carboni.[18]

News from Salerno was arriving by dispatch rider. Telephone links between Frascati and von Vietinghoff's headquarters had been sabotaged and the Italian engineers had taken care not to show the Germans how the lines worked. The mountains separating the two headquarters had the disturbing effect of cutting out all wireless communications as well.[19] Lack of up-to-date information of what was happening at Salerno 'left the Commander-in-Chief in a state of oppressive uncertainty' (Westphal). But Kesselring was not a man to hang around waiting for news. He spent most of 10 September planning defensive lines across Italy. If the 10th Army pushed the Allies into the sea at Salerno the lines could be scrapped. If the Allies secured a firm bridgehead the lines would become an essential part of the defence of Italy. The first would be an army in line abreast stretching right across Italy. A delaying action would be fought on it, giving German engineers time to destroy Naples harbour and all its public facilities. Naples would not be defended because it was of no strategic importance. Kesselring then pencilled in four more lines across Italy. The first ran along the Volturno and Biferno rivers. It would be known as the Victor Line, would have field fortifications made by the troops manning them, and would be held until 15 October. The second line, the Barbara, ran through the mountains north of the Volturno and the Biferno. Its main purpose, like that of the Victor, was to provide time for engineers and Todt workers* to fortify the third line, the Bernhardt. It was clear from the map that this was a far more formidable line than the others. The Abbruzzi mountains, flanked by the Garigliano and Sangro rivers, were much higher and more closely clumped together than the Neapolitan Alps south of them. Once fortified, the Bernhardt would present a powerful barrier to the advancing Allies and give time for the construction of an even stronger line behind it. This fourth line, later known as the Gustav, would begin at the mouth of the Garigliano, hinge on Cassino, and eventually become part of the Bernhardt.[20] Kesselring had studied reports of Italian manoeuvres and had seen the area from the air. Beyond Cassino the Liri Valley opened out. It was good tank country,

* Conscripted civilian labourers with German officers as overseers.

unlike most of southern Italy, and it led straight to Rome. If the Allied armour got to Cassino before it was properly fortified they would break through the town into the Liri Valley and capture Rome in a matter of days.

On 11 September Kesselring drew up a treaty making Rome an Open City. On 12 September he flew down to von Vietinghoff's headquarters. The Army Commander told him that the Allied landing force was being driven back towards the sea. Kesselring flew over the battlefield and returned to Frascati well pleased with what he'd seen. But on the same day Hitler, who had taken over overall command of the 10th Army, ordered Kesselring to supervise its retreat to Rome after the battle whatever its outcome. OKW had convinced Hitler that the Allies were pouring so many divisions into Italy that 10th Army would be smashed to pieces if it didn't make a rapid retreat to Rome and continue retreating northwards. In the same directive Hitler ordered Rommel to pick out defensive positions on the Pisa-Rimini line and prepare to fortify them. Kesselring does not record his feelings about the directive. He continued making flights over the Salerno bridgehead – the flights were 'not always . . . enjoyable'[21] – until he realized that the Allied naval bombardments and saturation bombing had scuppered von Vietinghoff's hopes of driving 5th Army into the sea before the British 8th Army divisions reinforced them. On 18 September von Vietinghoff disengaged from 5th Army and Kesselring sent his plans for defending Italy south to Rome to OKW. He included some very precise retreat schedules. Naples would be held until 30 September, the Victor Line until 15 October. The Bernhardt Line would not be occupied until 30 October. OKW passed the plans on to Hitler. The Führer, sensing that Kesselring's plans made sense, cancelled the order for 10th Army's retreat to Rome. It was to retreat to the Bernhardt instead.[22]

PART II

Lt-General Mark Clark and the Raising of the US 5th Army

Mark Clark had graduated from West Point in 1917. In December of that year he was assigned to an infantry battalion in France with the rank of captain. The battalion was moving up the Line when its CO became ill and Clark became acting CO. As the battalion neared the front a German battery fired two shells. One of them injured Clark so severely that when he left hospital he was invalided out of the infantry and assigned to the Army supply section. Such luck would have broken the spirit of most men but not Clark's. He performed his supply duties so efficiently that his commanding officer saw to it that he was promoted major, reassigned to the infantry and sent to the Army War College on a staff course. His instructor at the War College, Colonel Fred Walker, who had won the Distinguished Service Cross as a battalion commander in France, noted his potential. Colonel Walker's confidential report of Clark resulted in his becoming G3 to the US 3rd Division. In 1940 his handling of the division's amphibious exercises off the coast of California impressed General George C. Marshall, Chief of Staff, US Army. General Marshall had Clark promoted to Lt-Colonel and posted back to the Army War College, this time as an instructor. Early in 1941 Major-General McNair, Marshall's Chief of Staff, picked Clark as his G3, with the responsibility of training troops, and had him promoted brigadier. The US Army was in the process of mustering National Guard units* alongside its regular divisions. Clark had to lay down a training schedule that would bring the National Guard units up to the same standard as a regular division and make sure the schedule worked. Clark did an excellent job and was made GOC of the Army's Ground Forces. Soon after Pearl Harbor – December 1941 – Clark was promoted Major-General. An old friend, Major-General Dwight D. Eisenhower, invited him to visit the UK to meet their counter-parts in the British Army. The trip resulted in Clark being made commander of the first US Corps to be sent to Britain.

In the summer of 1942 Clark helped Eisenhower plan Operation Torch, the Allied landing in North Africa, and became his deputy commander. Eisenhower was worried about the possibility that the Vichy French forces in North Africa would oppose the landings and sent Clark to parley with General Mast, Chief of Staff of General Giraud, commander of the French Army in North Africa. Clark went to Algeria by submarine and met General Mast, who guaranteed that the French Army would oppose any attack by the German Army but warned Clark that Admiral Darlan, C-in-C French Forces in North Africa, might order the French Army to oppose Allied landings as well.

When the Allies landed in North Africa they encountered some resistance from French troops. Eisenhower sent Clark to Algiers to try and persuade Admiral Darlan to 'come over'. Darlan agreed and was issuing orders to all French Armed Forces to join the Allies when he was assassinated. General Giraud took his place and the Vichy French became the Free French.[23]

In December, 1942, Eisenhower received permission to raise a US Army

* The equivalent of British Territorial ones.

– the 5th – in case the Axis forces attacked the Allies through Spanish Morocco. Clark was made 5th Army Commander with the rank of Lt-General. He chose Major-General Alfred Gruenther as his Chief of Staff. Eisenhower thought this an excellent choice. (Gruenther, with the rank of full general, reorganized SHAPE* after the war.) The 5th Army originally consisted of Major-General George Patton's and Major-General Lloyd Fredenhall's task forces but these were quickly siphoned off to assist US forces hard pressed by Rommel's counter-attacks in Tunisia. For the time being the 5th was a skeleton army. Eisenhower, very much aware that Clark had never handled large bodies of troops in action, offered him the chance of commanding a corps on the Tunisian front. Clark turned down the offer, saying he was only interested in commanding an army. His decision angered Eisenhower. In a secret memorandum to General Marshall he wrote, 'This was a bad mistake on Clark's part'.[24]

When the Tunisian campaign ended, 5th Army was given the job of invading Italy. The Army was to be made up of three Corps, two US and one British. Although Clark was disappointed the 5th was not to be an all-American army, he thought highly of Lt-General Sir Brian Horrocks, the British Corps Commander, and was soon absorbed in picking his US units and preparing for the invasion. Originally the 5th Army's objective was Sardinia. Then it was changed to Taranto. Finally Salerno was chosen. Clark and his staff could at last settle down to the job of planning the landings. In between times he set about getting himself known to the press. Clark, who was six foot two, chose a GI as tall as himself to drive his jeep and two even taller military policemen to sit in the back. The sight of this entourage whizzing around army camps made a great impression on US correspondents, who filed long reports on Clark and the US 5th Army, just as Clark intended them to. Patton, now commanding the new US 7th Army with the rank of Lt-General, and who was receiving minimal press coverage, complained to Eisenhower about Clark's behaviour. In his diary Eisenhower wrote, 'Clark is indulging in too much self-promotion'.[25] His contingency

As Clark himself admits, Salerno was 'a near disaster'.[25] His contingency plans to evacuate US VI Corps on to the British X Corps bridgehead or vice versa alarmed Alexander as much as it did Eisenhower. Only a very inexperienced army commander could have suggested such a plan. The imminent arrival of the British 8th Army played a minor part in von Vietinghoff's decision to break off the battle. But a PRO at Alexander's 15th Army Group's HQ in Sicily put it about that the 8th Army had saved the 5th Army from defeat, and this was widely reported in the British press and

---

* Supreme Headquarters Allied Powers Europe. Unlike most US generals in 5th Army, Gruenther did not write his memoirs or keep a war diary. He wrote a book on bridge instead.

on the BBC. Clark was furious. He believed that Alexander[26] was responsible for the handout and never trusted him again. Alexander was not responsible, but during the Sicilian campaign he had been persuaded by General Sir Bernard Montgomery, commanding the British 8th Army, to issue a directive assigning General Patton's 7th Army the role of protecting 8th Army's rear whilst 8th Army did the fighting. Patton flew to Alexander's headquarters in Tunisia to protest. Major-General John Lucas, who was Eisenhower's personal observer in Sicily, made his own protest to the Supreme Commander.[27] Alexander at once changed his directive, allowing the US 7th Army their share of the action, but the damage had been done. Word got around among senior US generals that Alexander and Montgomery needed watching, and Clark was no slouch at watching. His conclusion that Alexander was responsible for the misinformation put out by the British PRO had its origins in Alexander's directive in Sicily. However, Alexander's letter-directive of 21 September, which ordered the 5th Army to advance up the western half of Italy, the 8th Army up the eastern, pleased Clark. The 5th Army had the direct route to Rome and Clark was determined that his army should take the capital. If Alexander tried to get 8th Army in first Clark was prepared to go to any lengths to prevent this happening. When the German 10th Army was at his mercy south of Rome in May, 1944, he ordered Major-General Lucian Truscott's VI Corps to take the capital instead of destroying the enemy.[28]

Ultra decrypts had picked up Hitler's directive of 12 September, but not his change of mind about 10th Army's retreat north of Rome. Alexander had no way of knowing that 10th Army was now retreating to the Bernhardt but he would have been well aware that Army Group B was preparing to fortify the Massa-Rimini* Line. In his 21 September letter-directive to Clark and Montgomery Alexander had suggested advance schedules. Rome and Terni, an important rail junction forty-five miles north of the capital, should be occupied by 7 November, Lucca and Ravenna by the 30th.[29] This reads more like a package tour than advance schedules. Ravenna is thirty miles north of Rimini. Leaving aside what sort of opposition 10th Army would offer north of Rome, did Alexander really believe Rommell would let the Allies through the Massa-Rimini Line without a fight?

Clark mistrusted Ultra decrypts. Eisenhower's efforts to persuade him that they were absolutely reliable and could provide 5th Army with invaluable information came to nothing. (Only when a decrypt warned Clark of a specific German counter-attack at Anzio did he change his mind.[30]) He told Eisenhower he preferred to rely on his own 5th Army Intelligence. This was

---

* Rommel had chosen to start what would eventually be known as the Gothic Line at Massa, twenty miles north-west of Pisa.

commanded by a Lt-Colonel Edward Howard. Apart from maintaining a remarkably detailed account of enemy movements on 5th Army's front, along with studies of German tactics during their retreat in Russia as well as North Africa, he occasionally slipped in reports that could only have come from Ultra.

PART III

The 10th Army's Retreat from Salerno
XIV Panzer Korp's Retreat to the Volturno
Hube and the Bernhardt Line

General von Vietinghoff had served in the Prussian Guards in the First World War and had a pride in his command not uncommon with Prussian generals. He had held command in a Panzer army korps in Russia for two years, giving and receiving some mighty onslaughts. He had then commanded 14th Army in Northern France. Vietinghoff tended to treat his men like numbers but had an excellent rapport with his Army generals and with General Westphal, who had been Rommel's Chief of Staff in North Africa. Von Vietinghoff's own Chief of Staff, Major-General Wentzell, had served with him in Russia.

Von Vietinghoff chose Hube's XIV Panzer Korps, which now consisted of the Hermann Göring Panzer Division, 16th Panzer Division, 15th Panzer Grenadier Division and one regiment of 3rd Panzer Grenadier Division (its other two regiments which had come south to fight at Salerno had returned to guard Rome airfields. Its third regiment would join them during the last week of September) to defend the western half of Italy whilst Lt-General Herr's LXXVI Panzer Korps – 26th Panzer Division, 1st Parachute Division and 29th Panzer Grenadier Division – defended the eastern half. The 1st Parachute Division was spread out between Salerno and Bari. It had to regroup near Foggia. General Herr's other two divisions would have to withdraw eastward until they reached their place in the line between XIV Panzer Korps and 1st Parachute Division. Von Vietinghoff had only just completed his plans for a very tricky operation when he was ordered to take over temporary command of Army Group B as Rommel had been operated on for appendicitis. Von Vietinghoff briefed Hube, who had just returned from sick leave himself and would be taking over temporary command of 10th Army, on how his plans were to be carried out. Much would depend on General Wentzell and the German rearguards. Hube chose the Hermann Göring Division and regiments from the 3rd, 15th, and 29th Panzer Divisions to delay the Allies while 10th Army re-grouped. It would need at least three days to complete the job. The rearguards held magnificently. The main body of the Army completed their task in spite of constant bombing of the Allied air forces. By 26 September it was in line abreast across Italy.[31]

XIV Panzer Korps retreated at its own pace, helped by persistent rain which impeded the Allied armour as well as grounding most of its planes. The Korps was commanded by Lt-General Hermann Balck, another general who had served with distinction in Russia. When Hube went sick OKW had sent him to take over temporary command of XIV Panzer Korps. Hitler had taken note of how well he had handled the Korps at Salerno and had marked him down for an Army command in Russia. OKW had refused all Kesselring's requests for fresh divisions and replacement of essential equipment but they certainly sent him good generals.

Von Vietinghoff returned on 28 September and found XIV Panzer Korps in such good order that he was able to send 16th Panzer Division and 15th Panzer Grenadier Division back to the Volturno to dig defences, leaving the Hermann Göring Division to hold up the Allies, who had the best part of five divisions in the hunt. Von Vietinghoff also sent Hube to reconnoitre the Bernhardt Line. Because both Kesselring and von Vietinghoff believed that the Allies' primary objective was Rome, and that the main thrust for the city would be bound to be up the western side of Italy Kesselring ordered von Vietinghoff to supervise Balck and Hube's handling of XIV Panzer Korps' retreat to the Bernhardt.[32]

The Neapolitan underground movement, who had molested the 3rd Panzer Grenadier Division on its way to Salerno, got wind of Kesselring's plan for the destruction of the city's harbour and public facilities and on 29 September they overcame the German garrison and manned the public facilities. Von Vietinghoff had to recall tanks and infantry from the 16th Panzer Division to deal with the uprising. By next day it was all over. 10th Army engineers could get on with the job, which they did with ruthless efficiency. The engineers and the Hermann Göring Division left Naples late on 30 September. The Allies entered it on 1 October.

On 30 September Kesselring and Rommel had been summoned to a conference with Hitler at his headquarters in Bavaria. The Führer had intended to discuss the defence of Foggia airfields, the biggest in Southern Italy, but they fell to Allies before the conference began. Hitler believed that once the airfields were in working order they would be used to support an Allied invasion of the Balkans. Allied disinformation and poor German counter-intelligence had convinced Hitler that the Allies' main thrust would come there and not in Italy. He asked his two Field-Marshals whether they thought the airfields could be recaptured. Rommel thought it unlikely. He could hardly have said anything else without appearing to back-track on his defensive policy for Italy. Kesselring was confident the airfield could be re-taken, provided 10th Army was given adequate support. Hitler was impressed by Kesselring's optimism and told him to send him a list of the support he would require. Kesselring asked for the Bernhardt to be fortified so that the line behind it – then known as the Gaeta-Ortona – could be made strong enough to hold up the Allies indefinitely. Rommel emphasized the importance of fortifying the Massa-Rimini Line.[33]

On 4 October Hitler authorized the fortification of both lines. He also ordered OKW to send two divisions from Army Group B to 10th Army. Two divisions from France would be sent to Army Group B as replacements.

By Highway 6 the distance between Naples and Capua, close to the Volturno, is twelve miles. It took 5th Army units operating on that road eight days to reach the river. The Germans had demolished mile-long stretches of road and early autumn rains had done the rest. Where the road wasn't blown it was flooded or covered with landslips. It was an engineers' nightmare and without British Bailey Bridges* the advance would have been held up indefinitely. British divisions operating on the coastal road to the west of Route 6 found their advance held up by demolitions and rearguard actions by the Hermann Göring Panzer Division. It took the British 7th Armoured Division seven days to reach the Volturno. The US 34th Division, up in the mountains east of Route 6, were held up by demolitions and the terrain. Projected Allied air strikes on the Volturno had to be abandoned because of the rain and mist. The planes were either grounded or unable to see the target.

Von Vietinghoff could hardly have asked for a more peaceful digging-in on the banks of the Volturno. But while the 5th Army was struggling towards the river 8th Army decided to make an amphibious landing behind the enemy lines at a small town called Termoli. A brigade of British Marine Commandos landed there on the night of 2 October. The entire German garrison was drunk but some German paratroop NCOs on a course in the town made the Commandos fight for it. Kesselring had only just got back from his interview with Hitler when he heard the town had fallen. He at once phoned von Vietinghoff and told him to dispatch the 16th Panzer

---

* They were made from strips of very strong tensile steel, light enough to be carried in a three-tonner, and simple to construct. Bailey Bridges built during the Italian Campaign are still in service in some parts of Tuscany and Umbria, and they are still part of Nato equipment (1990).

Division across Italy to re-take it. The Division would then join LXXVI Panzer Korps and remain with it permanently. The 3rd Panzer Grenadier Division would be sent from Rome to take the Division's place. The order shocked von Vietinghoff. The 16th was his best equipped Panzer Division. He would be hard pressed to hold the Volturno without them, and he would need them later in the hills behind the river. The thought of having the 3rd Panzer Grenadier Division in its place was deeply depressing. Von Vietinghoff knew a lot more about the 3rd Panzer Grenadiers than Kesselring did. They were an unreliable division. In a desperate ploy to hang on to the 16th Panzers he suggested that Kesselring send the 3rd Panzer Grenadier Division to Termoli instead. Kesselring told von Vietinghoff to stop quibbling and rang off. Von Vietinghoff, distraught at the thought of losing the 16th Panzers and furious at Kesselring's peremptory manner, decided not to pass on Kesselring's order to Major-General Rudolph Sickenius, the 16th Panzers' Commanding Officer. The division continued to dig in on the banks of the Volturno. It was only a chance call from General Westphal to General Wentzell late that night, 2 October, that blew the gaffe. Kesselring rang von Vietinghoff again and ordered him to get 16th Panzer Division moving 'in double quick time'. The 16th Panzers left in the early hours of 3 October, their Panzer Grenadier Regiment in the lead. The Divisonal quartermaster was playing games of his own. He'd only given half of the Division's vehicles enough petrol to get them to Termoli and into battle. He was relying on LXXVI Korps re-supplying the rest. The fuel saved would be put into divisional reserve.

16th Panzer Division's Grenadier Regiment and one battalion of tanks covered the seventy-five miles to Termoli in a little over twelve hours. With the support of some fighter bombers the combined force went straight into the attack. The Marine Commandos held their ground. The rest of the 16th Panzers had run out of fuel in the mountains. The Division's quartermaster discovered there was no chance of getting LXXVI Korps to refuel and had to organize the job himself. Allied air strikes at the stranded tanks made the re-supply a hard job. Another twenty-four hours passed before the rest of the 16th Panzers got to Termoli. By then they were under orders to split into two battle groups. One was to join in attacking Termoli, the other was to head south and support elements of LXXVI Panzer Korps under pressure from advancing 8th Army units. The Marine Commandos came under heavy attack on 4 October. Once more they held. Next day the enemy broke off the attack. The 16th Panzers retreated past Termoli with the rest of LXXVI Panzer Korps.[34]

Kesselring was furious at 16th Panzer Division's failure to retake Termoli. He considered von Vietinghoff's 'insubordination' to be its root causes. Von Vietinghoff believed that Kesselring had become obsessed with the idea of opposing all Allied landings, that the dispatch of 16th Panzer Division to Termoli was tactically inept, and that it should have been left at Volturno. He was almost certainly correct.

Hube returned from his reconnaissance of the Bernhardt on 8 October. He reported that the line was as formidable as the map indicated. He had chosen Minturno, at the mouth of the Garigliano River, as its western edge. It then ran along the Garigliano until it reached the edge of the Abbruzzi – the Camino Massif. The ground to the south and west of the Camino Massif was flat and the western slopes of the Massif were easy to climb. This was the Bernhardt's one weakness. (Kesselring quickly resolved it by having a large lake dammed and flooding the flat ground.) At the foot of the Camino Massif lay the small town of Mignano, twelve miles south-west of Cassino. The gap between the Camino Massif and the mountain east of Mignano, Monte Cesima, was one mile wide. Hube called this the Mignano Gap. The Naples-Rome rail line passed through the town and Highway 6 just outside it. There were areas of flat terrain beyond the town where the gap between mountains opened up to twon miles across. Although the narrowness of the Mignano Gap made it dangerous for tanks, it might tempt the Allies to use them just the same. Cassino and the Liri Valley were so close. Mignano Gap would be the focal point of XIV Panzer Korps sector of the Bernhardt. The Korps would also be responsible for defending the mountains north and east of the town of Venafro. The eastern half of the Bernhardt ran through the 6000-foot Maiella Mountains, past Castel di Sangro behind the River Sangro, and terminated at Fossechia.

Von Vietinghoff at once contacted the 10th Army's Chief Engineer, Major-General Hans Bessel, and gave him precise instructions on how he wanted the Bernhardt to be fortified. Bunkers for the infantry were to be sited behind the crests of the mountains and on the rear slopes so as to avoid the worst of the enemy artillery. Underground command posts were to be built on the rear slopes as well. No attempt should be made to construct a line. The defences should be in depth, enabling any enemy penetration to be sealed off. Rest centres were to be built close to the bunkers so the men could have breaks from the wet and the cold.[35] Kesselring had allotted two battalions of Todt workers and three battalions of engineers to General Bessel's command. General Bessel told Vietinghoff he was confident he could increase the work force by 4000-5000 men by offering local Italians high wages and three good meals a day. Vietinghoff thought this an excellent idea. Both generals were being a little naive. Italian males were being rounded up all over Italy to work for the Germans as official or unofficial Todt workers. Most local Italians steered clear of General Bessel's bait and local mayors refused to order their villagers to join in the scheme. Instead of 4000-5000 men General Bessel got 400. In addition to labour shortage he had to cope with lack of the right materials. He had no reinforced concrete or steel; presumably all available supplies were being earmarked for Cassino. His engineers were instructed to build bunkers large enough to hold about twenty-five men. Blasted deep into solid rock they were roofed with railway sleepers/ties, oak beams, loose rock and topped with concrete. Only three feet of the bunkers were above ground, making them virtually impossible for an Allied observer to spot. From an engineer's viewpoint they were model defensive positions. From an infantryman's they were a death trap. They were not sited to give mutual support. Attacking infantry could take them out one at a time. Once they were close enough to slip grenades through the bunker's loopholes it would be too late to surrender. And the sergeant* in charge of the bunker would be unlikely to allow any of his men to use the one exit before the infantry closed on the bunker. Similar bunkers were built on the western slopes of Monte Sammucro. A remarkable one-off job, a thirty foot tower, was erected on Monte Camino. The tower's ramparts could accommodate twenty men and its base was built with bevelled blocks of stone four feet long and two feet wide. Whoever had the idea of building such a Frederick Barbarosa type watchtower picked a winner.

General Bessel also had trouble getting hold of as many mines as he wanted. Most were being sent straight to the front. Bessel had to scrounge his share of them. Then he had to get them up the mountains. Mules could only take them so far. He had to use men to carry them up to the peaks. This took time, and time was another thing Bessel was short of. He only had three weeks to complete the job.[36]

* There were only two officers in a German infantry company. All platoons were commanded by sergeants.

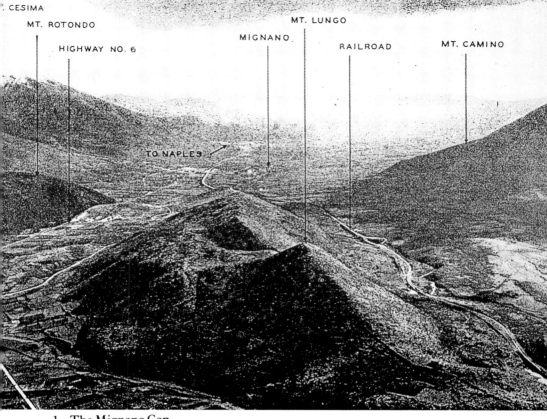

CESIMA
MT. ROTONDO
HIGHWAY NO. 6
MIGNANO
MT. LUNGO
RAILROAD
MT. CAMINO
TO NAPLES

1. The Mignano Gap

2. Eastern approaches to the Winter Line. The view that shook General Clark. Monte Sammucro, left, Monte Corno, and Monte Santa Croce.

3. Mignano, 4 November. The infantrymen are from U.S. 3rd Division.

4. The Camino Massif. Monastery Hill centre right, Monte La Defensa right. Photo taken from south east.

CHAPTER II

From the Volturno to the Winter Line

The facts about the Battle of Volturno are well known. The US 3rd and 34th Divisions made the most of easy crossings. Major-General Lucian Truscott, who commanded the 3rd Division, tricked the Hermann Göring Division into thinking his men were crossing opposite their centre, and sent his assault troops against their right flank instead. The 34th Division, faced with only one regiment of the 3rd Panzer Grenadier Division – another was still on its way from Rome – almost outflanked XIV Panzer Korps. Only well-directed artillery fire from Korps' guns prevented them from doing so. The total US casualties were less than 500. The British 46th and 56th Divisions had to cross the Volturno at two of its widest points and in areas where the flatness of the terrain gave the enemy – 15th Panzer Grenadier Division – an exceptionally clear field of fire. 46th Division established a bridgehead, but when their leading companies advanced they suffered nearly 1000 casualties. 56th Division was shelled in the start line and never crossed at all. It and British 7th Armoured Division, which had been making a diversionary display near the mouth of the Volturno, crossed the river on bridges erected by the US 3rd Division.*

The reasons why the British infantry divisions had such a bad time are laid out in Clark's autobiography. His version of events has been accepted as true because X Corps Commander, Lt-General Sir Richard McCreery, KBE, DSO, MC†, left no memoirs and X Corps' War diary, which might have been expected to record some details of the battle, restricts itself to trivia such as ration returns. McCreery opposed simultaneous crossings with the US Division on the grounds that the British infantry division had the harder job. McCreery wanted them to cross twenty-four hours after the US divisions so as to draw off the enemy fire from his own division. Clark insisted on simultaneous crossings. Or so he says.[1] In fact in his original plans for the

---

* A regiment from US 45th Division and a battalion of infantry from 26th Panzer Division fought a separate battle in the Upper Volturno Valley. The German infantry, who were defending XIV Panzer Korps' left flank, only retreated when the Korps withdrew.
† Later Commander British 8th Army and awarded the GCB.

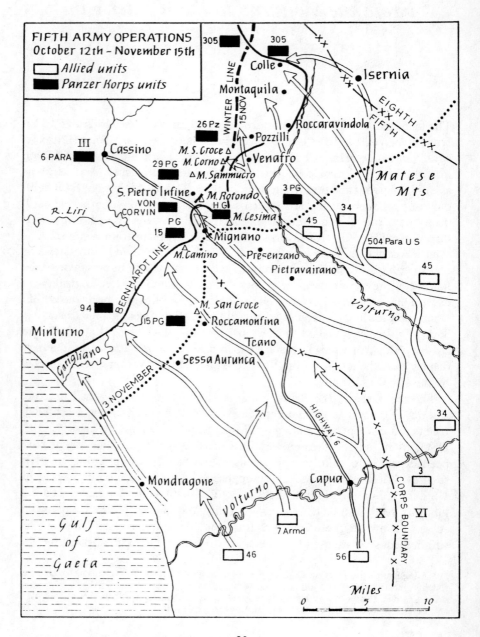

FIFTH ARMY OPERATIONS
October 12th – November 15th

☐ Allied units
■ Panzer Korps units

305 • Colle • Isernia
EIGHTH
FIFTH
• Montaquila
• Roccaravindola
WINTER LINE
15 NOV
26 Pz
• Pozzilli
M. S. Croce △
M. Corno △ • Venafro
29 PG △ M. Sammucro
△
III Cassino
6 PARA
3 PG
Matese
Mts
34
S. Pietro Infine M. Rotondo
VON H G
CORVIN △ M. Cesima
45
PG
R. Liri
15 • Mignano
504 Para U S
△ M. Camino • Presenzano
• Pietravairano
45
Volturno
BERNHARDT LINE
△ M. San Croce
94
• Roccamonfina
15 PG • Teano
Minturno •
HIGHWAY 6
3 NOVEMBER • Sessa Aurunca
Garigliano
34
3
• Mondragone
• Capua
CORPS BOUNDARY
Volturno
Gulf
of
Gaeta
X VI
7 Armd
46 56

Miles
0 5 10

20

crossing – Operations Instructions No. 6 – the British division *were* to cross after the US division (the 3rd). Clark had realized that McCreery's reasons for opposing simultaneous crossings made good sense.

McCreery was a very experienced soldier. As a subaltern he had served with the cavalry on the Western front from 1915 to 1918, being wounded and winning the MC. Like Alexander and Montgomery, he had been shocked by the way senior generals had used their front line troops and was determined that none under his command should be treated as cannon fodder. His regiment, the 12th Lancers, was among the first to be mechanized and, when he became its CO, McCreery earned a reputation for preferring tanks to horses, an unusual trait amongst British cavalry officers. In 1939 Alexander, then commanding British 1st Division, chose McCreery as his Chief of Staff. The 1st Division formed part of the BEF in France, Once there McCreery, who wanted the experience of handling armour in battle, persuaded Alexander to let him take command of an armoured brigade. During the BEF's retreat to Dunkirk the brigade formed part of its rearguard. McCreery's handling of his armour earned him the DSO. Back in the UK he was given command of one of the newly formed armoured divisions. Early in 1942 he went to the Middle East and became General Sir Claude Auchinleck's adviser on Armoured Fighting Vehicles. When Alexander succeeded Auchinleck as Commander-in-Chief, Middle East, he made McCreery his Chief of Staff. McCreery stayed with Alexander until Lt-General Sir Brian Horrocks, who had just taken over command of the newly formed X Corps, was wounded in a German air raid on Bizerta in July, 1943.

Prior to the crossing of the Volturno Clark had considered a number of options.[2] Replacing X Corps, whose heavy casualties* at Salerno had not been made good, with US II Corps† – 1st Armored Division and 36th Division, under the command of Major-General Geoffrey Keyes – was one of them. Clark had finally decided to reinforce X Corps and US 3rd Division – the only US division at the Volturno – by bringing up US 1st Armored Division. Alexander pointed out that, owing to its supply problems, 5th Army would be unable to support two armoured divisions. Clark, aware‡ that the Allied armour outnumbered the enemy's by about eight to one,

---

* 725 men were killed, 2,734 wounded and 1,800 were missing (most of them taken prisoner). US VI Corps casualties totalled 'about 3,500 men'. 10th Army lost 840 killed, 2,002 wounded and 630 missing: 8,679 5th Army casualties against 3,472 10th Army casualties.

† Two regiments of US 82nd Airborne Division, II Corps, were on police duty in Naples, whilst their 504th Regiment was moving up to protect 5th Army's right flank. In Sicily and at Salerno the 82nd Airborne had proved themselves the equals of British and German paratroopers. To use them to police Naples seems an extraordinary waste of talent. Ostensibly they were there because they had been earmarked to return to the UK on Operation Overlord, 'D' Day in Normandy. But British 7th Armoured Division was also earmarked for Overlord.

‡ Through Lt-Colonel Howard's selecting from the information from Ultra decrypts.

reluctantly abandoned the idea. On 12 October he drew up his 'definitive' plans – Operations Instructions number 6[3] – for the crossing. US 3rd Division would make simultaneous attacks with X Corps' 46th and 56th Divisions. British 7th Armoured Division would make a 'display' on the US 3rd Division's left flank. McCreery objected to the plans, for reasons already given, and Clark agreed to put US 3rd Division across twenty-four hours before the British Divisions.

When Major-General Lucas*, US VI Corps' new commander, informed General Truscott of the contents of Operations Instructions number 6 Truscott[4] objected to the plan as vigorously as McCreery had objected to the idea of simultaneous crossings, and on much the same grounds. If the US 3rd Division crossed by itself it would draw all the ememy's fire. Lucas reported back to Clark. Once again the Army Commander changed his plans. On the morning of 13 October he informed Lucas and McCreery that the US 34th Division would be brought into the attack and that VI Corps and X Corps would make simultaneous crossings that night.

The chopping and changing of Clark's plans delayed his attack almost as much as the weather. Truscott's crossing, which von Vietinghoff describes as 'a brilliant operation', outwitted and almost outflanked the Hermann Göring Division. The intense US pressure on both flanks of XIV Panzer Korps forced Hube to ask permission to withdraw. During the night of 14/15 October von Vietinghoff in turn asked Kesselring's permission. Kesselring, well content with the way his retreat schedule had been kept to – courtesy of the weather and Allied generals disagreeing among themselves – was confident enough to sanction XIV Panzer Korps' withdrawal without asking Hitler's permission.

The failure of the British 56th Division to cross the river highlights the importance of security in the approaches to a large river, and how ill-equipped 5th Army was to carry out such a crossing. The 56th Divisional Commander, Major-General D. A. H. Graham, had been badly injured in a road accident as the Division was moving up towards the Volturno. At the crossing the Division was under the temporary command of Brigadier L. O. Lyne, 169th (Queen's) Brigade. Brigadier C. E. A. Firth's 167th Brigade was to spearhead the assault across the river. During the night of 12/13 October their leading battalion, the 7th Ox and Bucks, moved into a factory close to the river. At Salerno one of the two battalions brigaded with the 7th Ox and Bucks had been overrun by the enemy, the other had withdrawn, leaving the Ox and Bucks to hld the line by itself. It had done so. After the

---

* Lucas had replaced Major-General Dawnay at Salerno. For a short time he had commanded a US corps in Sicily.

battle McCreery had visited Battalion HQ to congratulate the battalion's CO, a singular honour. On the morning of 13 October Brigadier Firth called an 'O' Group. Three senior officers of the Ox and Bucks had to leave the factory in full view of the enemy. They disguised themselves as peasants. Its one thing to dress like a peasant, another to walk like one. The 15th Panzer Grenadier Division, which was commanded by Colonel Baade,* was not fooled. It now knew where the crossing would take place, and the where-abouts of the troops who would lead it. Colonel Baade had his divisional artillery zero in on the factory and the length of river in front of it. At dusk on 13 October the Ox and Bucks filed out of the factory towards the river. The enemy artillery opened up on them. The battalion suffered eighty casualties within a few minutes. Their companies reformed, took to their boats and began crossing the river. Enemy guns blasted them out of it, causing another forty casualties and destroying most of the boats. Men Brigadier Lyne could replace, boats he could not. Like all Allied divisions in 5th Army, the 56th only had enough boats to equip one battalion. The crossing was scuppered. As Brigadier Firth reported the destruction of the boats, and Brigadier Lyne called off the crossing, 15th Panzer Grenadier Division sent a fighting patrol across the river. Slipping through 167th Brigade's lines, the patrol made its way to Capua, where Brigadier Lyne had his headquarters. The enemy shot up the town, then withdrew across the river.[5] The raid had the Baade touch. He wouldn't have led it, but he probably planned it: rubbing salt into the enemy's wounds.

The original 15th Panzer Grenadier Division, the 15th Light Division, had been lost in Tunisia. The ranks and junior officers of the new division had been raised from barracks in Sicily – replacements for the Afrika Korps. None of them had served together on manoeuvres, let alone in action. But they were young, German† and keen to show their senior commanders that they could match the exploits of the 15th Light Division in North Africa. (Both German and US Armies tried to instil a divisional pride in their men. The British Army relied more on a regimental one.) Senior commanders like Colonel Baade and the new Divisional Commander, Major-General Rodt – like all German divisional commanders in Italy he had served in Russia – played their part in putting the division through its paces, but it was Hube who ensured that the German ability to make bricks without straw was used to the full. From their very first action in the Sicilian Campaign the men of the 15th Panzer Grenadier Division fought like veterans.‡ One of their

* General Eberhard Rodt, the Divisional Commander, was away sick.
† In the Italian Campaign many of the division's replacements came from Eastern Europe.
‡ Veterans who weren't gun-shy. See British 7th Armoured Division.

Panzer Grenadier Regiments* suffered 40% casualties in an Allied air strike. When the Allied infantry pressed home an attack on the weakened regiment they were met with the same dour resistance that they had encountered before the air strike. A division that can take heavy losses and maintain its fighting spirit has come of age.

British 56th Division and 15th Panzer Grenadier Division encountered each other many times during the Italian Campaign. British 56th Division's two outstanding brigades, 201st (Guards) and 169th (Queen's), were given the job of breaking through the enemy rearguards in the high passes overlooking Salerno. The two brigades – 6th Grenadiers, 3rd Coldstream, 2nd Scots Guards and 2/5th, 2/6th and 2/7th Queen's Royal Regiment – were a formidable combination. The 3rd Coldstream and 2nd Scots Guards had been fighting since General Wavell's North African Campaign. Both battalions had outstanding records against Rommel's Afrika Korps. The 2nd Scots Guards held a ridge against the whole of the 21st Panzer Division. After the battle Rommel himself had paid tribute to their 'tremendous courage and tenacity'. The 3rd Coldstream were defending Tobruk when the enemy attacked. Two-thirds of the battalion were cut off but fifteen officers and 183 guardsmen fought their way out, supported by 200 troops from other regiments. The rest of the 35,000 garrison were taken prisoner.

After a rest and refit in Egypt the two battalions joined the newly formed 201st (Guards) Brigade in Tunisia. They soon showed they had lost none of their cutting edge. The 6th Grenadiers were fresh from the UK. Their first action was at the Mareth Line. Their objective was a ridge called Horseshoe. Divisional intelligence reported it lightly held. It was in fact part of the main position of the 90th Light Division, which had laid down two extensive minefields in front of Horseshoe. The three companies of Grenadiers who attacked the ridge suffered 70% casualties from anti-personnel mines and enemy mortaring but, closing ranks, they took their objectives. Realizing his men had suffered very heavy casualties in the minefields – he had been in them himself and blown to the ground – the Grenadiers' CO ordered the battalion's carriers to try and clear a way through the minefields so that the forward companies could be reinforced. All the carriers were detroyed. Enemy counter-attacks eventually forced the Grenadiers' infantry to retreat through the minefields, where they suffered more casualties. Within twenty-four hours the Battalion lost nine officers and sixty-seven guardsmen killed, five officers and eighty-three guardsmen seriously wounded and five officers and 104 guardsmen taken prisoner. It was probably the most terrible blooding suffered by any British battalion in the Second World War. Many

---

* The Division had 3 Panzer Grenadier Regiments. Later its 115th Regiment was attached to the Hermann Göring Panzer Division.

battalions would have been disbanded after such a disaster and it says a lot for the 6th Grenadiers and their CO that they kept going with skeleton companies until reinforcements brought them up to strength again. (By 1943 the Guards were the only infantry regiments in the British Army who could be sure of getting their own men as replacements. This was a big help in maintaining their role as crack troops.)

The first action of the Queen's Brigade had also been at the Mareth Line. Their leading battalion, 2/5th Queen's, took an objective that New Zealsnd infantry had failed to take – a real feather. And their casualties were relatively light, the best sort of blooding any CO could hope for. At Salerno the Queen's had been the only brigade in 5th Army to take and hold all its objective. At one point in the battle its 2/7th Battalion had broken through the enemy's front. If there had been any reserves to exploit the breakthrough the battle would have been over very quickly. The Queen's paid a high price for their successes. Its 2/5th Battalion was reduced to 150 men. Their casualties were all killed and wounded. They lost no prisoners.

In the high passes above Salerno two companies of the 6th Grenadiers attacked Pt 270 overlooking Monte Taborra. The enemy, two companies from 29th Panzer Grenadier Regiment, 3rd Panzer Grenadier Division, were in the process of withdrawing and the Grenadiers easily occupied their positions. But the Grenadiers' reserves of food, water and ammunition were miles to the rear. Their acting CO, Major Sir Hugh Cholmeley, decided it was too risky to leave his two companies out on a limb on Pt 270, and withdrew them to Monte Taborra. The enemy at once reoccupied their trenches.

The next day 3rd Coldstream attacked Pt 270. The enemy killed or wounded all the officers in its leading company. Company Sergeant Major P. Wright took command of the company. After wiping out three Spandau posts, he led the company to the summit. The Coldstream's other company also took their objective. The enemy kept firing until they were bayoneted or killed by grenades. CSM Wright was awarded the VC, but the attack cost the Coldstream 124 casualties. The battalion was bitter about the way the 6th Grenadiers' supply problems had resulted in many Coldstream losing their lives.[6]

Across the valley from Monte Taborra the Queen's were attacking Monte Stella, held by companies from 15th Panzer Grenadier Division. The leading company of 2/5th Queen's took and held the crest. They came under such accurate artillery and small arms fire that by the time another company relieved them they were reduced to one officer and eight men.* A private in the leading company was awarded the DCM, a rare honour.

---

* At full strength a British infantry company numbered 120.

On 28 October General Rodt paid 56th Division a remarkable compliment. He sent back an unwounded prisoner belonging to the division into US lines with a written message, assuring the recipient that all Allied wounded POWs were being well looked after, and passing on his congratulations to 'your friends on your left' – the 56th Division – on the way they were fighting. The US intelligence officer who received the message noted: 'Just what is the meaning behind this old-fashioned chivalrous approach is hard to tell.' It was a pity General Rodt was unable to pass on his 'old-fashioned approach' to his men. The rank and file of 15th Panzer Division was anything but chivalrous.

The US 3rd Division, the only regular US infantry division in the 5th Army, and one that provided more generals in the First World War than any other unit in the US Army, had taken part in the invasion of Sicily. Many of its best men had been sent as replacements to US infantry divisions fighting in the Tunisian Campaign. General Truscott, who had taken over command of the division in March, 1943, had his work cut out getting it into shape. It had been trained to march at only two and a half miles an hour. When Truscott upped this to four miles an hour* one of his regimental commanders waved the rule book at him. Two and a half miles an hour was the regulation pace, the Colonel said. Truscott told him to throw the rule book into a waste-paper basket.[7] In Sicily Truscott always made a point of finding out why an advance was being held up by visiting the 'sharp end'. Company commanders confronted by their divisional general asking awkward questions found their feet with remarkable speed. The division took thousands of Italian prisoners but the acquisition of 400 mules was of much greater importance. Realizing how valuable they would be for carrying supplies in the mountain country the division was fighting in, Truscott put the mules on divisional establishment. Other Allied generals showed no interest in mule trains. Major-General Troy Middleton, commanding US 45th Division, given use of Truscott's mules, returned them the next day, believing his men capable of portering the supplies needed. They found out too late that for every man fighting the enemy they needed two others to keep him supplied with food, water and ammunition. The US 3rd Division rapidly gained a reputation for advancing at speed. Their Army Commander, Lt-General Patton, referred admiringly to the 'Truscott trot'. But when he ordered Truscott to land one of his battalions behind the enemy lines and Truscott said he'd need twenty-four hours to plan the operation, Patton accused him of being afraid to fight.[8] Truscott reluctantly did a rush job. He dumped his battalion behind the enemy lines – and the enemy happened to be the crack 29th Panzer Grenadier Division. They all but

* This was later increased to 5 mph.

drove the US troops into the sea. Truscott never forgot the incident. When he took over command of 5th Army he always made sure his divisions had plenty of time to plan their attack.

The 3rd Division won the 'Messina Stakes', beating a patrol from 8th Army by a short head. Although Allied shipping backing up the Salerno bridgehead was at a premium Truscott contrived to get all his mules shipped over to the mainland.* Clark at once realized how important mule trains would be in Italy and ordered his commissariat to raise a further 1,300 mules. But the Germans had cornered the market. Only 300 mules were found. None of them was properly shod and none of them had saddles. Clark had to order shoes from North Africa and saddles from the States. Eisenhower did not share Alexander's optimism about the length of the Italian Campaign. On 1 September he had informed the US War Department that 5th Army would require 50,000 arctic combat suits and overshoes for the coming winter.[9] He also recommended Truscott as a future Corps Commander in a confidential report to General Marshall.

After 3rd Division had completed its part in the breakout from Salerno, Truscott noticed that his men looked in poor shape. Medical checks showed they were suffering from vitamin deficiency caused by the inadequate rations. (The US hard-pack rations were deficient in calories as well as vitamins, but this would not become known until early in 1944.) Truscott had vitamin pills issued to all his men. Other US divisional commanders didn't bother themselves about such things. As his division fought its way towards the Volturno supplies for 5th Army began drying up. The demolition of the Naples port facilities had seen to that. On 12 October the Army only had three days supply of petrol. There had been no cigarette or tobacco rations for over a week. Truscott noticed a worrying drop in his men's morale. A good smoke was one of the few comforts an infantryman had. Truscott asked Clark if he could help and Clark dispatched his own plane to Sicily. After it had made two trips the 3rd Division had enough cigarettes and tobacco to last until the Naples port facilities were in working order.

The Hermann Göring Airborne Panzer Division had been raised by Field-Marshal Göring himself, in place of the original division lost in North Africa. Like German paratroop divisions his men were Luftwaffe troops – on paper a most formidable combination of Airborne, Panzer and Panzer Grenadiers. But the new division, which had been trained by its commander, Major-General Conrath, had not lived up to its name in Sicily. Lt-General Frido von Senger und Etterlin, who directed the German divisions in Sicily – the Italian ones as well, in a diplomatic way – before Hube took over, had

---

* In warships.

27

replaced both* its regimental commanders. General Conrath was an able commander but unfuriated General von Senger by keeping in close touch with Göring, who told Conrath not to obey von Senger's orders if he disagreed with them. Von Senger suspected there was a Luftwaffe 'old boys' network between Göring and Kesselring. He may well have been right. The new regimental commanders and the transfer of 15th Panzer Grenadier Division's 115th Regiment to the division enabled General Conrath to bring it up to scratch. Its 40% causalties in Sicily were made up before Salerno, thanks to Göring's intervention, and during the battle it fought with great spirit. It continued to do so throughout XIV Panzer Korps' retreat to the Bernhardt. Göring had every reason to be proud of his new 'eagles', and continued to watch the retreat as closely as Hitler did. Now that Kesselring was overall commander of the 10th Army Göring could no longer give General Conrath *carte blanche*, but the Field-Marshal was ready to intervene if he thought his pet division was taking too heavy casualties or in danger of being trapped by the Allies. He was not going to let the division get the chop in Italy as well as in North Africa.[10]

The original 3rd Panzer Grenadier Division had been lost at Stalingrad. Its officers were pukka Germans, its rank and file drawn from what had been Polish Silesia, and were made up of Silesian Germans and Poles. Each company had 60% Germans, 40% Poles. The proportion of Germans to Poles always remained the same. If a company lost more Germans than Poles in a particular action other Germans were drafted into the company. Whilst this arrangement made sense to the powers that be, it created a very bad atmosphere in the companies. Germans distrusted Poles and vice versa. Neither nationality could obtain promotion until they had served a period of probation. Company officers decided how long this period should last. Back in Silesia the families of the Polish element in the division were harassed by Nazi officials. Letters from home, usually a boost for morale, often had the opposite effect on the unfortunate Poles.

The Division's first action took place at Salerno. Their 29th Panzer Grenadier Regiment was ordered to take part in the 10th Army's main counter-attack on the Allies. Von Vietinghoff saw to it that the Regiment was temporarily commanded by Colonel Schmalz, Hermann Göring Division, whose battle group in Sicily had fought hard. The 29th Regiment took their initial objective in a night attack, but next morning had to advance in full view of Allied artillery observers. A heavy naval and artillery barrage destroyed two of the 29th battalions' headquarters and broke up the rifle companies' attack. The remaining battalions pressed home their attack without success. The 29th Regiment's casualties were heavy but a large

---

* The division was only two regiments strong in Sicily.

number of missing men turned up after the battle. Von Vietinghoff dubbed the Regiment 'unreliable'. Considering that the Regiment had never been in action and had encountered the full weight of the Allied firepower, this seems a little hard. But in one way von Vietinghoff was right. Neither he nor the Allied units who encountered the 3rd Panzer Grenadier Division's two infantry regiments ever knew what sort of opposition to expect. Although one of the 29th Panzer Grenadier Regiment's companies had fought to the death in the high passes above Salerno, another company in the same battalion made only token resistance and had to be 'covered' by a company from the 15th Panzer Grenadier Division.

It was somehow appropriate that the 3rd Panzer Grenadier Division should be commanded by a general so badly crippled with war wounds that he had to hobble around on crutches. Major-General Graeser was proud of his men. He made regular visits to the front in a small car, encouraging them to fight hard. But as von Senger observes, 'Although the personality of the leader can contribute vitality to the spirit animating a division it cannot eliminate every deficiency'.[11]

The US 34th Infantry Division, National Guard (Major-General Charles Ryder), drew all its junior officers* and ranks from Iowa, North and South Dakota and Minnesota, with the exception of the 1st Battalions, 133rd Regiment, which was made up of Hawaiian Japanese who'd become naturalized Americans. It was the first US Division to be sent overseas and took part in the Allied landings in North Africa. At the Kasserine Pass its 168th Regiment was exposed to the full force of Rommel's counter-attack. In three days' fighting the Regiment suffered 75% casualties. The Division was withdrawn from the line to reform. It then took part in the Allied Tunisian offensive. Although the 34th took all its objectives it adopted a 'softly, softly, catchee monkey' approach to the enemy, which, after the Kasserine Pass, was hardly surprising, and their Corps Commander, Major-General Patton, took umbrage. His comments on the Division's performance were noted by Clark, and certainly tipped the balance in favour of the 36th Division being chosen for the Salerno bridgehead. This was hard on General Ryder and those men in the 34th who wanted another chance to show how they could fight. However, they had someone at hand who believed they typified 'GI Joe'. Ernie Pyle was making a name for himself as a war correspondent. His reports on the 34th in North Africa put them on the map back home. It was fitting that when Hollywood made a film about Ernie Pyle they chose a former battalion commander from the 34th as military adviser.

The US 45th Division, National Guard, was recruited from Oklahoma,

---

* When the 34th Division was inducted into the US regular army all its senior officers were replaced by regulars.

Arizona and New Mexico. About 30% of its men were full-blooded Red Indians.* Under their first class commander, Major-General Troy Middleton, the Division fought well in Sicily. At Salerno its performance had disappointed Clark.† Like the 34th, the 45th Division had something to prove.

The British 7th Armoured Division were the original 'Desert Rats' (so called because of the jerboa on their divisional flash). Its splendid fighting record on the Desert had not been matched in Tunisia. On a number of occasions it had showed 'excessive caution',[12] when making attacks, a not unusual characteristic of a division which had been too long in the field. McCreery found most veteran divisions stale and gun-shy, and much preferred to use fresh, inexperienced divisions eager to win their spurs.[13] X Corps Intelligence compiled a list of all the divisions serving in 10th Army, showing that their original formations had all been lost at Stalingrad or in Tunisia. (To prove they'd done their homework they named all the original formations. In the case of the 29th Panzer Grenadier Division they got it wrong.) Presumably the object of the exercise was to try and convince X Corps divisional commanders they were only up against 'retreads'. The divisional commanders could have told them that most of the 'retreads' were fighting with the skill and determination of their original formations. In front of Naples the 7th Armoured Division had treated the enemy rearguard, the Hermann Göring Panzer Division, with considerable respect. General Conrath made scathing comments about an enemy being unable or unwilling to press home its attacks.

The British 46th Division (Major-General J. L. I. Hawksworth) were an unlucky formation. Although they had three very good brigades – three battalions of Hampshires, three North Country, and three Midland – they always seemed to be in the wrong place at the wrong time. They never produced the same results as the British 56th Division and McCreery tended to use the 46th in back-up roles.

Colonel William Darby's Regiment of Rangers‡ were waiting in the wings. They and the British Marine Commandos had secured 5th Army's left flank at Salerno and had taken heavy losses. They had also had a particularly exhausting Sicilian Campaign, always out in front of Patton's 7th Army and never getting more than a twenty-four hour rest. The original Ranger battalion,§ the 1st, had been raised by Darby when he was a Lt-

* Commenting on the improved performance of the US Divisions at Mignano Gap, General Wentzell referred to 'their Red Indian tactics'.

† During the 45th's low advance in the upper Volturno Clark suggested to General Lucas that he 'light a fire' under General Middleton.

‡ The Rangers were named after a guerrilla force which had fought in Canada during the war between the British and the French in the 1750s.

§ Only 400 at full strength compared to a US infantry battalion's 800 men.

Colonel based in Scotland. His battalion had trained with the British commandos, who Darby admired, and on who he based the Rangers. The 1st Rangers had landed with other US Forces in North Africa in 1942. The ease with which they had sliced through Vichy French troops earned them headlines in the *New York Times*. In Tunisia they had acted as rearguard when the US division had retreated during Rommel's counter-offensive. General Patton had been so impressed by the way they had carried out their job that he acceded to Colonel Darby's request that the Rangers be allowed to choose when to wear steel helmets. This was a time when Patton was trying to get Army surgeons to wear steel helmets when they were operating on wounded men. When the US division went on the offensive the Rangers were out in front. For their part in the action at El Guettar, where they were up against German paratroops fighting as infantry, as well as the best Italian troops, the battalion was awarded the Presidential Unit Citation.* When the campaign was over and Patton learnt he was to command the US Army which was to invade Sicily, he decided he needed more Rangers, so he authorized Colonel Darby to raise two more battalions. Whilst Darby made recruiting speeches, his officers and sergeants went round bars and barracks in Oran selecting recruits. Too many volunteers for the 1st Rangers Battalion had turned out to be below Ranger standard so Darby was now creaming off the best men in other units, something deeply resented by the units' COs, but there was nothing they could do about it. Darby had the go-ahead from Patton himself.[14]

The Rangers Regiment won all their battles in Sicily. Colonel Darby was awarded the DSC and offered the command of a Regiment in the 45th Division. He turned down the promotion. He had no intention of leaving his beloved Rangers. His popularity with them, always high, knew no bounds after that.†

The Rangers always had their own way of going about things. In Sicily it was customary for troops first into town to welcome the runners-up with ironic cheers. (The US 3rd Division did this to Montgomery. He was not amused.) The 3rd Rangers upped the ante. Realizing that the US Division to which they were attached had no idea that they had taken the town of Porto Empedocle – the two groups were out of radio contact – Rangers Sausen, Jackson and Stanton decided to pass themselves off as the Mayor and deputies of Porto Empedocle. They dressed up in black suits nicked from a mortician, helped themselves to a case of brandy from a wine merchant and assembled on the steps of the town hall. When Major-General

---

* The US Army had the excellent idea of awarding companies and battalions citations for gallantry. The Presidential Citation was the highest award.

† Darby was promoted full Colonel for the Rangers' action at Salerno, which earned 1st and 3rd Rangers another Presidential Citation.

Collins, commanding the US Infantry Division, drove into town Ranger Sausen made him a speech in Italian and presented him with the case of brandy. General Collins replied in pidgin Italian, assuring the 'Mayor' that his troops would not loot the town. He must have been very surprised when the 'Mayor' and his deputy suddenly took to their heels.[15]

On 16 October the 2nd Battalion, 135th Regiment, US 34th Division, attacked an enemy-held mountain on the far side of the Volturno. The divisional artillery was still on the other side of the river and they had to rely on battalion heavy mortars and machine guns for support. The mountain was criss-crossed with ravines and woods, making it ideal terrain for the defending enemy, who were thought to be 120-140 strong. It took the battalion two days to capture the crest of the mountain. By then it knew that the enemy consisted of one platoon of forty men. Thirty-five of them belonged to the 3rd Panzer Grenadier Division. The other five, who had been taken prisoner, were from a Nebelwerfer battery. The enemy had tricked the US battalion into thinking they were up against a substantial number of troops by frequent changes of position. From the rear slopes of the mountain the thirty-five Panzer Grenadiers, aided by an SP gun, held up over 500 US troops for a further twenty-four hours. When they finally withdrew the US battalion commander discovered that the mountain's north-eastern spur stretched for miles. Just how many miles he couldn't determine because he had no large-scale map. He could choose between sending out patrols to find out if the spur was occupied by the enemy, something that would hold up his battalion's advance for hours, or order his companies to advance down the mountain and risk being enfiladed by enemy troops. He chose to advance.[16]

On the same day as the 34th Division's battalion began its attack the US 3rd Division tackled a hill held by about 250 men from the 3rd and 15th Panzer Grenadier Divisions. Colonel Harry Sherman committed the whole of his 7th Regiment to the assault. When the leading companies of his 1st Battalion were half way up the hill they were counter-attacked by the enemy and forced back. Colonel Sherman replaced the 1st Battalion with his 2nd and 3rd Battalions. Their companies suffered exactly the same fate as those of the 1st Battalion. They reformed and attacked again. The fighting continued into the night, with the enemy still holding the crest of the hill. Colonel Sherman decided to withdraw his men and mount another attack the following morning. By then the divisional artillery would be across the Volturno and they could lay down a support barrage for his men. But during the night the enemy withdrew from the hill. At low cost to themselves they had inflicted heavy casualties on the 7th Regiment and had only retreated when ordered to.

Both enemy rearguard actions were copybook examples of how such affairs should be carried out. They had two things in common: the presence of the 'unreliable' 3rd Panzer Grenadiers, who had shown the two US divisions they could fight as skilfully and as ferociously as the very best German infantry, and the lack of US artillery support. The absence of artillery support was thought to be a temporary drawback. 5th Army intelligence knew that the Army's guns outnumbered XIV Panzer Korps by about three to one. And the Naples port facilities were now in full swing. Allied gunners could fire as many shells as they liked. German gunners had to husband every round unless the infantry they were supporting was attacked. German battery commanders knew that if they lost any guns they would not be replaced. OKW's persistence in turning a blind eye to Kesselring's requests for replacements put a very great strain on German artillery officers and ranks, a strain that was increased when, on or around 18 October, Kesselring ordered* that all Korps' artillery should be withdrawn to the Bernhardt.[17] The Allied artillery held all the cards on paper, but their forward observers soon discovered what the CO of the 2nd Battalion, 135th Regiment, US 34th Division already knew – that the mountains north of the Volturno stretched for miles. They weren't very high – 2,000 feet at most – but they were riddled with crests. This posed a severe technical problem for the Allied artillery. How to make sure support barrages landed on the right crest, the one which the infantry was attacking. If the weather had been kinder US spotter planes – Piper Cubs – could have done the job. But it kept on raining.† When their airfields were in a condition to allow them to take off they usually found the target obscured by mist of low clouds. The Allied gunners had to rely on their Forward Observers. These very brave men who risked their lives more often than the infantry did – Forward Observers were always up front – sometimes had easy targets. Enemy retreating in daylight.‡ Often they were not sure whether they could direct their guns on to the right crest, or where the right crest was. Rather than risk subjecting their infantry to 'friendly fire' they told their guns they could not direct them on target. Allied infantry had to rely on battalion weapons, heavy mortars and machine guns, to give them support when they attacked an enemy position. The mortars, US 81mm, British 3", provided the main support. This held good for the German infantry as well. German 81 mm mortars, which were very accurate, caused more casualties to Allied infantrymen than any other

* He also ordered the Luftwaffe not to carry out any more offensive strikes. The Luftwaffe and Korps guns were reserved for the defence of the Bernhardt.
† On 25 October 5th Army Operations reported laconically, 'It did not rain'.
‡ German prisoners who had fought in Russia were unanimous in saying that Allied shelling was far more devastating than anything they had experienced in Russia. A German MO taken prisoner remarked bitterly, 'You people expend artillery ammunition but mine expend only the bodies of men.'

weapon.* The infantrymen were also keenly aware of the German Spandau.† Belt-fed, it had a rate of fire of 1,300 rounds a minute. Men on the receiving end were impressed by the whip-like crack of its bullets. The British Bren gun, firing 600 rounds a minute, sounded like a pop gun in comparison. So did the US Browning automatic rifle, which had an even slower rate of fire. But Allies infantrymen who survived Spandau bursts at short range quickly realized that it was a far less accurate gun than their own weapons. The Spandau rate of fire gave it an exceptionally heavy recoil. This made it very hard for the gunner to fire really accurate bursts. Spandau gunners who could cope with its recoil made it a most murderous weapon. General Sickenius had noted that Allied infantrymen 'had an exaggerated respect for the Spandau'. He could have added that their respect for the German Nebelwerfer, a multiple-barrelled mortar, was even more exaggerated. Unlike the German 81 mm mortar, whose bombs‡ simply made a 'whoosh' just before landing, the Nebelwerfer could be heard from the moment it was fired. Its projectiles took between 60 and 90 seconds to arrive on target. The six bombs the mortar put up made a curious 'wurr-ra, wurr-ra' to begin with. As the bombs neared the target the sound changed to a howling roar. The build-up of fear in the minds of the men on the receiving end could be catastrophic. The first time they were targeted by Nebelwerfer the whole of the US 34th's Hawaiian Japanese battalion panicked. It took the rest of the day for them to reform.§ By then many of its men had discovered that the Nebelwerfer's bark was much worse than its bite. Unlike the German 81 mm mortar it was a most inaccurate weapon. Its projectiles straddled an area of several hundred square yards. Most Nebelwerfer batteries – 150 mm – fired bombs weighing 75 pounds. A few heavy batteries – 210 mm – fired ones that weighed 248 pounds. US troops nicknamed the Nebelwerfer 'screaming meanies', British troops called them 'moaning minnies'. Each sobriquet referred to a particular part of the Nebelwerfer's flight path. The Allied equivalent of the Nebelwerfer was the 4.2" mortar. It was a US invention and why they calibrated it in inches is something of a mystery. All other US mortars and guns were calibrated in millimetres. The 4.2" mortar was copied by the British. But the British 4.2" mortar fired different projectiles to the US 4.2" mortar. At Salerno Darby's Rangers received British rounds and were unable to fire them. Although a battery of 4.2" mortars could lay down twelve tons of shells in one minute they were as

* In World War II 60% of all casualties in all armies were caused by shells. Guns had a range of 20 miles or more.
† It was actually a Mauser, the MG42. The German infantry had nicknamed it Spandau because its specially tapered bullets were made in the town of Spandau, near Berlin.
‡ US shells.
§ The battalion went on to receive the Presidential Unit Citation for gallantry, and won more decorations than any other US battalion in 5th Army.

inaccurate as Nebelwerfers. The tail-fins of British bombs often fell off, causing them to fall short.

The retreating Germans, given enough time, held up the Allied infantry with anti-personnel mines. The Germans excelled in this particular field. The shrapnel-filled 'S' mine, which came on stream in 1942, was the most deadly. Anyone treading on one set off an initial charge that propelled the mine five feet into the air. Then the main charge exploded, causing an air-burst that killed or severely wounded anyone in the area. The 'S' mine could be found by mine detectors. The wooden Schu mine could not. It had to be located with a bayonet. Anyone who trod on one lost a foot. Advancing infantry didn't have the time to fiddle around with bayonets and British battalions never went into action carrying mine detectors. US battalions had their own specialized pioneer platoons who worked alongside the leading infantry platoons using mine detectors. The Allied infantry also had to cope with Box mines – booby-trapped anti-tank mines with their steel casing removed so as to make them proof against mine detectors. At the beginning of the retreat German pioneers attached them to trip wires. By the end of it they had perfected the 'tread wire'. The wire was now out of sight and buried just below the surface of the earth.*

Mountain warfare puts a severe strain on troops unused to it, particularly on advancing infantry who suffer more casualties than the defending enemy, the psychological strain of 'false' crests – what seems to be the top of the mountain turns out to be just another crest – as well as the physical strain of slogging up one mountain after another making long approach marches, and then having to go straight into the attack. Towards the end of October at least one British battalion was issued with Benzedrine to keep its men going. The Allied and German infantry shared the same fear that if they were badly wounded it would take them hours to receive treatment from a medical officer. It took stretcher bearers† twelve hours to carry a severely wounded Scots Guard major to the nearest Aid Post. He survived the trip. Others didn't. Allied and German infantry also suffered from skin complaints and blood poisoning caused by there being no time or facility to enable them to wash properly or change their underclothes.[18]

Although the German infantry were able to rest up on top of one mountain after another, they were under much greater psychological strain than Allied infantry. They had been on the retreat ever since Salerno. Kesselring and von Vietinghoff encouraged their divisional commanders to visit the troops in the line as often as possible. There's nothing like seeing the 'Brass' at the 'sharp end' to cheer up the infantry, and German divisional commanders

* For other weapons used by German and Allied infantry see Appendix B.
† US litter bearers.

35

considered it part of their duty to visit them. (Apart from Truscott, Allied divisional commanders rarely put in an appearance at the front.) They found their men's morale remarkably good. They were more worried about their thinness on the ground. At the beginning of the Sicilian Campaign a German infantry battalion had had a fighting strength of 500-600 men. By the third week of October they were down to 175-250.* In a rather desperate effort to make the most of his resources, von Vietinghoff ordered all German platoons to be split in two. Each squad was commanded by a sergeant. Two letters intended for Germany but ending up with US Intelligence give a good idea of how the German infantry were reacting to the retreat. One was written by a corporal† in the 71st Panzer Grenadier Regiment, 29th Panzer Grenadier Division,‡ and reflects the Regiment's pride in its achievements. (It had been the 71st Regiment, led by divisional tanks, that had almost pushed US VI Corps into the sea at Salerno.) 'We are retreating very slowly, a fact that ought to make the enemy feel ashamed, to our winter quarters. We are inferior in men and material. None dare sleep at night or he might find himself a prisoner. My men are so spread out that by the time I have visited them all I feel exhausted. Despite desperate conditions, we inflict heavy losses whenever the enemy attacks or we retreat. They are talking about relieving us on 31 October. I don't believe it.' The writer's division *was* relieved on 31 October but by then he was dead. His letter is remarkable in that it shows how freely German troops were allowed to describe what was happening to them. Allied troops were forbidden to even say what country they were in, let alone talk about the fighting. All letters were censored by platoon officers. The second letter that failed to reach its destination was short and to the point: 'I am slightly wounded in the thigh. But that's enough to get me out of the shit!'

To begin with Allied Intelligence officers were surprised there weren't more German deserters. Between 15 and 31 October there were only eighty-four German infantrymen listed as bona fide deserters. (It was sometimes difficult to distinguish deserters from POWs.) Most of these came from the 8th and 29th Panzer Grenadier Regiments, and they were mainly Poles. One of them remarked that he believed the whole division would desert were it not for the fact that all rank and file had been warned that if they did reprisals would be taken against their families. Deserters and POWs all talked freely,§ unlike Allied prisoners who rarely gave any information

---

* The fighting strength of 15th Panzer Grenadier Regiment, 29th Panzer Grenadier Division, totalled 526.

† German Corporals were the equivalent of US and British sergeants.

‡ Although this division belonged to General Heer's LXXVI Panzer Korps, they came over to XIV Panzer Korps' front to help out the 3rd Panzer Grenadiers Division.

§ For an example of how much information a good interrogation officer could get out of a prisoner see Appendix C.

except the laid-down 'name and number'. Von Vietinghoff got to know of the difference and was bitter about it. One battalion in the 15th Panzer Grenadier Regiment, 29th Panzer Grenadiers, had been nicknamed 'The Woodchoppers' – *Holz Hacker* – because all rank and file had set their hearts on being taken prisoner and sent to Canada as lumberjacks. All German prisoners who were interrogated, including officers from the Hermann Göring Division, said that they believed the war to be lost, a view shared, it seemed, by the fanatical Nazis in the various regiments. It might be expected that the Woodchoppers' battalion would only put up token resistance. Instead they continued to fight as hard as the other infantry battalions in their division. US interrogation officers concluded that the 'Woodchoppers' were backing themselves both ways. If the war ended suddenly they'd get back to Germany a good deal quicker than if they were sent to Canada. 'They hesitate to come across the line, because, as they see it, this might keep them away from home much longer than if they continued fighting.' Such calculations were not the prerogative of the German infantry. An officer in the 29th Panzer Grenadier Division, whose battle group had held up the divisions of the 8th Army making their way to Salerno, wasn't in the least surprised that the British armour and infantry hadn't pressed home their attacks. They all knew the war was already won, so why should they risk their lives unnecessarily? He was right. From 1943 onwards many British plans adopted the 'softly, softly catchee moneky' approach to the enemy that had gone down badly with Patton. The historian Cyril Falls discovered that the longer the Italian Campaign went on the heavier the artillery barrage needed to get British infantry to attack.

In October, 1943, most of British X Corps' infantry was fighting a good deal harder than 8th Army had on its way to Salerno. Their problem was lack of replacements. After Salerno they had received only 1,500. From 22 September to 31 October their rifle companies had suffered over 2,000 casualties.* At full strength a British infantry battalion totalled 801, but some 300 of these were 'specialists' – mortar-crews, anti-tank gunners, heavy machine gunners, pioneers, signallers, fitters, and admin. Its four rifle companies had a strength of around 500. By late October most of British X Corps infantry battalions were down to three rifle companies instead of four, and each company averaged around 100 men. X Corps had had no replacements since Salerno and there were none in the pipeline. Operation Overlord had seen to that. Newly trained infantry in the UK was being held back for the Normany landings. The shortage of infantrymen, particularly in the British 56th Division, was a cause of deep concern to McCreery.

* Between 7 October and 15 November British X Corps suffered 2874 battle casualties, US VI Corps 6843. Between 11 October and 10 November XIV Panzer Korps suffered 4514 battle casualties.

When he heard that the British 50th Division was leaving 8th Army for Operation Overlord he managed to secure one of its brigades – 168th* – which had formed part of the 56th Division in Tunisia, and bring up the division's strength to four brigades.

US VI Corps had no problems with replacements. The three rifle companies of their infantry battalions were being kept up to full strength. (Each company had five officers and 180-200 men.) For the time being it did have a problem with deserters. An article in the 5th Army's newspaper *The Stars and Stripes* saying that all US Air Force personnel would be rotated back to the States after serving a certain period overseas resulted in a 'grapevine' request from VI Corps GIs that they be rotated too. When they were told this was not on, whole squads of men, up to one hundred in a single day,[19] began walking back to Naples. At first Clark let them off with a caution but when the 'Naples trot' continued he had them court-martialled for desertion. Truscott suggested that one way to stop the desertions would be to open leave centres in and around Naples and rotate VI Corps GIs to them instead of to the States. Clark took up the idea. This combination of stick and carrot ended the US desertions. There were no leave centres for X Corps. Every man was needed in or behind the line.

Occasionally the weather was good enough for XII Air Support Command, 5th Army's air support, to fly, but cooperation between them and the troops on the ground was very poor. The XII Air Support Command insisted that all demands for its service should be made at least twelve hours in advance. On 13 October, when the US 45th Division was advancing up the Upper Volturno Valley, General Middleton asked for support. His leading battalion had been bombed by twenty enemy planes as well as being held up on the ground. On 13 October XII Air Support Command informed General Middleton that 'the weather had interfered with the detailed execution of the above programme'. It hadn't interfered with the Luftwaffe's programme. Between 14 and 17 October General Middleton put in four more requests for fighter-bomber support. They were all turned down. The reasons given varied from 'all fighter-bomber airdromes unusable' to 'weather reported impossible'.[20] XII Air Support Command made similar excuses to US 3rd Division. On 23 October Truscott sought out their commander, General House, who reluctantly agreed to try out a scheme of Truscott's called Forward Ground Control. Two pilots would be seconded to the 3rd Division to work with divisional forward observers. The scheme was first tried out on 31 October. The weather was good and the strike went in as planned. 'Against an experienced, alert enemy in prepared positions . . . it proved to be the most effective air support we ever received. The bombing was

* 1st London Scottish, 1st Irish Rifles, and 12th Royal Berkshires.

accurate . . . it contributed greatly to the advancing troops' ability to seize their objective on schedule and with light losses. Nevertheless, this was the only instance in which we ever had air support with Forward Ground Control during the entire campaign.'[21]

In an undated paper* entitled 'Analysis of Tactical Attacks on Bridges and Viaducts, Italy', XII Air Support Command noted that it had taken thirty-four heavy bombers two hundred sorties to hit a bridge, twenty-four medium bombers fifty-nine sorties to hit one, and twenty-four fighter-bombers nineteen sorties. Clearly XII Air Support Command needed all the specialized bombing practice it could get, but General House's failure to implement Forward Ground Control as one of its permanent features is an indictment of his command.

German Enigma signals intercepted on 1 October and decrypted by Ultra on the 2nd revealed everything that had been said at Hitler's conference with Kesselring and Rommel. A decrypt of 5 October disclosed Hitler's decisions to fortify both the Bernhardt and the Massa-Rimini Lines. A decrypt on 7 October identified the 65th and 305th Infantry as the two divisions which were to be transferred from Army Group B to 10th Army. On 8 October three more decrypts revealed 10th Army's defence plans for the Bernhardt, as well as part of its geographical area – it passed close to Cassino – the boundaries between XIV and LXXVI Panzer Korps, and the fact that the Luftwaffe was referring to the Bernhardt as 'The Winter Line'.† The German strategy for the defence of Italy had changed completely. Both 15th Army HQ and the US Anglo Joint Intelligence Committee in Algiers were concerned about the proposed movement of the two German divisions from Army Group B to 10th Army. They believed that 10th Army might be preparing to counter-attack. When another decrypt reported that the 65th and 305th Infantry Divisions had begun moving south 15th Army Intelligence section prepared a bulletin sayng that the enemy could switch divisions from the Russian front to Italy, although a decrypt of 19 October had made it clear that OKW were preparing to *withdraw* divisions from Italy.‡ 15th Army Intelligence section went ahead and issued their bulletin. On 24 October Alexander sent a signal[22] to Eisenhower saying he believed the

* Held in US Department of Defense Archives in a file marked 'Air, Miscellaneous' the file contains some interesting accounts of the way carrier pigeons were used in the Italian Campaign. US 504 Parachute Regiment, who were way out on the 5th Army's right flank, discovered they were unable to contact Lucas's HQ by wireless and used pigeons instead. During the Battle of the Rapido the US 36th Division also used pigeons. The Germans captured one and sent it back with a message in English: 'Herewith a messenger pigeon is returned. We have enough to eat and what's more we look forward to your next attack. The German troops.'

† The Allies also decided to call it The Winter Line.

‡ The Adolf Hitler SS Panzer Division, the 16th Panzer Division and the 24th Panzer Division all began moving out of Italy in November.

enemy were capable of increasing their divisions in Italy from 24 to 60. Eisenhower asked Joint Intelligence Committee what they thought of Alexander's forecast. JIC, a very capable unit which did not manipulate facts to suit a brief, issued a communiqué describing the forecast as 'contrary to all evidence'. They added a rider to the effect that, for the foreseeable future, the enemy in Italy would not be reinforced at all. They were right.[23]

When Kesselring discovered that one of the two infantry divisions moving south was the 94th Infantry he was angry. The 94th had been on coastguard duty near Livorno and, as far as Kesselring was concerned, coastguards were about all its men were fit for. The division had originally been raised to man the Atlantic Wall being built on the coast of France and the Low Countries, a sedentary job to suit men whose average age was around forty. It was the nearest thing to a 'Dad's Army' division in Italy and more of a liability than a reinforcement, as far as Kesselring was concerned.* The only place for it was out of harm's way behind the Garigliano. Both Kesselring and von Vietinghoff were confident that the 5th Army would not attempt to cross the river at the same time as it attacked the Mignano Gap sector, providing the defences of the Garigliano were brought up to scratch. The sort of ad hoc defences that the 94th Division would dig themselves would not do. Kesselring told von Vietinghoff that the 10th Army engineers working on the Mignano Gap defences would have to be transferred to the Garigliano. Von Vietinghoff pointed out that the defences round Mignano and Monte Cesima were not complete, and asked Kesselring to delay the engineers' departure until they had finished them. Kesselring said the troops occupying Mignano and Monte Cesima would have to finish the defences themselves and the engineers went off to the Garigliano.

Kesselring liked what he'd heard about 305th Infantry Division. Although it had never been in action it had been raised in the Wurtemberg-Baden area of Germany, which had a reputation for producing good infantrymen, its rank and file were young and its senior officers hand-picked by an experienced commander, Major-General Haag. The 305th Division would be placed on XIV Panzer Korps' left flank, and would be allowed to occupy their positions at the Bernhardt as soon as they began arriving.

Kesselring also told von Vietinghoff his plans for the rest of XIV Panzer Korps at the Bernhardt. 15th Panzer Grenadier Division, who were on the Korps' right flank, would occupy the Camino Massif, leaving the Allies a clear run to the Garigliano. The Hermann Göring Division would be withdrawn for a rest and refit. The 3rd Panzer Grenadier Division would take over from the Hermann Göring in XIV Panzer Korps' centre, and be

* The 94th would show Kesselring how well a 'Dad's Army' division could fight when X Corps crossed the Garigliano in January, 1944.

responsible for the defence of Mignano and Monte Santa Croce. The prospect of the 3rd Panzer Grenadier Division manning Monte Cesima and the Mignano Gap appalled von Vietinghoff. He told Kesselring the division was understrength,* unreliable, and had suffered very heavy losses during the retreat. The Hermann Göring's two Panzer Grenadier regiments, which had suffered relatively light losses – like all good infantrymen they knew how to look after themselves in a retreat – should be kept in the line and man the Monte Cesima and Mignano Gap defences. Kesselring insisted on the Hermann Göring Divisions being withdrawn but agreed to place two of its Panzer Grenadier battalions in Army Reserve along with III/104th Panzer Grenadier Regiment, 15th Panzer Grenadier Division. He also promised to reinforce the 3rd Panzer Grenadier Division with a battalion of paratroopers who were training near Cassino. Kesselring himself had to fight off a 'try on' from OKW, who sent a signal ordering him to release 15th Panzer Grenadier Division and send it back to them as soon as the 94th and 305th Infantry Divisions had arrived. Kesselring informed OKW that the 15th Panzer Grenadier Division formed an essential part of XIV Panzer Korps' defence of the Bernhardt's Mignano Gap sector and that he had no intention of releasing the Division. OKW did not press the matter.[24]

The 94th and 305th Infantry Division began arriving early in mid-October. Ultra decrypts sent on from 15th Army Intelligence section to 5th Army Intelligence informed them of the positions taken up by the fresh divisions. 5th Army Intelligence also made full use of British Y Force. This was a special signals unit which had cracked the German's front line VHF code in North Africa. In Sicily the enemy had changed their VHF frequency and Y Force had been unable to home in on it. By October they had succeeded in doing so and could follow all orders issued by German regimental and battalion commanders. 5th Army Intelligence also received on-the-spot information about enemy fortifications and headquarters from Italian civilians and escaped POWs. 10th Army never issued any Intelligence reports. This wasn't surprising. They had to rely on their forward observers and Allied POWs – who didn't talk – and occasional wireless intercepts, to work out what the Allies were up to. The Germans had no equivalent of Y Force, but the Allies' wireless discipline was lax. At Salerno 10th Army signallers had cottoned on to Clark's provisional evacuation plans. 10th Army commanders whose units were retreating to the Bernhardt had to rely on forward observers to guess what the Allied Commanders' plans were.

On 22 October Kesselring sent Hitler a list of the units the 10th Army would need to retake Foggia: 3-4 Panzer Grenadier Divisions, 2 Mountain Divisions, 2 Fighter Groups, 1 Fighter Bomber Group and 1 Anti-Aircraft

---

* III/8th Panzer Grenadier Regiment was on coastguard duty at Civitavecchia.

Regiment. Kesselring must have known that the odds on getting such reinforcements were remote. But he also knew his Führer. An optimistic forecast about retaking Foggia backed up with impeccably kept retreat schedules would go down very well indeed. The timing of Kesselring's 'shopping list' could hardly have been better. On 17 October Hitler had ordered OKW to draw up a document appointing Rommel as Supreme Commander.[25] A friend of Rommel's at OKW sent him a secret message telling him about the document. Rommel naturally presumed that his role as Supreme Commander was to be made official. But when OKW returned the document to Hitler he didn't sign it. On 21 October he summoned Kesselring to his headquarters in East Prussia. There is no record of their conversation in OKW archives but on 27 October Hitler ordered OKW to draw up another document appointing Kesselring as Supreme Commander. Kesselring returned to Frascati knowing that, barring a serious hitch in the 10th Army retreat schedules, the job was his.

The first thing he did on his return was to ring von Vietinghoff and stress the importance of keeping to all the retreat schedules. There were schedules within schedules. Each division in the 10th Army has one of its own. On 23 October British 56th Division had almost broken through part of 15th Panzer Grenadier Division's fifteen-mile front, forcing the units defending that section of the Barbara Line – which consisted of field works erected by the division itself – to retreat twenty-four hours before they were scheduled to do so. Kesselring reprimanded von Vietinghoff for failing to ensure that Hube had kept to the retreat schedule. Von Vietinghoff reprimanded Hube, who doubtless passed on the message to General Rodt, now back in command of 15th Panzer Grenadier Division.

On 2 October Alexander had issued a directive to Clark, ordering him to target Venafro-Isernia-Sessa Arrunca as the 5th Army's objective prior to its advance on Rome. Clark had had a good look at the map and had realized the importance of Cassino in relation to the Liri Valley and Rome. But XIV Panzer Korps' dogged resistance north of the Volturno and reports from Lt-Colonel Howard about the enemy's intention to make a stand on the Winter Line made it clear to Clark that he would have no easy passage to Cassino. He would have to make a frontal assault on the Winter Line or carry out an amphibious landing behind it. On 21 October he discussed the possibilities of such a landing with General Gruenther, Brigadier John O'Daniel, the Army's Chief of Amphibious Operations, and Colonel Dan Brann, Clark's G3. Clark plumped for Gaeta, and said an amphibious landing 'was vital'. Later that day Eisenhower arrived at Clark's headquarters at Caserta, and Clark discussed the matter with him. On 24 October Brigadier O'Daniel informed Clark that the beach west of Gaeta was impracticable for a landing, but that the beaches east of the town were ideal. Clark said that these beaches were too far from base to support, i.e. that the bridgehead troops could not be sure of receiving adequate air cover. For the time being plans for an amphibious landing were shelved. On 26 October Clark held another conference with General Gruenther and Colonel Brann.[26] He proposed an armoured strike against XIV Panzer Korps' left flank. Tanks from the US 1st Armored Division* would attack along the Venafro-San Pietro road, move on to Highway Six, and turn the enemy's left flank. Using the secondary Venafro-San Pietro road instead of Highway Six would take the enemy by surprise. The scheme must have taken General Gruenther and Colonel Brann by surprise. The US 1st Armored Division had been caught off guard at Kasserine Pass in Tunisia. Rommel's Panzers had destroyed almost a thousand of its vehicles in a single day.[27] The Venafro-San Pietro road was overlooked by high mountains at Venafro. Its route to San Pietro zig-zagged its way through a pass with mountains on either side of it. If the 1st Armored Division tried to make its way through the pass before the high ground overlooking it had been taken, the enemy would take it out with anti-tank mines, 88s, and solid shot from heavy artillery. Presumably General Gruenther and Colonel Brann pointed this out to Clark because he dropped the scheme. The fact that he considered it at all shows how little Clark knew about handling armour – and how much he could have profited if he had accepted Eisenhower's advice and commanded a Corps in Tunisia. Truscott, who succeeded Clark as 5th Army's commander, considered that Clark lacked 'the feel of battle' that all top flight army commanders must have.[28] He lacked it because he had never handled a division or Corps in action.

The trickiest part of XIV Panzer Korps' retreat would be the realignment of its divisions and the occupation of their Mignano Gap positions. Hube had chosen excellent ones. Seen from the lower Volturno the rock 'wall' of Monte Sammucro-Monte Corno-Monte Santa Croce would give any invader food for thought. Monte Sammucro is more of a massif than a mountain. 3,953 feet high and with spurs stretching several miles, it dominates the Mignano Gap. Its eastern slopes have a string of peaks and pinnacles that would look well on a cathedral. The last thousand feet of the mountain is trackless. Its broken rock gives good cover for attacking troops but once they had taken the main peaks they would be faced with three others on its western slopes.

The Camino Massif is eight miles long and four miles wide. Its highest mountain, Monte Camino, is 3,158 feet high. Its second highest, Monte La Difensa, is 2,958 feet. The two mountains differ considerably in character. Monte Camino can be climbed relatively easily up a mule track on its south-

* There were now enough supplies to support two Allied armoured divisions in Italy.

43

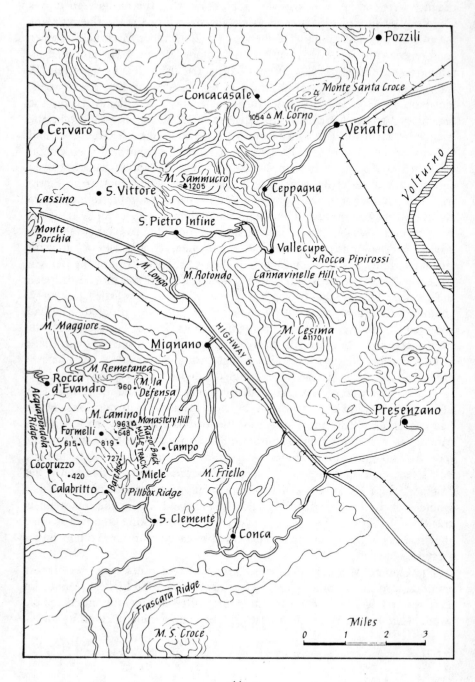

eastern face and up a path on its southern flank, and if an attack on it was made up either of these two approaches the defenders would be hard put to it to prevent an enemy reaching a plateau 700 feet below the summit. But the plateau is overlooked by a labyrinth of small peaks and ridges, as well as by the main peak. Small numbers of attacking troops would be at the mercy of the defenders above them. Only simultaneous attacks by large bodies of troops could hope to prove successful. Monte La Difensa, as its name suggests, favours its defenders even more. High up on its eastern and northern flanks there is a curving line of cliffs accessible only to trained mountaineers with ropes. There is an easy way up, a gully running down its eastern face, but no experienced troops would ever attempt to climb it. The open terrain would expose them to direct enemy fire. But if the attackers did manage to scale the cliffs and take the peak the mountain was theirs – unlike Monte Camino, Monte La Difensa has no subsidiary peaks – and they would be in a good position to attack Monte Rementea, 2,985 feet high. Once Monte Rementea had fallen an assault on the massif's remaining mountain, Monte Maggiore, 1,673 feet, would be relatively easy.

Tucked in between the Camino Massif and Monte Sammucro are two small mountains, Monte Rotondo, 1,223 feet, and Monte Lungo, 1,154 feet. They would, if necessary, act as 'last ditch' defences of the Mignano Gap. Apart from the Camino Massif and Monte Sammucro it was protected by a rolling mass of mountains to its north that culminated in the 3,872 foot Monte Cesima. Monte Cesima was the most sensitive point in Mignano Gap's defences. Not only was it the gateway to the Gap from the east but from its summit an enemy observer could overlook all the other German lines of communication and defences in the Mignano valley. Unlike the Camino Massif and Monte Sammucro, Monte Cesima has no precipitous cliffs or peaks. It's an easy climb all round the clock. Hube had emphasized the need for Monte Cesima to be thoroughly fortified. The other mountain that needed watching was Monte Corno, 3,451 feet. Its summit was split in two and its terrain did not need fortifying. But it was essential to have staunch defenders occupying it because if the Allies captured either of the two peaks they could overlook all German lines of communication, as far back as Cassino.

The occupation of XIV Panzer Korps' Mignano Gap positions would have to be carried out without Hube, who would be leaving for the Russian front on 28 October. His deputy, General Balck, would accompany him.* Westphal had recommended Lt-General von Senger as Hube's successor and Kesselring, remembering how well von Senger had done in Sicily and

---

* Hube took over command of the 2nd Panzer Army, Balck the reformed 6th Army. For Hube's remarkable career as an Army Commander see Appendix D.

elsewhere, approved the choice. When the Axis broke up von Senger had been sent to Corsica to supervise the surrender of the four Italian divisions occupying the island. The divisions refused to surrender. Using the one German regiment available – SS troops – von Senger attacked them. After a week's skirmishing the Italian Corps Commander surrendered. Von Senger received a telegram from Hitler ordering him to shoot all the Italian officers in both divisions. Like Kesselring, von Senger ignored the order. Then Corsica was invaded by the Free French. Von Senger evacuated his forces, which included 10,000 men from the Luftwaffe, to the mainland. Allied bombers harried the convoy and sunk several ships, but Hitler received a report saying that all German troops had reached the mainland safely. Hitler sent von Senger another telegram, congratulating him on the way he'd handled the evacuation, but blacklisted him for failing to obey orders to shoot the Italian officers. This didn't surprise von Senger. He had never joined the Nazi party and had little time for Hitler. He much preferred his friends in the UK. In 1912 he had won a Rhodes scholarship to Oxford. During his two years there he became deeply attached to England and Englishmen and remained an Anglophile for the rest of his life. In 1914 he returned to Germany, joined the Army and was given a temporary commission in an infantry regiment. He saw enough trench warfare to realize what infantrymen had to endure. In 1916 he was given a regular commission, promoted captain and attached to staff headquarters. After the war he transferred to the cavalry because he liked riding. Soon after Hitler came to power von Senger became a lay Benedictine. Shortly before the Second World War he was promoted Colonel and joined the General Staff. In 1940 he had himself transferred to Rommel's armoured division and commanded one of his regiments in the invasion of France. Later that year he was sent to Italy as chief German liaison officer on the Franco-Italian Armistice Commission. In 1942 he was promoted Major-General and given command of 17th Panzer Division in Russia. His Division formed part of the German attempt to break their way through the Russian 'ring' round Stalingrad. During the Russian counter-attack early in 1943 his Division formed part of the German armies' rearguard. Besides being a very good general, von Senger was something of a dreamer. When XIV Panzer Korps cracked during the Fourth battle for Cassino he did all he could to avert its destruction, then issued invitations for a final tea on the lawn of the 14th century villa he had made his headquarters. His guests were Baade, now a Major-General but still wearing his kilt, and an English fighter pilot who'd been shot down earlier in the day. Tea on the lawn. Just like Oxford.[29]

Von Vietinghoff and von Senger quickly established an excellent rapport. Von Vietinghoff remarked to his new Korps' Commander, 'You can't fight and dig defences at the same time. They don't really understand that at the top.' On or around 29 October the two generals inspected the Mignano Gap's defences. Those on the all-important Monte Cesima were hardly begun, let alone completed.* On the Camino Massif and Monte Sammucro von Senger noted 'the futility of our positions, which consisted of single strongpoints, all weak and uncoordinated'. The loss of such positions would not be so important as the loss of the shelters built near them. Von Senger knew from his experiences in Russia just how important such shelters were in winter. 'If troops are unable to find shelters they will not defend their positions well . . . they always think that conditions in the rear are bound to get better. This frame of mind is always disastrous.'[30] Ironically 10th Army engineers and the Todt workers had made an excellent job of Mignano Gap's *second* line of defences. On Monte Rotondo and Cannavinelle Hill they had constructed inter-connecting bunkers well protected with barbed wire. The sheer size of the Camino Massif and Monte Sammucro and lack of time would account for the failure to build a large network on these mountain masses, but why they had been ordered to complete the defences of Monte Rotondo and Cannavinelle Hill before starting on Monte Cesima is inexplicable.

Von Senger at once put in a priority order for dynamite, crowbars and spades – Italian ones bought on the open market. German-issue spades had proved ineffectual during the retreat, so that all infantry units in XIV Panzer Korps occupying the mountains would be able to make their own defensive positions.

During the last week of October the 15th Panzer Grenadier Division re-aligned itself in front of the Camino Massif, and the bulk of the Hermann Göring Division withdrew from the Line. 3rd Panzer Grenadiers' 8th Panzer Grenadier Regiment took over the defences of Mignano and Monte Cesima; the boundary line between them and the 29th Panzer Grenadier Regiment passed over the crest of Monte Sammucro. Each regiment considered the responsibility for defending it lay with the other. In the end a disgruntled platoon from the 29th Regiment occupied it and the 3rd Battalion, 6th Parachute Regiment, moved up to support the Division.

British 7th Armoured Division, which was advancing towards Mondragone, and British 46th Division, on their right, encountered only light rearguard opposition. As 15th Panzer Grenadier Division units opposite them retreated towards their positions on the Camino Massif the two British Divisions suddenly found they had no enemy on their front at all. By 31 October patrols from both divisions had reached the Garigliano. They reported extensive defences on the enemy's side of the river. British 56th

---

* In his report 'Fortifying the Bernhardt Line' General Bessel admits that at best only 50% of the defences were completed and in some places only 25%.

Division, which had three of their brigades – 168th, 169th and 201st – in the Line ran into much tougher opposition. But on 30 October 168th Brigade broke through 15th Panzer Grenadier divisional rearguards at Teano and chased them back to Roccamonfina, which they took on 1 November. Kesselring blamed von Senger for this 'dent' in the Line. On 2 November 168th Brigade took the 3,297 foot Monte Santa Croce (not to be confused with the mountain of the same name north east of Monte Corno) and the last of the 15th Panzer Grenadier divisional rearguards retreated towards the Camino Massif.

The two battalions already occupying the massif – III/129th Panzer Grenadiers on Monte Camino and I/104th Panzer Grenadiers on Monte La Difensa – had made good use of their 'do-it-yourself' kit. Von Senger, who visited the battalions shortly before the Allies attacked, was delighted by the way the troops had blown themselves dugouts out of the rock 'shaped like swallow nests', then covered them with railway ties/sleepers and rock. The small bunkers had a much wider field of fire than those made by General Bessel's engineers and were well coordinated.

In VI Corps Sector General Lucas was playing himself in. At Anzio the British war correspondent Wynford Vaughan-Thomas described Lucas as a 'nice old pussycat'* and entries in his diary back up the description. He was very concerned for the welfare of his men. His appreciation of 5th Army's strength at Mignano Gap was much sharper than Clark's. Clark was always worrying about German counter-attacks. Lucas was confident that, if they came, US artillery would break them up. He was right. After he had briefed his divisional generals on his plans for VI Corps' attack on Mignano Gap, and they had objected to them, he called them 'primadonnas . . . of great combat experience'. Lucas was prepared to let his generals have their head if they could persuade him they were right. His plans for the attack on Mignano Gap were straightforward. Truscott's 3rd Division was heading straight for Mignano Gap and would continue to do so. 4th Rangers would attempt to infiltrate behind the enemy lines in the 3rd Division's sector and aid its attack. US 34th and 45th Division would cross the Volturno again and attack XIV Panzer Korps' left flank. The 45th Division would take Venafro then head for the village of Pozzili, which Lucas believed to be the key point of the enemy's defences. The 34th Division would attack the villages and mountains north of Pozzili, right on the boundary between the 3rd Panzer Grenadiers and 305th Infantry Division.† (10th Army commanders were always concerned at the way both 5th and 8th Army Divisions attacked the boundaries between their divisions. They thought it inspired

* His generals called him 'Old Foxy'.
† Which Ultra decrypts had disclosed.

guess-work.) 504 Parachute Regiment would cut the Venafro-Isernia road and protect VI Corps' right flank.

The US 3rd Division began its advance into Mignano Gap on 31 October. 8th Panzer Grenadier Regiment had a desperate time trying to contain them. The 3rd Division's 15th Regiment, commanded by Lt-Colonel Ashton Manhart, swept them off the 2,000-foot mountain behind the village of Pietravairano then advanced up the Teano-Venafro road. Here they were held up by a large road block. As soon as they had captured it they were driven out by a counter-attack. It took the 15th Regiment's leading companies the rest of the day to retake the block. Both sides used the bayonet.*

On the 15th Regiment's left flank Colonel Sherman's 7th Regiment crossed Highway Six and took Monte Friello. It was not defended but the local inhabitants warned the US troops that the Germans had spent days mining the mountain. Pioneers from the 7th's 1st Battalion removed 3,000 S-mines from its slopes. The company of the 8th Panzer Grenadier Regiment defending the area retreated into another minefield nobody had warned them of and suffered a number of dead and wounded. With McCreery's permission Truscott ordered 7th Regiment to swing left into X Corps' zone of advance and attack the lower slopes of Monte La Difensa.

Von Vietinghoff had kept to Kesselring's retreat schedules most admirably. The Bernhardt positions had not been occupied until the night of 30/31 October, but fighting patrols from Lt-Colonel Manhart's 15th Regiment entered the Mignano Gap during the night of 1 November. When von Vietinghoff informed Kesselring of their presence the Field Marshal was furious. On 2 November he sent von Vietinghoff a signal addressed to 'The Commander of the 10th Army'. The signal began: 'The last two days have proved to me that the Command is not being carried out with the energy and far sightedness required by the situation. My own personal intervention was necessary to point out the shortcomings of the work on the Bernhardt positions.† In spite of my repeated observations it has not been possible up till now to develop the most important artillery positions in the manner which would have been necessary and feasible'. Kesselring went on to criticize the way the 10th Army was continuing to use units he had earmarked for Army reserve, and von Vietinghoff's failure to prevent US troops entering Mignano Gap.

Von Vietinghoff's reaction to the signal had a touch of Verdi about it. In

---

* The enemy holding the road-block may have belonged to the Hermann Göring Panzer Division. Two battalions of its III/8th Panzer Grenadier Regiment, commanded by Colonel von Corvin, were still in the line and did not withdraw to Army reserve until 1 November. Kesselring had decided to reinforce 3rd Panzer Grenadier Division with its III/8th Panzer Grenadier Regiment.[32]

† The main reasons for the 'shortcomings' was Kesselring's insistence that the Army engineers be moved to the Garigliano sector.

a long letter to Kesselring he rebutted all criticisms in considerable detail, to his own and any uninterested party's satisfaction. He then informed Kesselring he was taking six weeks' sick leave and would leave for Germany on 4 November.[31]

The III/8th Panzer Grenadier Regiment had been given the task of defending Monte Cesima. The battalion had never been in action but it was exceptionally strong – 508 rifles. The combined rifle strength of I and II/8th Panzer Grenadier Regiment totalled 447. The CO of the III battalion positioned one of his companies on the summit of Monte Cesima and placed the rest on the ridges of the eastern approaches to the mountain.[32]

During the night of 2/3 November the whole of Lt-Colonel Manhart's 15th Regiment advanced through Mignano Gap, outflanking the enemy companies round the base of Monte Cesima and forcing them to withdraw to new positions on Monte Lungo.

Communications between III/8th Panzer Grenadier Regiment and XIV Panzer Korps headquarters broke down. Von Vietinghoff spent the morning of 3 November discussing the defences of Mignano Gap with von Senger, emphasizing the importance of Monte Cesima.[33] Von Senger noted in his war diary: 'It was certainly right to hold the Bernhardt Line as long as possible, thereby gaining time for building up the Gustav Line'. It was only during the afternoon of 3 November that von Senger discovered that Monte Cesima was now held by a single company of the III/8th Panzer Grenadier Regiment. When he informed Kesselring, the Commander in Chief made scathing remarks[34] about how easily one company of troops could be 'swept away' and ordered III/6th Parachute Regiment to fight their way through to the summit of Monte Cesima. The counter-attack would go in at first light on 4 November.

Von Vietinghoff's letter arrived at Frascati on 4 November. His announcement that he was taking six weeks' sick leave must have come as a considerable shock to Kesselring. He had lost his Army Commander when he most needed him. III/6th Parachute Regiment's counter-attack had been broken up by US artillery. The battalion had taken heavy losses and was in no state to mount another attack. Von Senger had no other troops available to take III/6th Parachute Regiment's place. It was only a matter of time before Monte Cesima was captured. The way in which von Vietinghoff had answered Kesselring's strictures – his precise explanations of why things had not gone according to plan, explanations that Kesselring had not waited to hear – made Kesselring belatedly aware that his Army Commander was much better informed than he had been. Instead of sacking von Vietinghoff for what was clearly a diplomatic illness, Kesselring informed OKW that his Army Commander was taking sick leave and asked for the best available

5. Monte Camino. The left-hand ridge is Bare Arse and culminates in Point 727. Point 819 and its 'twin' are further to the right. Razorback begins below the right-hand point. The first pimple is Pip, the second Squeak, the third Wilfred. The peak on the extreme right is Monastery Hill.

6. Frascara Ridge. General Templer is explaining his plan of attack on Monte Camino to General Truscott. General McCreery is standing on the right.

7. German mortar bombs exploding on Bare Arse ridge. Photo taken from near Calabritto.

8. A private from a British patrol releasing a carrier pigeon. It is on its way back to Battalion HQ. In the mountains carrier pigeons were much more reliable than wireless sets.

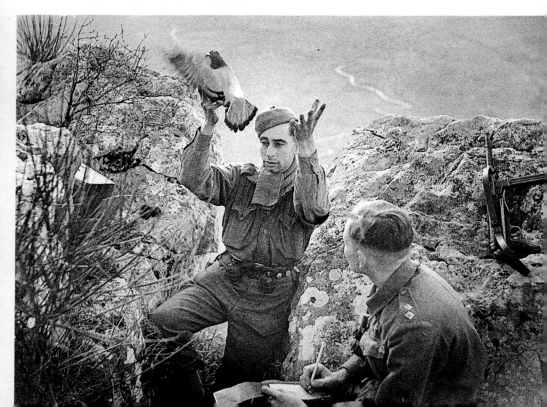

general to act as 10th Army's temporary commander. In the meantime Kesselring took over command of the Army himself.*

During the night of 4/5 November the company of the 8th Panzer Grenadier Regiment defending Monte Cesima slipped through the US 3rd Division's lines and joined the rest of their battalion on Monte Lungo.†

The loss of Monte Cesima sent shock waves through the whole of 10th Army. When General Wentzell rang Westphal and told him that the paratroopers attack had failed, Westphal exclaimed, '*Mein Gott!*' 'Yes, even the most aggressive troops fail sometimes,' Wentzell remarked. Wentzell's conversation with Colonel von Bonin, von Senger's Chief of Staff, went as follows. Colonel von Bonin: 'How the position was lost is unknown to Graeser'. Wentzell: 'It must be investigated to see if those people fought at all. I'm under the impression they have all stopped fighting.' Colonel von Bonin: 'That's highly possible'.[35]

Later that morning, 4 November, XIV Panzer Korps' headquarters had another shock. 4th Rangers appeared at the bottom of Cannavinelle Hill like dragons' teeth springing up overnight. With the aid of Italian guides the Rangers had infiltrated the enemy lines and were preparing to attack the mountain, held by II/8th Panzer Grenadier Regiment. German fighting patrols from other units who were sent to sort out the Rangers suffered heavy losses. At 11 am the Rangers attacked Cannavinelle Hill. They soon discovered that they were up against a resolute enemy in well-prepared positions. When they were half way up the mountain the Panzer Grenadiers counter-attacked and forced the Rangers to retreat, but not before they had killed or wounded thirty of the enemy. The Rangers dug in at the bottom of the mountain. They had lost seven men killed, nineteen wounded and twenty-two missing. Known enemy dead totalled forty-two.[36]

On the night of 3/4 November the US 34th and 45th Divisions had crossed the Volturno for the last time. The 179th Regiment, 45th Division, drove back elements of III Battalion, 6th Parachute Regiment, who were having a bad day, in front of Venafro, brushed aside opposition in the town, then took to their vehicles and raced up the Venafro-Pozzili road. In Pozzili they took out several Spandaus, then charged the battalion of the 29th Panzer Grenadier Regiment who were defending the hill overlooking the village. Von Senger, who happened to be visiting the battalion, was impressed by the way the US troops pressed home their attack. They were no longer afraid of hand-to-hand fighting, as they had been in Sicily. But as the Panzer Grenadiers withdrew from the hill and von Senger headed back to his

---

* Lt-General Joachim Lemelsen, who had commanded a Panzer Korps in Russia, replaced von Vietinghoff on 6 November.
† on Monte Cesima.

headquarters at Roccasecca he knew that XIV Panzer Korps was in trouble.[37] Lucas had been correct in assuming that Pozzili was the key point in the Korps' left wing, and there were no other troops between Pozzili and Cassino. Back at Roccasecca von Senger discovered that the situation was much graver than he'd realized. The US 34th Division had turned the flank of the 305th Division, just as Lucas had hoped it would. The 34th and 45th Divisions could now mountaineer their way to Cassino, assisted by 504 Parachute Regiment, who had entered Isernia without meeting any opposition. Von Senger contacted Kesselring and informed him that XIV Panzer Korps' left flank was wide open. Kesselring at once ordered Major General Count von Lüttwitz to switch his 26th Panzer Division from the Adriatic sector to Mignano Gap. The 29th Panzers were the best armoured division in Italy. And it possessed two Panzer Grenadier Regiments. It could, and did, turn its reconnaissance battalion into infantry as well. Its leading Panzer Grenadier Regiment reached the Pozzili sector in the late afternoon of 5 November. They at once counter-attacked. The attack was broken up by US artillery but by the following morning the 26th Panzers had seven infantry battalions in the line. The crisis on XIV Panzer Korps' left flank was over. Von Senger could concentrate on the one building up in its centre.

Late on 4 November a patrol from 1st Battalion, US 15th Regiment reported Monte Cesima clear of the enemy. Forward observers who took up positions on top of Monte Cesima reported that they could see for miles. XIV Panzer Korps centre's second line of defences – Monte Lungo, Monte Rotondo, San Pietro – was open to inspection, as were the enemy's lines of communications. Clark and Truscott went up Monte Cesima to see things for themselves. Clark, still looking for ways of using his armour, noted the 'flat lands' beyond San Pietro – 'flatter lands' would have been more like it – and decided that San Pietro was the key to the enemy defences. It would have to be taken before he could use his tanks. So would Monte Rotondo and Monte Lungo. Truscott, whose 15th Regiment had discovered that Cannavinelle Hill had also been abandoned by the enemy, saw Monte Rotondo as the enemy's second Monte Cesima, its one surviving barrier to stop his division's advance. Truscott decided to use his 15th Regiment to take Monte Rotondo and Monte Lungo and then unleash his 30th Regiment, back in reserve, to exploit the breakthrough. He put the plan to Lucas later that day and Lucas approved it. But as Truscott was setting things in motion, briefing Colonel Manhart for an attack on the two mountains on 6 November, Clark also visited Lucas's headquarters. Lucas told him that Truscott was preparing to attack Monte Rotondo and Monte Lungo, but not that he planned to use the 30th Regiment to exploit any breakthrough. Clark suggested simultaneous attacks – the 15th Division approaching from the south east and the 180th Regiment, 45th Division from the north-east.

Lucas, who wanted to use the 180th Regiment to attack Monte Corno and Monte Santa Croce, suggested that Truscott's 30th Regiment should be bussed round to the 180th's sector and carry out a simultaneous attack with the 15th Regiment and Clark agreed to the change of plans.[38] When Lucas rang Truscott to tell him the news Truscott realized from Lucas's nervous tone of voice that something was wrong. Lucas told him that Clark had decided on simultaneous attacks and that he had ordered the 30th Regiment to be bussed round to 180th Regiment's sector. Truscott was distraught. He reminded Lucas that he had approved his plans for the 30th Regiment and that Clark's plan would wreck his division's chances of exploiting any breakthrough. He asked permission to plead his case with Clark. Lucas said, 'That would put me in a helluva position'. It certainly would have. Truscott, who never discovered that it was Lucas who had queered his pitch and not Clark, had to accept the fact that his plans 'were all shot'. But he pointed out to Lucas that it would take at least forty-eight hours to mount simultaneous attacks on Monte Rotondo. The need to keep up the pressure on the enemy was paramount. Truscott asked Lucas to let him attack Monte Rotondo on 6 November, using one battalion from the 30th Regiment, whilst a battalion from 15th Regiment tackled Monte Lungo. Lucas agreed to the plans. On the night of 5/6 November the 30th Regiment was bussed round to the 180th Regiment's sector. There would be no time for them to reconnoitre Monte Rotondo before they attacked it, something Truscott was bitter about even before his men went in.[39] After a run-of-the-mill support barrage the 2nd Battalion, 30th Regiment attacked the mountain on the morning of 6 November. The battalion defending Monte Rotondo – II/8th Regiment Panzer Grenadiers – called for DF. It was the heaviest the US troops had ever encountered but they kept going. There was a touch of the Somme about the attack. When the GIs closed with the enemy they found them in deep inter-connecting dugouts protected by uncut barbed wire. After suffering heavy casualties from small arms fire they broke. The 1st Battalion, 15th Regiment's attack on Monte Lungo was equally unsuccessful.*

At nightfall, as both US Regimental Commanders were planning further attacks and the 2nd Battalion, 30th Regiment were sleeping things off near the LOD a strong enemy fighting patrol made its way down Monte Rotondo. After cutting the 2nd Battalion's communications wire they slipped past some dozy sentries and shot up men asleep in their bivouacs. They then

* There are no After Action reports on the 30th Regiment's action on Monte Rotondo, and no detailed casualty reports. But 5th Army casualties for 6 November list 65 men killed in action, 276 wounded and 29 missing. All US Divisions except the US 3rd Division were on the defensive. Nearly all the casualties would have come from its regiments, and most from the 2nd Battalion, 30th Regiment.

withdrew. But the patrol had by no means finished with the 30th Regiment. Its 1st Battalion was occupying Cannavinelle Hill. The enemy patrol, who knew the exact lay of the land, moved up the mountain, crept past some more sleepy sentries, then used up their ammunition on other doughboys sleeping in their bivouacs. Such a magnificent raid shows what the 3rd Panzer Grenadier Division was capable of at its best. All honour to the men who made it. Staff officers like Colonel von Bonin were ignorant in more ways than one.

The failure of the attacks on Monte Rotondo and Monte Lungo, the retributions exacted by the enemy, and intelligence reports quoting first-hand descriptions of the enemy's defences on Monte Rotondo, brought home to Truscott what the regiments were up against. He told Lucas he would need very heavy artillery support for his second attack on Monte Rotondo. Three battalions of divisional artillery would be nothing like enough. He wanted six battalions of 155 MM and two battalions of Corps 240 mm. Truscott, at his most demanding,* was a hard man to argue with. Lucas agreed to his requests. Truscott, still not happy about simultaneous attacks on Monte Rotondo – one of his battalions could end up shooting the other – said he still wished to use the 30th Regiment to attack Monte Rotondo whilst the 15th Regiment dealt with Monte Lungo. Lucas agreed to let him do so.

By now Lucas had realized that his 34th and 45th Divisions had broken through the enemy front at Pozzili on 4 November. In a diary entry of 6 November he attributes the failure of the divisions to exploit their break-through to 'too few and too tired troops'. He had yet to learn that it had been the arrival of the 26th Panzers that had prevented his divisions mountaineering their way to Cassino. In an afterthought to his 6 November entry† he remarks that the stalemate that followed 'allowed the Germans to develop the Cassino defences into ones of formidable strength'. It was not inappropriate that the order confirming Kesselring as Supreme Commander came through on 6 November. Hitler sent Rommel to supervise the building of the Atlantic Wall.

At 8.45 am on 8 November 98 guns opened up on Monte Rotondo. The barrage lasted a quarter of an hour. The shells from the 240 mm dented the

---

* When his division was in full cry after the crossing of the Volturno Lucas ordered him to halt until the US 34th Division was abreast of the 3rd. Truscott, seeing his chances of outflanking XIV Panzer Korps slip away, told Lucas his divisions 'could take Berlin' if only Lucas would leave it alone. 'This was a rash statement', Lucas noted in his diary.

† On the same day Lucas and Clark left VI Corps HQ near Venafro to have a look at the 'castle walls' of Monte Sammucro, Monte Corno and Monte Santa Croce. Lucas noticed that Clark seemed 'quite overcome at the ruggedness of the terrain and the fact that the enemy were looking down our throats'. This was the area through which Clark had wanted the 1st US Armored Division to advance.

enemy's strongpoints and made gaps in the barbed wire protecting them. The 2nd and 3rd Battalions, 30th Infantry made the most of their chances. By 9.20 they had fought their way to the summit. If they could hold on to it there was still a good chance of Truscott being able to drive through XIV Panzer Korps' centre. The 3rd Battalion, 15th Regiment's attack on Monte Lungo only secured a toehold on it and lost a number of prisoners. 'Those people' Wentzell and Colonel von Bonin had condemned were proving their worth to General Graeser, if nobody else in XIV Panzer Korps.

Chapter III

First Time Up

On the Camino Massif the 7th Regiment, US 3rd Division, was preparing to mount an attack on Monte La Difensa. By 4 November it had cleared the enemy from the lower slopes of the mountain and its patrols were reconnoitring routes to the summit, trying to find a way round Monte La Difensa's cliffs, and testing its defences. Although the 7th Regiment had whipped elements of the Hermann Göring Division at the Volturno and Colonel Sherman had been singled out for special praise on the way he had handled the regiment's advance on the Winter Line, he never underestimated the ingenuity of the German infantry, particularly when they were in prepared positions. Instead of mounting a one-battalion attack on Monte La Difensa, Colonel Sherman intended a simultaneous attack by two battalions, one coming in from the east, the other from the north. The attacks would go in on the night of 6 November.

On the British 56th Division's front a patrol from 168th Brigade's leading battalion, 1st London Irish, reached the south-eastern approaches to Monte Camino on the evening of 4 November. There was a mule track leading up a corrie. This looked to be an excellent route to the summit, difficult to defend in depth, but the patrol reported that the track was impassable.

Clark had been receiving reports of extensive demolitions around the perimeter of Cassino. The enemy were clearing the decks prior to fortifying the town. Speed was more essential than ever if 5th Army was to reach Cassino before its defences were really strong. US VI Corps had made remarkable gains on the Army's right flank and in the Mignano Gap. Colonel Sherman's 7th Regiment was already moving up Monte La Difensa, while the British 56th Division appeared to be lagging behind. McCreery told Clark that the easiest route up Monte Camino was blocked. 56th Division would need time to find another route up the mountain and to probe the enemy's defences. Clark said there was no time for that and ordered McCreery to time his attack on Monte Camino for the night of 6 November, the same night that Colonel Sherman's 7th Regiment was to launch their attack on Monte La Difensa.

On 5 November McCreery told General Templer to plan 56th Division's attack for the following night. There would be no time for patrols. Both generals believed Monte Camino would be strongly defended by the enemy. X Corps' and British 56th Division's intelligence reports for the period are sketchy. They must have relied heavily on Ultra decrypts, Y Force reports and 5th Army Intelligence for providing details of the enemy's strength, whereabouts and identification. During the first week of November there were no Ultra decrypts that concerned the Camino Massif, Y Force was not yet in position below the Massif and 5th Army Intelligence concentrated all its reports on the enemy facing the US divisions and on the enemy activities around Cassino. On 5 November British 56th Division Intelligence reported that civilians had said Monte Camino was 'lightly held'. Civilian reports were often accurate. This particular report was so inaccurate that it seems probable that it referred to the wide open spaces leading to the Garigliano, to the south of Monte Camino. When 201st (Guards) Brigade was briefed for the attack and told that Monte Camino was 'lightly defended' they had one word for the report: Horseshoe.

Early on 5 November 201st (Guards) Brigade had moved down the slopes of Monte Santa Croce and taken up positions on Frascara Ridge, looking on to Monte Camino. The ridge was about four miles from Monte Camino's summit. Later that morning McCreery, General Templer and Brigadier Gascoigne walked through 6th Grenadiers' position. Lieutenant Michael Wheatley, a platoon commander in 3 Company, 6th Grenadiers, watched them come and go. Such a clutch of 'senior commanders spying out the land was always a bad sign'.[1]

That afternoon Colonel Hugh Kingsmill, CO 6th Grenadiers, held an 'O' group on the ridge. 6th Grenadiers, four companies strong, would lead the brigade's assault on Monte Camino. He told his company commanders and other senior officers that there would be no time to probe the enemy's defences or to reconnoitre a route up the mountain. As the mule-track up the corrie had been reported impassable, the battalion's attack would have to go in elsewhere. Colonel Kingsmill and his officers had a good look at Monte Camino through binoculars. There were only two feasible routes up it – one along a very long and exposed ridge on its southern approaches, the other up a ridge to the north-east of the corrie. Although this second ridge led right up to the base of Monte Camino's peak it was too jagged for Colonel Kingsmill's liking. He called it Razorback and the long exposed ridge Bare Arse. The Grenadiers would assault Monte Camino up Bare Arse. Just below Monte Camino's pyramid-shaped peak there was a small monastery.* Colonel Kingsmill called the peak Monastery Hill. Between Pt 727, Bare

* It turned out to be a chapel.

Arse's summit, and Monastery Hill there were twin peaks, Pt 819 and another very close to it. Colonel Kingsmill decided that his battalion should aim at securing Pt 727 and Pt 819 peaks. To attempt to take Monastery Hill as well would be asking too much of his battalion. Monastery Hill would be pinched out. Once the battalion had secured its objectives 2nd Battalion Scots Guards would pass through it and take Pt 648, behind Pt 819. 167th and 168th Brigades would then take up the attack. The 3rd Battalion, Coldstream would attack the village of Calabritto, near the base of Bare Arse, at dusk so as to secure the Grenadiers' left flank. They were scheduled to take it at 20.00 hours. Once they had done so 6th Grenadiers would move on to Bare Arse and begin the assault. South of the Camino Massif the 46th Division would carry out a feint attack at the Garigliano, with the object of drawing off some of the enemy in the area of the Massif. Colonel Kingsmill told his officers that greatcoats would be left at Battalion's HQ. Although the previous night had been very cold, Colonel Kingsmill had decided that his men would have their work cut out getting to Pt 727 before daylight without being clobbered with greatcoats. It was a shrewd decision. Colonel Kingsmil's assessment of 6th Grenadiers' assault at Monte Camino had the hallmark of a man who knew his job very well indeed.

As Colonel Kingsmill was returning to his headquarters his jeep drove over a small cliff. Although no bones were broken he was too badly shaken to continue in command. The Grenadiers' second-in-command, Major Sir Hugh Cholmeley, took over. The accident was doubly unfortunate. The Grenadiers were deprived of an excellent CO and those officers and Guardsmen who believed in omens found this an exceedingly bad one, almost as bad as the 'lightly held' intelligence report. Guardsman W. Chadwick, 2nd Scots Guards, taken prisoner at Salerno, where he won the DCM, had escaped from POW camp near Cassino. He had rejoined the battalion on 2 November. His description of how the enemy were geligniting themselves into the solid rock in and around Monte Camino was 'illuminating'. A friend of Lieutenant Wheatley from 2nd Scots Guards, Lieutenant David Fyfe-Jamieson, MC paid him a visit. 'You've had it,' he told Wheatley. 3 Company Grenadier platoon officers 'were, as usual, in excellent heart and being frightfully funny', Lieutenant Wheatley noted. 'But they knew a blood bath was imminent.' Guardsman Len Sarginson, 19, who joined 6th Grenadiers after Salerno and was now in Lieutenant Wheatley's platoon, summed up Monte Camino as 'steep solid rock leading God knows where'.[2]

At midday on 6 November a volunteer patrol from 3rd Coldstream reconnoitred the route to Calabritto. It spotted enemy pillboxes on a ridge at the base of Bare Arse. At dusk the 3rd Coldstream set off for Calabritto and Pillbox Ridge in single file. A heavy support barrage was going down on Calabritto. When 4 Company reached Pillbox Ridge they were held up by

Spandaus. Their leading platoon dealt with two of them but reported that a third was on the edge of a pit. They couldn't get at the crew. The battalion mortar officer, Lieutenant P. H. Wyld, filled his haversack with grenades and dealt with the Spandaus. Another of 4 Company's platoons advancing along the road to Calabritto ran into an anti-personnel mine field. They lost their officer and a number of men badly wounded. The rest of the platoon shot up an enemy section close to the minefield and took a prisoner. A German-speaking NCO told him to show them an unmined route to Calabritto. When he refused to do so the NCO jabbed him in the back with a bayonet. The German changed his mind, but the safe way to Calabritto 'entailed a dreadful climb through dense undergrowth and past enormous rock boulders.' Fires started in the undergrowth by the enemy or the shelling quickly spread 'until the long line of the company became clearly silhouetted to form admirable targets for enemy Spandaus'. And the route 4 Company was taking was 'all round the houses', the long way to Calabritto. 4 Company's advance fell behind schedule. 2 Company, advancing along the road, had not been warned about the minefield. They walked straight into it. Their advance stopped altogether.[3]

Major Sir Hugh Cholmeley and 6th Grenadiers, who were following the attack from the valley between Frascara Ridge and Monte Camino and noting just where the exchange of small arms fire was taking place, as well as the bush fire blazing at the foot of Bare Arse, realized that the attack was falling behind schedule. At 21.30 hours Major Cholmeley decided he could not afford to wait any longer. Better to risk losing men on the approach march to Bare Arse than for the battalion to be caught on it in daylight. After the company commanders had aligned their men in single file Major Cholmeley led them across country to Bare Arse. They reached it at 22.30 hours. Once the battalion began climbing the track leading up the ridge they were silhouetted by the flames from the burning undergrowth. Major Cholmeley ordered the battalion to leave the track and climb up Bare Arse's eastern flank. The Grenadiers found themselves in the same 'boulder country' as the Coldstream had encountered. The stones were scattered around like pebbles on a beach. In places the Grenadiers could squeeze between them. Often they had to climb over them. They were 'as big as a house' in Guardsman Sarginson's memory. As he and the rest of the battalion forced their way over and through them Sarginson lost all sense of time. The boulders seemed to go on for ever. When the Grenadiers did finally get clear of them they found themselves wading ankle deep in shale on a sloping ridge. The angle of the ridge, the shale, and the weight of the Guards' equipment made it very hard for them to keep their feet. They kept on falling over. It took the battalion an hour to cover a quarter of a mile. Sarginson's mind became numb. His legs seemed to keep going of their own accord. He heard his platoon sergeant, 'Topper' Brown, shouting encouragement. 'Well done, lads! Keep it up, lads!' The Guards were making so much noise that it was pointless to try and maintain the usual silence on an approach march. Sarginson remembered his company commander, Major Thomas Cook's own particular war cry. 'Lead on my warriors!' The overwhelming relief that Sarginson felt when his company halted for a rest was blotted out by the physical and emotional pain of starting up again. The Grenadiers' officers, whose equipment was quite light, had something else to worry about. They knew their men were marching as fast as they possibly could, but would it be fast enough for the whole of the battalion to reach Pt 727 before daylight? And what sort of state would the Guardsmen be in when they reached Pt 727? The prospect of their men having to go straight into an attack after such a terrible forced march dismayed them. And the sound of their support barrage going down on Pts 727 and 819 when they were only about three-quarters of the way up Bare Arse rubbed things in. They would have to attack without any support at all.

The battalion's order of march was 4, 3, 2, 1, HQ Companies. 4 Company would attack Pt 727. 3 and 2 Companies would pass through them and make simultaneous attacks – 2 Company on Pt 819 and its twin peak, 3 Company on a small wood at the base and slightly to the east of the two peaks. 4 Company would then secure the head of the corrie, where Razorback linked up with Monastery Hill. 1 Company would be in reserve.

4 Company reached Pt 727 at 05.30 hours. It was not defended. At 06.30 3 Company's leading platoon, Lieutenant Wheatley's, caught up with 4 Company. The rest of 3 Company 'straggled out for about 750 yards'. Its second platoon reached Pt 727 at first light. Spandaus on Razorback opened up on its third platoon and Company HQ, pinning them down. Captain Ralph Howard, OC 2 Company, re-routed his men and arrived at Pt 727 ahead of 3 Company's third platoon and Company HQ. It was now dawn.* Spandaus were firing from Monastery Hill as well as Razorback. To wait for the rest of 3 Company to catch up was out of the question. Lieutenant Wheatley, whose platoon had flushed out three of the enemy – 'like a grouse drive' – had a quick word with Captain Howard. The two companies deployed in open formation, then charged across a quarter of a mile of open ground. Lieutenant Wheatley's men found their objective undefended. As they built themselves sangars or dug slit-trenches – in most places the ground was too rocky to dig – they kept an eye on 2 Company charging up the bushy slopes of Pt 819 and the smaller peak. Captain Howard's men went in very quickly, making full use of the cover provided by the bushes.

---

* The Coldstream were storming Calabritto. They took 18 prisoners. The operation had cost them 7 killed and 15 wounded.

The way they raced up the slopes rattled the enemy, who fired wildly. 2 Company took both peaks at a cost of one officer mortally wounded, Lieutenant Grenville Cholmondley, and two guardsmen slightly wounded. But once on the summit 2 Company came under intense fire from Monastery Hill, Razorback, and Pt 819's rear slope. Guardsman Alan Phillips, who was sharing a slit trench with two German wounded POWs, was more concerned with his own field of fire. There were bushes growing a few yards in front of his trench. If the enemy counter-attacked they'd be on top of him before he could open fire.

The enemy did counter-attack. Lieutenant Wheatley heard Brens firing, and the crunch of a DF barrage falling on the enemy held slopes. 2 Company had the battalion's artillery forward observer with them. Some time later Captain Howard walked into the wood. He told Lieutenant Wheatley that 2 Company only had about thirty men left. Lieutenant Wheatley at once ordered 3 Company's second platoon, under Sergeant Young, to go to 2 Company's assistance. It was the last he saw of the platoon. Some walking wounded from 2 Company came in. One of them, Lieutenant Rodney Wace, had been shot in the chest and had lost two fingers. Major Cook and the remainder of 3 Company arrived in the wood soon afterwards. As Major Cook went to confer with Captain Howard a burst of Spandau mortally wounded Major Cook and smashed Captain Howard's left knee cap. Another burst from the same Spandau killed two guardsmen from 3 Company HQ and severely wounded two others. Captain Whatman, 3 Company's second-in-command, survived the massacre because he had been 'caught short'. By the time he arrived in the wood the Spandau had temporarily ceased firing.

Back at Pt 727 4 Company deployed for their advance on the head of the corrie. But the intensity of fire from Razorback and Monastery Hill – heavy mortars as well as heavy Spandaus – pinned them down. Major Cholmeley, who was at Battalion Tac HQ just below Pt 727, with 1 Company alongside, ordered 4th Company to make themselves temporary positions on Pt 727. This wasn't necessary. Pt 727 was honeycombed with caves and 4th Company moved into them.

Captain Howard contacted Major Cholmeley by wireless – there had been no chance to lay down signals cable* and establish contact by phone – and told him that his combined force was coming under fire from Pt 819 as well as Razorback and Monastery Hill. 2 Company was in danger of being overrun. He also informed Major Cholmeley that Major Cook had been killed and he himself wounded. 3rd Company was now under his command.

Major Cholmeley phoned Brigadier Gascoigne. The Brigade Commander promised to send up the 2nd Battalion Scots Guards to Pt 727 as soon as it

* US 'wire'.

was dark. In the meantime it was essential that Pt 819 be held. Brigadier Gascoigne alerted the Scots Guards and they prepared to climb up Bare Arse that night – 7/8 November. But early in the afternoon there was a cloudburst. The ground in the valley below Monte Camino was turned into a quagmire. Major Cholmeley had told Brigadier Gascoigne the difficulties the Grenadiers had encountered on Bare Arse. The brigade commander, afraid that the downpour would make another ascent even more difficult and that the Scots Guards might be caught on Bare Arse in daylight, postponed the move up the ridge for twenty-four hours. By one of those quirks of fate that decide battles the order to postpone the march up Bare Arse never reached F Company, Scots Guards. Led by their commander, Major H. N. S. Rathbone, the company set off up Bare Arse as soon as it was dark. It was three officers and one hundred and five guardsmen strong. They carried only four boxes of rations instead of the usual ten. (The remaining six boxes were on their way with the order to postpone the march up Bare Arse.) Although the company was wearing greatcoats Captain Richard Coke, MC, second-in-command, noted that the north wind cut through them like a knife. Then came the boulders. 'One had to choose each foothold and sometimes climb with hands and knees. It was necessary to have frequent rests. 200 yards or so was as much as we could manage at a time.'[4]

In the wood below Pt 819 the combined force of 3 and 2 Companies were being harried by German patrols. They withdrew at first light. Lieutenant Wheatley then made his own check of those 'present and correct' and the force's casualties. Within the perimeter of the Guards ring of defences there were three unwounded officers and about sixty guardsmen, a number of whom were wounded. Three officers had been killed, two severely wounded. Guardsmen killed and missing totalled one hundred and twenty. The missing included the Guards forward observer. The Grenadiers in the wood would be unable to call on any artillery support.

Major Cholmeley must have been relieved as well as surprised when F Company, Scots Guards arrived at his Tac HQ. He ordered Major Rathbone to take up temporary positions behind Pt 727 and join the Grenadiers in the wood as soon as it was dark. Once there F Company would, if necessary, retake Pt 819. F Company made themselves sangars then finished off the four boxes of rations.

At 1600 hours Captain Howard reported that the handful of Grenadiers holding onto Pt 819 had probably been overrun.* He also said his force was

---

* The Grenadier Guards history has it that Pt 819 was held throughout the action fought on Monte Camino. Lieutenant Wheatley's manuscript and 15th Panzer Grenadier Division's daily reports make it clear that Pt 819 was recaptured on 7 November. F Company Scots Guards After Action report makes it equally clear that all organized resistance on the twin peaks had ceased by the time the company joined the Grenadiers' ring.

taking casualties from mortars and Spandaus. Shortly afterwards the wireless went dead.

When Major Cholmeley contacted Brigadier Gascoigne the brigade commander said that Pt 819 and its adjoining peak must be retaken 'at all costs'. The rest of 2nd Battalion Scots Guards would climb Bare Arse that night. Major Cholmeley, worried about his men having no greatcoats – it had been near freezing during the night – asked if they could be portered up at the same time as the Scots Guards climbed Bare Arse. Brigadier Gascoigne said that the Basuto porters would only be able to carry up food, water and ammunition. He'd try and find other porters for the greatcoats. There were none available. General Templer ordered 169th (Queen's) Brigade, who were resting fifteen miles behind the line, to provide a battalion to porter up the Guards' greatcoats. These arrived on Monte Camino on the night of 9/10 November.

At 1800 hours on 8 November F Company Scots Guards set off for the Grenadiers' wood, accompanied by stretcher bearers carrying rations. When the party arrived it was just light enough for Captain Coke to see the Grenadiers' ring of sangars. The stretcher bearers returned to Pt 727 carrying Lieutenant Wace and some severely wounded guardsmen. Although Captain Howard's wound was causing him great pain, he refused to be evacuated. He told Major Rathbone that several of 2 Company's wounded, including one officer, had had to be left behind on Pt 819. Major Rathbone said he would send out a patrol to try and find them. He added that his company would not attack Pt 819 until it had some sleep. Its positions near Pt 727 had been continuously mortared. All enemy mortaring had now ceased. Their Spandaus had also stopped firing. As the Scots Guards mingled with the Grenadiers, Captain Howard had the rations shared out amongst the Grenadiers. Major Rathbone told Captain Howard that F Company had had nothing to eat for twelve hours. Captain Howard said there were only enough rations for the Grenadiers.[5]

Major Rathbone scheduled F Company's attack for 04.15 hours the next morning (9 November). Because the Scots Guards were going into the attack there was no need for them to build themselves sangars. While Lieutenant Fyfe-Jamieson went out on a patrol to Pt 819 to test its defences as well as look for the Grenadiers wounded, the rest of the Scots Guards got what sleep they could. When Lieutenant Fyfe-Jamieson returned he reported that his patrol had been unable to find any of the Grenadiers wounded and that Pt 819 was strongly held. He spent the night in Lieutenant Wheatley's slit trench and was 'his usual amusing self'.

When F Company's officers and NCOs began assembling their men for the attack it was too dark to tell Scots Guards from Grenadiers. The attack was postponed until dawn. In the meantime Captain Coke took out another patrol to Pt 819 to find the best route up it. The more cover the better. The patrol was fired on by several Spandaus at the base of Pt 819. The enemy had moved down the peak in the night.

At first light Major Rathbone told Captain Howard that, while his men were prepared to attack Pt 819 in daylight, he would not order them to make the attack until they had had something to eat. As the two officers were arguing a Spandau opened up from close range.[6] Other Spandaus began firing from the summit of Pt 819 and Monastery Hill. There was no longer any question of F Company making an attack. Major Rathbone had to align his men in and around the Grenadiers' ring. All the Guards stood to, the Grenadiers in sangars and slit trenches, nearly all the Scots Guards out in the open. Three sections of them were covering the Grenadiers' right flank. Captain Coke, who was lucky enough to be sharing a sangar with Captain Howard, made a very exact appreciation of the lay of the land. Guards' wood was on a slope. 'The position held was about the highest part of the wood, the ground very rocky.' The rocks built up to a small crest facing Monastery Hill as well as Pt 819. 'This meant that the ground immediately behind the crest was dead. The enemy could operate there unseen. The field of fire was limited in most cases to between twenty and thirty yards.' Spandaus found gaps in the crest and began firing at point blank range. The Guards returned the fire with Brens and rifles. Between 0800 and 0900 hours Guards' wood was heavily mortared. When the barrage lifted the enemy counter-attacked from the direction of Monastery Hill and Razorback. They overran the three sections of Scots Guards outside the ring. Elsewhere they were held. Major Rathbone, deeply concerned for his men, went round to the right flank of the ring to reorganize their position. As he did so he was hit in the chest and mortally wounded. At about the same time Lieutenant Fyfe-Jamieson got a bullet through the thigh. 'A clean flesh wound,' Lieutenant Wheatley noted. 'He took it as you would expect him to, a few muttered curses but otherwise not a word.' Lieutenant Wheatley was under friendly surveillance from Guardsman Sarginson, who had built himself a sangar next to Lieutenant Wheatley's slit trench. Sarginson had taken part in several attacks but this was the first time he'd been under attack himself. He was glad of Lieutenant Wheatley's lively presence.

The enemy's capture of the ground which had been defended by the three sections of Scots Guards added to the pressure on the ring. The enemy now had additional dead ground to operate in. More Spandaus opened up at point blank range. Firing back at them with Brens was good for morale but not much else. The only way the Guards could get at the unseen enemy was to use platoon 2″ mortars. These were pretty ineffectual weapons – their bombs had less lethal fragmentation than '36' grenades – but they could at least land bombs on the ground held by the enemy. Guardsman 'NAAFI' Hollis, 3 Company, was firing a 2" mortar with his mate, Guardsman George Beale. Beale was a bit of a recluse. When his section went out drinking he stayed behind to mend their socks and bone up their best boots. Hollis had three bombs left when a Scots Guardsman next to his sangar, who was also firing a 2" mortar, shouted out that he was out of bombs. Could Hollis spare any? Before Hollis could answer Guardsman Beale jumped up shouting, 'Those things are no fucking use!' He clambered out of the sangar waving his entrenching tool. 'I'm going to get the bastards with this!' he yelled. As he charged towards the crest he was shot by a Spandau. As he fell Hollis saw two mortar bombs land right beside him. Hollis ducked. When he looked up he was horrified to see there was no trace of Beale's body. It had literally been blown to bits.[7]

At around midday a second enemy counter-attack came in, from Pt 819 as well as Monastery Hill and Razorback. Making skilful use of the dead ground, the enemy infantry closed up behind the Spandaus firing through the gaps in the crest and began pelting the Guards with grenades. Fragments from them wounded Lieutenant Wheatley in one eye, blinded his batman in both eyes and temporarily blinded Lieutenant Fyfe-Jamieson. An English-speaking officer or NCO shouted at the Guards to surrender. A Grenadier officer yelled out, 'Any man who attempts to surrender will get detention!' A Guardsman in a sangar close to the enemy put his hands up. Lieutenant Wheatley shouted, 'Give the buggers hell!' and flung two grenades at the enemy. The Guards, cheering loudly, threw more grenades. The screams from behind the crests showed they had found their target. Captain Coke expected the enemy to come again. He was doubtful if the Guards could withstand a third attack: 'Our men very thin on the ground', and those still on their feet had used up most of the ammunition and grenades. Lieutenant Wheatley was equally doubtful if the Guards could cope with another attack. He reckoned the Scots Guards, caught in the open, had lost about 50% of their men. He had a word with Lieutenant John Brocklebank, another of 3rd Company's platoon commanders, who was in the slit trench next to his. Lieutenant Brocklebank didn't answer. He continued to stare at the crest. For a moment Wheatley thought he was shell-shocked. Then he saw he'd been shot through the head. A little later, when the enemy mortars opened up again, Wheatley saw a guardsman in his platoon get a direct hit from a bomb. 'His right leg was smashed but still joined to him by a piece of trouser and bone, and lay beside him on the parapet of his slit trench and when he saw it he went off his head. Thank God he died before the hour was out.' Captain Howard's right knee was smashed by another bomb. Using the Scots Guards' 69 wireless set Captain Howard told Cholmeley that the situation was critical and asked for reinforcements, ammunition, grenades, food and water. Major Cholmeley promised to send them up as soon as it was dark.

The attack that Captain Coke and Lieutenant Wheatley dreaded never materialized. Captain Coke thought that the enemy* had 'probably had enough'. This may well have been true but the dead ground that had proved so advantageous to the enemy also posed a severe hazard. The invisible enemy infantry who had got close enough to throw grenades had kept their heads down for a very good reason. If they attempted to charge over the crest they would have popped up like snap targets on a range, with the difference that they would have been at a distance of twenty to thirty yards and not three hundred, a target impossible to miss.

As the mortaring and the Spandauing died away and it became clear that for the time being the enemy was not massing for another attack, the Guards had something to eat. The Grenadiers shared what rations they had left with the Scots Guards. Dead men's rations and water came in handy. It was pouring with rain – it had been raining all day – and it was very cold. Captain Coke 'kept trying to inject the morphine into him [Captain Howard] but owing to the cold and wet, fingers wouldn't always do the job properly'.[8] But he managed it in the end.

At around 1600 hours the mortaring and Spandauing increased in intensity. The Guards stood to. Sergeant Brown ordered Guardsman Sarginson to leave his sangar and cover the dead ground lost by the Scots Guards. Sarginson was quite glad to stretch his legs, but as he ran towards the dead ground a mortar bomb blew him to the ground. 'It felt like a sledgehammer hitting me in the buttocks.' A medical orderly crawled over to him; there weren't many left. (Two orderlies wearing Red Cross armbands had been shot dead whilst tending the wounded.) He dressed the wound and they shared a cigarette. The orderly told Sarginson that as soon as it was dark he would be picked up and evacuated.

As it grew dark guardsmen carried Sarginson to the centre of the ring and placed him with other severely wounded men. Those still defending the ring were cheered by a coded wireless message: the rest of the Scots Guards were on their way. But shortly afterwards a fire fight broke out to their rear. Spandaus kept firing long after Brens had ceased to. The enemy had infiltrated between Guards' wood and Pt 727. The Guards' ring was

---

* II/104th Panzer Grenadier Regiment attacked the Guards. They lost 10 men killed. Those who died of wounds would only be included in XIV Panzer Korps casualty returns issued every ten days. It is sometimes possible to track down the number of wounded suffered by a German battalion in an attack by checking divisional daily reports or casualty returns. In the case of II/104th Panzer Grenadier Regiment's attack on the Guards the number of wounded is not recorded. It is worth mentioning that all 15th Panzer Grenadier Division's battalions on the Camino Massif were still wearing summer kit. The Guards at least had battle-dress.

surrounded. Unless the reinforcements Major Cholmeley had promised fought their way through to them their wounded could not be evacuated. As the Guards watched and waited, Captain J. I. V. Snell, HQ Company, staggered into the ring with a box of ammunition under one arm, a box of rations under the other. Each box weighed around forty pounds. He told Captain Howard that the platoon from 4 Company coming up as reinforcements had been ambushed by the enemy and forced back to Pt 727. No further attempts to break through to Guards' wood had been planned. The enemy now controlled all the ground* between the wood and Pt 727, and the Scots Guards had postponed their ascent up Monte Camino until first light the following morning.

The Guards in the ring had plenty to think about. The fact that their wounded could not be evacuated and would have no protection against the cold during the night preyed on their minds. 'It was terrible to know we could do little or nothing for them.'[9]

As Sarginson lay with the other Guardsmen he had a mystical experience that sometimes happens to those facing death. He felt as if he was being shielded by invisible hands. 'It was sweet and I seemed to lose all fear for the first time during the ordeal.' Later he became aware of two men standing near him. An officer said quietly, 'Is there anyone here still alive?' 'Over here, Sir!' said Sarginson. Nobody else replied.† The officer, Captain Whatman, and 3 Company's CSM examined Sarginson's wounds. Captain Whatman told him his right buttock was bleeding badly and that they had no means of staunching the wound. Did he think he would walk back to Pt 727? Realizing that if he didn't make the attempt he'd bleed to death, Sarginson said 'Yessir!' Captain Whatman and the CSM helped him to his feet and led him over to a party of fifteen walking-wounded guardsmen in charge of Lieutenant Fyfe-Jamieson. As the party moved off a gale sprang up. The wind almost blew the men off their feet. As Sarginson hung on to rocks for support and noticed the Scots Guardsman in front of him lifting his unwounded arm in the air to help him keep his balance, he felt, for no apparent reason, that the gale would save his life. It probably did. If, as seems likely, the wind was blowing away from the Panzer Grenadiers who had ambushed the platoon from 4 Company, they would not have heard Lieutenant Fyfe-Jamieson's party making their way to Pt 727. It wasn't long before Sarginson began feeling faint from loss of blood. He nearly keeled over but he knew if he did he'd never get up again. 'I mustn't give in,' he thought; 'must keep going.' And his Guards training to 'keep going regardless' ensured that he did. The party reached Pt 727 safely. Whilst

* called the Saucer.
† 12 of the wounded died during the night.

Sarginson and some of the other wounded were being stretchered down Bare Arse Lieutenant Fyfe-Jamieson gave Major Cholmeley an on-the-spot report of the situation in Guards' wood. After having his wounds dressed at the RAP near the bottom of Bare Arse, Sarginson was driven back to Naples General Hospital in the back of a three-tonner. Shell craters in the road made it a very bumpy ride indeed, the last thing anyone with a wound in the buttocks wanted. But Sarginson 'rode' the pain and made a complete recovery in hospital. Within three months he was back in the line. Lieutenant Fyfe-Jamieson's 'clean flesh wound' went bad on him. He died on 12 November.

The Scots Guards' ascent of Monte Camino had been postponed because their patrols had discovered that the corrie mule track was not 'impassable'. It was good for mules as well as men. The order for them to march up Bare Arse was cancelled. They were climbing up the corrie instead. To what extent the 1st London Irish patrol's incompetence affected the outcome of the Guards action on Monte Camino is impossible to determine, but it certainly didn't make things any easier for them.

The Guards in the wood were now down to three officers and about fifty men. As another cold and wet dawn, 10 November, broke over the battlefield they prepared to face another counter-attack. The enemy between the wood and Pt 727 had withdrawn during the night. They would add that little bit extra weight to a counter-attack. The awareness that their wounded had died during the night weighed heavily on the Guards' morale. They had had nothing to eat for eighteen hours. They were soaked to the skin. Many of them were wounded. They would go down fighting. No doubt about that. But one more determined counter-attack would almost certainly scupper them.

The enemy mortars and Spandaus were unexpectedly silent. At first the Guards were suspicious. They knew from some of their own attacks how silences could occur just before they went in. But as time went by and the enemy still didn't open fire the Guards began to realize something was afoot. Just what it was they weren't sure. Perhaps the enemy were re-grouping. The longer they took to do it the better.

The enemy *were* re-grouping. II/104th Panzer Grenadier Regiment had reinforced III/129th Panzer Grenadier Regiment on the night of 7/8 November. On the night of 9'10 November II'129th Panzer Grenadier Regiment joined the other two battalions as a floating reserve.[10] The various realignments taking place among the enemy would have ruled out any attacks on 10 November. But why they failed to maintain any sort of harassing fire on Guards' wood is curious. They had no shortage of ammunition or mortar bombs. The battalion who relieved the Guards would find this out quick enough. The only harassing fire the Guards received was 'friendly'. The divisional artillery had been told that the Guards had withdrawn from the wood and, presuming that the enemy was now occupying it, the gunners were trying a 'map shoot'. Fortunately for the Guards all their shells fell short.

During the morning the Guards were tremendously heartened by the sounds of Brens taking on Spandaus down in the corrie. The Scots Guards were on their way. Captain Howard was in no condition to share the Guards' elation. By now he was too weak from his wounds to continue to command. He handed over to Captain Whatman, who determined to have him evacuated as soon as it was dark.

The Scots Guards' leading company – Right Flank – were climbing up the corrie mule track 'taking out Spandaus and corpses like rabbits out of a hat'. Right Flank OC, Captain R. S. P. Howe, and his two leading scouts, Guardsmen G. H. Connor and H. J. Spraggon, accounted for most of the nine Spandaus taken out in the corrie.[11] The firing got closer and closer. The Guards in the wood relaxed. As soon as it was dark the Scots Guards would relieve them. They were not to know that the two companies of the Scots Guards climbing the corrie were under orders to secure the top of the corrie and then attack Razorback. General Templer had decided to use the 7th Ox and Bucks to relieve the Guards in the wood early on 11 November. But nobody told the Ox and Bucks that. They were under orders to recapture Pt 819 'and the wood below it'. The 3rd Battalion, Coldstream* would relieve the Grenadiers at Pt 727. They had been having a very unpleasant time half way up Bare Arse. They had lost two officers and nineteen guardsmen killed through enemy shell fire and had discovered that splinters of rock could be as deadly as shrapnel. They had also lost their commanding officer, Lt-Colonel David Forbes, killed by shrapnel on his way to visit Calabritto. He was the last of the officers who had been with the battalion since its early days on the Desert.

As dusk fell Guards' wood was surrounded by the enemy instead of Scots Guards. The effect on the Guards' morale must have been terrible. Instead of being relieved they were being shot up by the enemy. Major Cholmeley, who knew the 7th Ox and Bucks would be relieving the Guards at 3 am the following morning, was reluctant to pass on the news by wireless in case the enemy intercepted the message. Instead he dispatched a runner, Captain A. D. S. Adair, who slipped through the enemy ring and delivered the message to Captain Whatman. When Captain Whatman told him he wanted to try and evacuate Captain Howard, Captain Adair said he'd help carry him. The carrying party was ambushed as soon as it left the wood. Adair and one

* Their place at Calabritto had been taken by 1st London Scottish and 10th Royal Berkshire, 168th Brigade. 1/129th Panzer Grenadier Regiment, which had been driven out of the village, fought their way back into it. They were only driven out again after some very hard fighting.

guardsman managed to carry Captain Howard back to the wood. He then went hunting for the enemy who'd ambushed the carrying party. He was never seen alive again.* Whatman sent a coded wireless message back to Major Cholmeley, indicating that he knew the relief was on the way. The rest of the Guards knew it too, providing they were still there when it arrived. Excited by their two successful ambushes the enemy closed right in. Spandaus began firing through the gaps in the crest of the wood. The Guards were ordered to hold their fire. What ammunition they had left would be needed to beat off the night attack that seemed inevitable. But once again the enemy decided not to risk an all-out attack and confined themselves to harassing fire and, when the three companies of the Ox and Bucks arrived at 03.30 hours – remarkably punctual – they quickly withdrew. The Ox and Bucks were very surprised to find the Guards still in the wood. It says a lot for the discipline of their leading company that they didn't mistake the Guards for the enemy and open fire on them.

The Guards took the corrie mule track down Monte Camino, carrying some of their wounded. For the survivors of 2 and 3 Companies, 6th Grenadiers and F Company, 2nd Scots Guards, it was the most terrible battle in the whole of the Italian Campaign. Captain Coke remembers it 'as a very unpleasant spot indeed, and certainly the worst few days and nights I experienced in the war'.[11] The casualty figures in his After Action report compiled a few days after the battle are very exact. Of the 108 men who had gone up Monte Camino one officer was killed, one died of wounds, seven guardsmen were killed, twenty-one wounded, five sick and seventeen missing. One missing guardsman had run for it and turned up after the battle. The rest had belonged to three sections overrun on the Guards' right flank. The 6th Grenadiers After Action report has no detailed casualty figures. The Grenadier Guards history settles for a flourish: 'Four hundred and eighty-three Grenadiers had gone up Camino, and only two hundred and sixty-three returned.' Details of the Grenadiers casualties can to some extent be worked out from the appendices in their history. Five officers and thirty-nine guardsmen were killed or died of wounds, five officers were severely wounded and seventy-three guardsmen taken prisoner. The number of guardsmen wounded is unrecorded. Captain Howard, who lost both legs above the knee, received the DSO for his part in the action, Captain Whatman the MC. The enemy had not quite finished with 201st (Guards) Brigade. On 15 November Brigadier Gascoigne was severely wounded by shell fire and Colonel Kingsmill assumed temporary command of the brigade.

*

* The War Graves Commission found his body near the wood early in 1944.

As A and B Companies of the Ox and Bucks advanced on Pt 819 and its 'twin' they were heavily Spandaued from Razorback. The Ox and Bucks had been told it was held by the Scots Guards. Right Flank, Scots Guards, had only managed to get a toehold on it, losing eight guardsmen killed in daylight attacks and subsequent shelling. After a hurried conference between Major J. P. R. Montgomerie, OC A Company and Captain J. P. P. Wright, DSO, OC B Company, it was decided that B Company should attack Razorback whilst A Company went ahead with its attack on Pt 819. B Company captured Razorback, killing and wounding a number of the enemy, and took twenty-three prisoners. A Company pressed home its attack on Pt 819 and captured the summit. B Company, who suffered about twenty casualties in their attack on Razorback and had to send other men back to Tac HQ with their prisoners, then attacked the smaller peak. They gained the summit but were at once counter-attacked and forced off it. The Company were now down to about 60% strength. Captain Wright decided not to make another attack against the 'twin' peak. Instead he ordered his company to reinforce A Company on Pt 819. For some unexplained reason A Company were unable to site their Brens on the enemy's side of the slope, making it hard for them to withstand a sudden counter-attack.

At first light the combined companies came under heavy fire from Monastery Hill and Razorback. The enemy had reoccupied the ridge. As Spandaus and mortars picked off his men Major Montgomerie tried to evacuate the more seriously wounded. But carrying parties with Red Cross armbands were shot up by the enemy. The wounded had to be left in the open.

At dawn the enemy behind Pt 819 counter-attacked and forced the Ox and Bucks off the summit. The two companies now numbered one hundred men. Major Montgomerie ordered them to withdraw to Guards' wood. As Captain Wright was organizing his company's withdrawal he was shot dead by a sniper. Soon after the two companies had linked up with C Company in the wood they were attacked from the rear. The enemy had infiltrated into the Saucer. But as the enemy attacked the wood they were counter-attacked by a party of Ox and Bucks from Battalion Tac HQ near the head of the corrie. The enemy fled.

As soon as it was dusk Major Montgomerie took up fresh positions between the wood and Tac HQ, making it impossible for the enemy to get behind his companies. In twelve hours' fighting the battalion had lost four officers and twenty-one other ranks killed or died of wounds, three officers and sixty-five men wounded and twenty-one men missing.[13] II Battalion, 129th Panzer Grenadier Regiment, counted forty dead and wounded on the two peaks.

Early next morning, 11 November, a company of Royal Fusiliers and a platoon of heavy machine gunners from the Cheshire Regiment arrived at the Scots Guards Tac HQ, also near the top of the corrie. They were unsure of what they were supposed to do. General Templer contacted Brigadier Firth, 167th Brigade, and ordered him to prepare to send the rest of the 8th Royal Fusilier battalion up Monte Camino. But on 12 November McCreery went up Monte Camino to see things for himself and realized it was no longer possible to take Monte Camino with a crippled division. He ordered General Templer to stop sending any more troops up the mountain and told Clark that 56th Division's attack had failed. He would be withdrawing all troops from Monte Camino and Calabritto.*

The news came as a shock to Clark, who had already received reports from Truscott that Colonel Sherman's attack on Monte La Difensa had also failed. The luckless men of the 7th Regiment had been unable to find a way up Monte La Difensa's cliffs. Trapped at the bottom of them, they had taken a terrible beating. The enemy had Spandaued and mortared them at will. The Regiment was withdrawn from Monte La Difensa on 10 November. It had lost two officers and eighty-nine ranks killed or died of wounds, nineteen officers and 519 ranks wounded and an unrecorded number of officers and men suffering from exposure and trench feet. No detailed account of this action exists. 15th Panzer Grenadier Division casualties totalled ten officers and 234 ranks killed or died of wounds, ten officers and 537 ranks wounded, two officers and 194 ranks missing, two officers and 501 ranks sick.[14] Although the Division had won an outstanding defensive victory, their losses, particularly in officers – twenty-two out of thirty in their rifle companies – were severe. Von Senger mentioned this in a personal message of congratulations to General Rodt.

On 8 November a conference had been held at XIV Korps' HQ. This was attended by Kesselring as well as General Lemelsen. Von Senger said his piece in no uncertain terms. The defences of the Bernhardt at Mignano Gap were totally inadequate, there weren't enough men to man them, and Kesselring's policy of keeping battalions in Army reserve instead of Korps reserve was wrong. Furthermore the 3rd Panzer Grenadier Division had taken such heavy losses that it was no longer a cohesive fighting force. It needed replacing as quickly as possible. General Lemelsen agreed with von Senger on all points. Kesselring, no longer so sure that he knew better than his generals, agreed that all the battalions in Army reserve should be moved up to Korps reserve. But he hedged about replacing the 3rd Panzer Grenadier

* British 56th Division withdrew from Monte Camino and Calabritto on the night of 14 November. The withdrawals were carried out so skilfully that the enemy didn't realize that they had taken place. Their artillery continued to shell Guards' wood and Pt 727 until 17 November. On 19 November XIV Panzer Korps' diarist reported triumphantly, 'We have retaken Pt 727 and Calabritto!'

Division. He only had two-thirds of the Hermann Göring Division and the 29th Panzer Grenadier Division in reserve. He was not going to commit the rest of the Hermann Göring Division to the battle – he may have been under pressure from Göring not to do so – and the 29th Panzer Grenadier Division had hardly had time to rest let alone refit.*

II/8th Panzer Grenadier Regiment had launched several counter-attacks on Monte Rotondo on 8 November. The US 3rd Division's historian described their counter-attacks as 'uncoordinated'. This was hardly surprising. By nightfall the strength of the battalion was down to thirty men.† It was amalgamated with III/8th Panzer Grenadier Regiment on Monte Lungo. Von Senger, desperate to re-take Monte Rotondo, ordered III/104th Panzer Grenadier Regiment, now released from Army reserve, to capture it 'at all costs', a phrase that was to become depressingly familiar to Allied as well as German infantry. Von Senger also ordered von Corvin's battle group to take up positions close to San Pietro.

During the night of 8/9 November III/104th Panzer Grenadier Regiment passed through III/8th Panzer Grenadier on Monte Lungo. This battalion still held the US prisoners taken during 3rd Battalion, 15th Regiment's unsuccessful attack on 8 November. III/104th Panzer Grenadier Regiment's C.O. decided that if his battalion was to retake Monte Rotondo 'at all costs' then the ends justified the means. He took charge of the US prisoners and told them that they would be forced to advance in front of his battalion when it attacked Monte Rotondo. This barbaric ploy was put into effect at 08.45 hours on 9 November. The two leading companies of III/104th advanced up the eastern slopes of Monte Rotondo. driving the US prisoners in front of them. The mountain was defended by three understrength companies of the 3rd Battalion, 30th Regiment, US 3rd Division. Its Company L was down to fifty-seven men. The enemy overran a US platoon and forced their prisoners to advance in front of them. Finding a gap between Companies K and L, they attacked Company L in the flank. The US prisoners, acting as a human shield, yelled 'Don't shoot!' L Company's commander, Lieutenant Britt, shouted back. 'We're going to shoot! Fall flat! You won't be hurt.' The US troops opened fire – what happened to the US prisoners is not known – the enemy returned it, then got among the US troops. Their short delay in opening fire had allowed the Panzer Grenadiers just the opportunity they wanted. As the two sides fought it out with bayonets, submachine guns and Bars Lieutenant Britt jumped from one position to another, yelling encouragement to his men. The enemy couldn't seem to hit him. A company

---

* It had been withdrawn from the line on 31 October.

† XIV Panzer Korps battle casualties 1–10 November totalled 339 killed, 1088 wounded and 652 missing. 3rd Panzer Grenadier Division's share totalled 161 killed, 556 wounded, and 357 missing. Figures that Colonel von Bonin should have studied.

commander impervious to point blank fire does wonders for his men's morale. They kept fighting hard and the enemy suddenly broke. As they retreated down the mountain Lieutenant Britt collapsed. He had been wounded four times. The enemy left sixty-five dead and wounded behind them.

At 09.30 hours on 10 November III/104th Panzer Grenadier Regiment made a second attack on Monte Rotondo, under cover of heavy mortar and Nebelwerfer fire. This time they made skilful use of terrain instead of US prisoners. They climbed up the eastern slopes of Monte Rotondo and hit Company E so hard that it broke. The enemy had a clear run to the summit barred only by one man, Private Floyd Lindstrom, and his Browning heavy machine gun weighing 112 pounds. When a Spandau opened up at him from behind a bank Private Lindstrom picked up the Browning and charged the Spandau, firing from the hip. Having killed the crew he picked up the Spandau and several belts of its ammunition and returned to his position. A sergeant from E Company ran over and took charge of the Spandau. As the two men fired flat out at the enemy, other members of E Company, their courage restored by Private Lindstrom's example, kept the Browning supplied with ammunition. The concentration of fire from the two guns broke up the enemy's attack. Once again they retreated down the mountain. Private Lindstrom and Lieutenant Britt both received the Medal of Honor.[15]

III/104th Panzer Grenadier Regiment had only taken 30% casualties, but they were not asked to make another attack. Instead Monte Rotondo was subjected to intense harassing fire. The enemy used Korps as well as divisional artillery and many batteries of Nebelwerfers. The momentum of the barrages built up steadily until it became a question not of when the enemy batteries were firing but when they weren't. To the men of the 3rd Battalion, 30th Infantry, another enemy counter-attack seemed inevitable. But von Senger no longer expected to retake Monte Rotondo. Perhaps Colonel von Bonin thought that III/104th Panzer Grenadier Regiment's claims to have almost taken the mountain were exaggerated and said as much to von Senger. XIV Panzer Korps' commander, well satisfied with the way things were turning out on the Camino Massif, was concentrating his mind on events taking place on Monte Corno and Monte Santa Croce.

The 2nd Battalion, 180th Regiment, had begun working its way up the mountains on 6 November. On 8 November their leading company captured a number of prisoners along with an enormous cache of food – whole hams, fresh potatoes, as opposed to the dehydrated ones dished out to Allied troops when they got a hot meal, fresh bread, cheese, tinned salmon and tinned pilchards. The GIs had seen nothing like it since they left the States. (Along with the food were parcels of silk underwear and stockings ready to be sent back to Germany.) The temptation to sit down to a real meal and to hell with the war must have been strong, but, encouraged by their officers and non-coms, the company continued to fight their way up the mountain. On the night of 9/10 November it captured the peak of Monte Santa Croce. It then worked its way along the ridge towards Monte Corno, ambushing twelve of the enemy and on the night of 10/11 November it captured both peaks of Monte Corno. For a single company to capture two mountains within twenty hours was a great achievement.[16] Whilst it was being relieved by 1st Rangers the battalion of the 29th Panzer Grenadier Regiment which had been dislodged from both peaks of Monte Corno put in its counter-attack and retook the higher one. Colonel Darby realized that one battalion of Rangers could not possibly hold both mountains. Guessing that Lucas might prevaricate,* Colonel Darby, accustomed to going straight to the top, contacted Clark directly. Clark promised to send up a battalion from 504th Parachute Regiment to take over Monte Santa Croce. The Rangers were to consolidate on Monte Corno's lower peak, and then capture its higher one. But its lower one gave the US observers just as good a view of the enemy lines of communications. They could see as far as Cassino. Kesselring described this as 'a tragedy . . . now all the important heights are gone'.[17] He said Monte Corno must be retaken at all costs. Von Senger told him that the battalion of the 29th Panzer Grenadier Regiment holding onto the higher peak of Monte Corno had shot their bolt. They were too few on the ground to launch any more counter-attacks. The best they could hope for was to hang on to the higher peak. If Kesselring wanted it retaken he would have to relieve the battalion with a fresh one. Von Senger knew very well that the only fresh battalions available were those of the von Corvin battle group. Although it was now under his command he still had to have Kesselring's permission to use it. Von Senger had the Commander in Chief in a corner. Kesselring had to choose between bringing up a fresh battalion – one from von Corvin's battle group – or he could take von Senger's earlier advice and relieve the whole of the 3rd Panzer Grenadier Division. Kesselring telephoned Major General Walter Fries, Divisional Commander 29th Panzer Grenadiers, and ordered him to move up the line that night – 11/12 November – and begin relieving 3rd Panzer Grenadier Division.

The feelings of the men of the 29th Panzer Grenadiers when told they were going back into the line straight away are summed up by Regimental Sergeant Major Finke, II/15th Panzer Grenadier Regiment: 'They promised to give us three weeks' rest. All we got was nine days.'[18]

The Division, originally the 29th Motorized, had been raised in Hesse and Thuringen, north of Bavaria, in 1936. Throughout the Second World War it managed to get most of its replacements from its own training depots, a remarkable achievement for a division lacking the clout of an SS or Luftwaffe

* Colonel Darby was right. Lucas considered the reinforcements as 'unnecessary'.

75

formation. Getting replacements from its own depots played an important part in maintaining the division's reputation as one of the hardest fighting units in the Wehrmacht. Its performance in France in 1940 so impressed General Guderian that he chose it to lead his Panzer Army's drive into Russia in 1941. The division lived up to his expectations. It had the better of all Russian divisions it encountered until Stalingrad. Even then it partially avoided the fate of most German divisions trapped there. It had enough of its wounded flown out and linked up with men wounded in other battles in Russia to form an entire regiment. When the division was reformed under General Fries, who had commanded its 15th Panzer Grenadier Regiment before the war, it drew enough replacements from its own depots to make up its own Panzer regiment. The new division was reinforced by a regiment from the 345th Bavarian Infantry Division. General Fries split it up amongst the veterans of his own division and during the Italian Campaign replaced Bavarian wounded with men from Hesse and Thuringen. Von Senger had noted the way the division had fought in Sicily and had heard about its outstanding performance at Salerno.* He was delighted to have it under his command again. He rated General Fries highly: 'Being warm-hearted toward his troops he could demand much of them.' Although the division had not had the rest it was promised it had received its full quota of tanks and a good many infantry replacements. Its Panzer Grenadier Battalions had a fighting strength of around 400 men.

On 10 November 4th Rangers began reconnoitring the northern slopes of Monte Sammucro. Both Lucas and General Middleton, commanding US 45th Division, were concerned about the gap between his division and US 3rd Division, and they decided to plug it with the Rangers. Major Roy Murray, 4th Rangers Commanding Officer, would have 180th Regiment, 45th Division, as a back-up force. Major Murray ordered his patrols to find out if Monte Sammucro's three eastern pinnacles – Pts 570, 630 and 670 – were occupied by the enemy. The terrain allowed the Rangers' scouts to get close to the pinnacles in daylight without being spotted. They reported that Pt 630 was occupied by a strong force of the enemy. Major Murray sent A Company (three officers and forty-three other ranks) to occupy Pt 570. Early on 11 November F Company (one officer and forty-two other ranks) supported by B Company (two officers and forty-three other ranks) moved up to Pt 570. After a short artillery and 4.2" mortar barrage the Rangers attacked Pt 630 at 12.00 hours. It was a 'milkrun'. The battalion of the 29th Panzer Grenadier Regiment defending the crest caved in. The Rangers took five officers and over one hundred other ranks prisoners. The Rangers lost

* Whilst Colonel Kruger's 71st Panzer Grenadiers and the division's tanks were pushing one wing of the 5th Army towards the sea, Colonel Ulrich's 15th Panzer Grenadier Regiment was smashing US attacks against the key town of Altavilla.

one man killed and one wounded. But they came under heavy fire from Pt 670. The remnants of the enemy battalion had occupied it. At 0430 hours on 12 November A and D Companies (two officers and thirty other ranks) took Pt 670 without loss, capturing another forty prisoners.

On the night of 11/12 November the 29th Panzer Grenadier Division began relieving the 3rd Panzer Grenadier Division. The III/15th Panzer Grenadier Regiment took over from them on Monte Lungo whilst their I and II Battalions occupied Monte Sammucro.

12 November was a hard day for Kesselring. He had to cope with Hitler as well as XIV Panzer Korps' crumbling centre. The Führer was following every move that 5th and 10th Armies made on a large-scale map of the area. During the day General Lemelsen heard about eighty stragglers from the battalion of the 28th Panzer Grenadier Regiment, knocked off Pts 630 and 670, had reached San Pietro. He visited the village and was dismayed by the men's condition. They were in no state to fight. He phoned Kesselring and asked permission for the men to withdraw to San Vittore, two miles west of San Pietro. Kesselring, who considered San Vittore as good a 'blocking' point as San Pietro, said that, providing the Führer agreed to the withdrawal, it could take place. Late that evening Kesselring rang General Lemelsen and told him 'the Führer has given us a free hand concerning San Pietro'. The battalion of 29th Panzer Grenadier Regiment holding San Pietro were allowed to withdraw to San Vittore. Early on 12 November Westphal rang General Lemelsen to say that Hitler had changed his mind. San Pietro was to be held indefinitely.[19] General Lemelsen rang Kesselring to ask if he should order the battalion of the 29th Panzer Grenadier Regiment in San Vittore to re-occupy San Pietro. They decided that one of 15th Panzer Grenadier's Regiment on Monte Sammucro should be switched to San Pietro instead. Colonel Ulich, Commanding Officer, 15th Panzer Grenadier Regiment, ordered Captain Helmut Meitzel's II Battalion to occupy the village.

Hitler then made his second intervention. The pinnacles on the southern slopes of Monte Sammucro were to be retaken, and Monte Rotondo attacked from the north. When the orders reached Colonel Ulich he chose his II Battalion to make the attack. It would be supported by I Battalion. When Ulich briefed Captain Meitzel for the attack, scheduled for dawn on 13 November, and told him that the orders came from 'the highest possible authority' Captain Meitzel could well believe it. The orders were crazy.[20] Captain Meitzel could see from the map that retaking the pinnacles was a reasonable proposition, but to swing south in daylight and attack Monte Rotondo would result in his battalion being broken up by US artillery.

But Captain Meitzel was not someone to question orders. He had fought in Poland, France and Russia, where he'd been made a company commander. He'd collected five medals on the way, including the Iron Cross, first class, and a Gold one for close combat. Captain Meitzel always led from the front. He had been wounded five times and his fifth wound, a severe one, saved his life. He was evacuated from Stalingrad on one of the last planes to fly out of the city. In August, 1943, when he was still only twenty-three, he was made Commanding Officer, II/15th Panzer Grenadier Regiment. Impressed by the way Russian infantry went into attack yelling their heads off, and the effect this had on his own men, he had trained his reformed battalion to go into an attack using their own particular battle cry. It had proved very effective at Salerno. Colonel Ulich promised him that his battalion would receive an exceptionally heavy support barrage for its attack on the pinnacles. In addtion to their own generous supply of shells the divisional artillery hasd taken over a stock-pile left behind by the 3rd Panzer Grenadier Division. For the foreseeable future the division would be able to fire as many shells as it liked. The strict rules applied to all other divisional artillery in XIV Panzer Korps did not apply to the 29th Panzer Grenadiers Division.

At 0630 on 13 November II Battalion's support barrage went down on Pts 670, 630 and 570. It lasted three-quarters of an hour. The II Battalion, who had been crouching behind a ridge overlooking both San Pietro and the pinnacles, set off on their attack as soon as the barrage lifted. RSM Finke, who was taking part in the attack, had noticed that the pinnacles had been shrouded in mist all the previous day. He was hoping the same thing would happen again. But as the 2nd Battalion moved towards the pinnacle the mist lifted and the sun came out. 'We cursed it!' RSM Finke remembers. It was his last coherent memory of the action. Captain Meitzel, who once again was up front, prefers not to talk about it. Considering what happened to his battalion during the action, this is understandable. Interestingly enough 4th Rangers' second-in-command, Captain Walter Nye, remembers taking the pinnacles from the battalion of the 29th Panzer Grenadier Regiment, but not the enemy counter-attack.[21] Sergeant James Altieri, who received a field commission for his part in the action, prefers to rely on his written account of it, as full of sound and fury as RSM Finke's, and a good deal more boastful. He makes a wild stab at the identity of the enemy: 'an SS unit . . . the most elite formation in the German Army'. Fortunately Major Murray[22] and Captain Robert Davis[23], 180th Regiment, both wrote excellent After Action accounts of the battle.

Within a quarter of an hour of their support barrage lifting II Battalion had bundled the Rangers off Pts 670 and 570 as easily as the Rangers had bundled the enemy off them. Although the barrage had caused few casualties it had kept the Rangers' heads down. When the shelling lifted and the Rangers looked over their parapets the sight of hundreds of enemy charging towards them giving their own version of the 'Rebel yell' caused them to delay opening fire for a few seconds. By the time the Rangers had begun firing the Panzer Grenadiers were already advancing up the pinnacles very quickly indeed. As they closed in the Rangers ran for it.

Leaving Spandaus on Pts 670 and 570 the whole of II Battalion began attacking Pt 630. The company already climbing up it had found it hard going. It was much steeper than the other two pinnacles and, although the very rocky terrain gave good cover, it had also slowed down their attack. Major Murray, who was commanding the two companies of Rangers – F and D – holding Pt 630 had had time to get his men to bring down well-directed small arms fire on the advancing enemy. But when they were joined by two more companies and began climbing up the rear slopes of the pinnacle as well as the forward ones, supported by Spandau fire from Pts 670 and 570, the situation rapidly deteriorated. At 07.15, just half an hour after II Battalion had launched its attack, Major Murray sent a wireless message to Rangers Tac HQ at Ceppagna, saying that two of his companies had been overrun and the situation for the Rangers defending Pt 630 was critical. Reinforcements were urgently needed, so was 4.2″ mortar support. Major Murray asked for one to be laid down a hundred yards from the summit. The Rangers' officer alerted their Chemical company – 4.2″ DF went down within minutes – and then rang General Middleton to ask for reinforcements. General Middleton rang Colonel Dulaney, commanding 180th Regiment, and ordered him to send up reinforcements as quickly as possible. Somewhere along the line the message '2 companies of Rangers overrun' became '4th Rangers' battalion overrun'.

The 4.2″ DF slowed down II Battalion's advance, but they kept on coming. Major Murray was unable to ask his Forward Observer to call for artillery support because his lines of communication had been destroyed during the enemy's support barrage. British and US artillery could never be contacted by wireless.

Down in the valley Colonel Dulaney set out to find where 4th Rangers had been overrun. He had not been told that they had been holding Pts 570, 630 and 670. He was accompanied by his battalion's commanders and the commanding officer of the Regiment's Chemical company, Captain Robert Davis. As they were climbing up Monte Sammucro they were caught in a 4.2″ mortar barrage laid down by the Rangers Chemical company. Luckily the Rangers were firing phosphorous shells. None of the officers suffered any ill effects. Captain Davis had had reports that phosphorous shells were ineffective on rocky ground owing to poor fragmentation. He now knew the reports were accurate. Colonel Dulaney told his battalion commanders to find out where the enemy positions were, and he and Captain Davis returned to Regimental HQ.

It was now around 1030. Colonel Ulich, who could see that the II Battalion attack had been slowed down by the mortaring, ordered his I Battalion to support their attack. As soon as it began climbing down Monte Sammucro its companies were pinned down by intense US shell fire. Major Murray noted with relief that the enemy attacking Pt 630 had now gone on the defensive. 'Our situation was such that one more coordinated attack would have overcome us', he noted. 'At 13.00 hours under the "protection" of two improvised white flags the enemy began withdrawing down the hill'. White flags are a sign of surrender, not of retreat. Major Murray directed the fire of his men and his 4.2″ mortars onto the retreating enemy. Away from the cover of the rocks Captain Meitzel's men were a soft target. After the action the War Graves Commission counted eighty dead on one side of Pt 630, twenty-one on the other. Those of II Battalion who made it to the bottom of the pinnacle had to climb back up the ridge down which they had advanced. They were harried by artillery and 4.2″ mortar fire, and ambushed by Company K, 180th Regiment, who had worked their way round to the south of Pt 630. Twenty-nine of the enemy surrendered. After the action 180th Regiment counted a further twenty-four enemy dead on the ridge.

Both Captain Meitzel and RSM Finke made it back to San Pietro. Buoyed up with the elation that follows a close brush with death, Finke remarked, 'We had survived the day!' As Captain Meitzel was questioning his men, trying to find out who were definitely dead and who were missing, a shell-burst slightly wounded him in one cheek. It was his eighth wound, one he could grin about. But there was nothing else to find comfort in. His battalion had been smashed. When I Battalion sent out stretcher bearers to pick up II Battalion's wounded the US artillery and Chemical companies held their fire. By nightfall seventy-six of II Battalion wounded had been evacuated. The proportion of dead – 125 – to wounded was unusually high, terribly high for Captain Meitzel. As soon as it was dark a hot meal and real coffee were brought up to San Pietro. As always a good meal cheered everyone up. They could take pride in their attack. The grieving for dead comrades would come later.

4th Rangers, who were replaced by a battalion from 180th Regiment, had won a remarkable victory, at a cost of only five Rangers killed and thirty-five severely wounded. They and their Chemical company had proved that even the bravest of men have a breaking point. Although 4th Rangers received a 5th Army commendation for their action, official records* state '4th Rangers overrun on Monte Sammucro', something that 4th Rangers veterans are none too happy about.

The failure of II Battalion's attack – Hitler's own – had a devastating effect on morale at XIV Panzer Korps' HQ. Von Senger told Kesselring that its centre – III/104th Panzer Grenadier Regiment – was disintegrating under

* VI Corps' historical records.

constant enemy harassing fire. Rather than commit the von Corvin battle group to the US 'mincing machine', Kesselring obtained Hitler's approval for XIV Panzer Korps to retreat to the Graeser Line a mile behind Monte Rotondo. XIV Panzer Korps' diarist begins his entry for 13 November with a summary of the II Battalion, 15th Panzer Grenadier Regiment's unsuccessful attack on Pts 570, 630, 670. He concludes it with the sentence, 'Die Engländer have won the Battle for Mignano Gap'.

Kesselring and his generals may have thought that 'Die Engländer' had won it, but on the same day as XIV Panzer Korps' diarist made that entry Clark decided to call off the battle. He told Alexander that X Corps had failed to take Monte Camino, that the situation in the centre was stalemate and not much better on the Army's right flank. His men were exhausted. They needed to rest, reform and be reinforced before making another attack. Alexander approved his breaking off the battle.

By midday on 13 November it became apparent to the long-suffering 3rd Battalion, 30th Infantry,that the enemy were withdrawing from their positions in front of Monte Rotondo.[24] Battalions from the 15th and 30th Regiments went after them, forcing III/104 Regiment to fight a rearguard action. So much for 'exhausted troops'. During the night of 13/14 November the enemy disengaged. Early on 14 November fighting patrols from the 15th Regiment reported blown bridges, well fortified positions abandoned without a fight and a long line of traffic moving up Highway Six towards Cassino. Alarmed by the US 3rd Division's attacks Kesselring had ordered a general retreat to the Gustav. The Graeser Line had been abandoned.[25]

Aerial reconnaissance carried out later on 14 November confirmed[26] the reports from 15th Division's patrols. The enemy was pulling back to the Gustav. There were now only three artillery pieces left in the Mignano Gap area. Just what Clark made of these reports is anybody's guess. On 12 November he had considered replacing the British 56th Division with the US 36th Division. But he made no move to reinforce US 3rd Division's drive towards Cassino. Instead he ordered all units in 5th Army to go on the defensive. The 15th and 30th Regiment's battalions pulled back to their jump-off positions around Monte Rotondo. As soon as he heard they had withdrawn Kesselring realized that XIV Panzer Korps had been let off the hook. He countermanded orders for a retreat to the Gustav. The von Corvin battle group was shunted back to its positions near San Pietro, I/15th Panzer Grenadier Regiment took over positions in front of Monte Rotondo, and as dusk fell another long line of traffic moved south from Cassino. It had been a very close-run thing indeed.*

* By 16 November Lucas at least had realized this: 'The German situation in the centre was desperate when we were forced to halt. The enemy thus avoided a great disaster.'

Chapter IV

Interlude

As 5th Army and XIV Panzer Korps regrouped contact between them was mainly limited to patrolling, air strikes, air surveillance, harassing fire and counter-battery fire. Full-scale fighting continued only on Monte Corno.

Cassino and the rest of the Gustav Line had begun being fortified on 10 November. On 15 November Westphal was summoned to a conference by Hitler. Generals Jodl and Warlimont of OKW were also present. Additions to the Gustav Line were planned and all three generals stressed the importance of holding the Bernhardt Line for as long as possible so that the Gustav's defences could be completed before the Allies broke through the Bernhardt. Another addition, on 29 November, to the Gustav included Monte Cassino, hitherto left out of the line because of the Benedictine Abbey on its summit. Westphal asked for two more infantry divisions to be sent to XIV Panzer Korps. Hitler approved the dispatch of the Austrian 44th Infantry Divisions, which arrived between 29 November and 14 December, and the 5th Mountain Division, which began arriving on 17 December.[1]

10th Army engineers who were in charge of building the defences of Cassino went about their job in their usual methodical fashion. This wasn't good enough for Kesselring. In the third week of November he appointed Colonel von Corvin as town commandant and promised him a force of 44,000 Todt workers. Colonel von Corvin evacuated Cassino's 20,000 inhabitants, the Todt workers moved in and worked a dawn-till-dusk schedule. Von Corvin selected a number of key strongpoints, which included the station and the Continental Hotel, both built of solid marble, and had the engineers demolish the buildings around them so as to give a clear field of fire. The Todt workers strengthened all strongpoints with reinforced concrete and strips of railway lines. They also fixed custom-built steel emplacements for tanks on ground floors and lined all cellar walls with steel. Three-ton steel pillboxes were erected between the strongpoints and round the periphery of the town, each with a charcoal burner to keep the occupants warm. The Todt workers also built a maze of underground rest bunkers that connected

9. Terraces on top of Monte Camino. Point 819 and its 'twin' are to the left and part of Guards Wood is at the top of the terraces facing the two points. Monastery Hill is centre right. The top of Razorback — Wilfred — is next to it. The mule track is in the foreground to the right.

10. German prisoners taken near Calabritto being escorted to an interrogation centre.

11. Coldstream Guards after their withdrawal from Monte Camino.

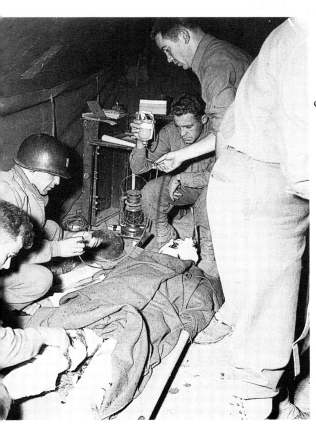

12. A U.S. surgical unit operating on a man wounded by a S. mine.

13. Mud

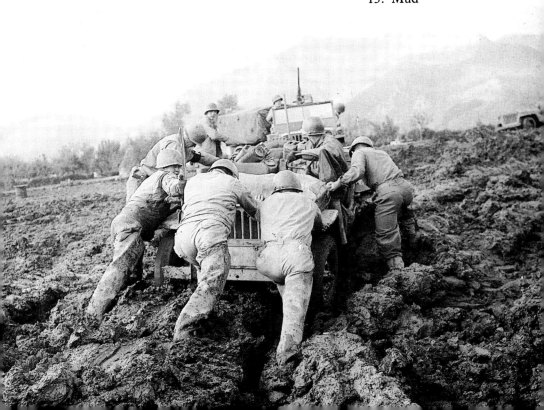

14. British engineers surveying a demolition.

15. British engineers manhandling a Bailey bridge across the demolition.

up with the strongpoints. Each bunker contained twenty-four double-tiered bunks.[2]

Every division in the 10th Army was responsible for fortifying its section of the Gustav. The 29th Panzer Grenadier Division's line of retreat ran straight through Cassino so their engineers took a hand in fortifying part of the town. The division evacuated all the villages in their zone of combat except San Pietro infine. The San Pietrans had evacuated themselves.

San Pietro, a large 11th century walled village*, lay on the lower northern slopes of Monte Sammucro. The walls surrounding the village were two feet thick, between eighteen and twenty feet high and had six towers. (A seventh had been destroyed in an earthquake.) Its walls and ravines – immediately to the west of the village there is one several hundred feet deep, to the east a smaller one – would have made it a hard place to take in the period when its inhabitants were citizen soldiers. But in October, 1943, the Germans slipped into the village by night. A Gestapo snatch squad carried off the village priest from his sick bed. He was never seen again. The same week a convoy of German lorries pulled up at the village. Two hundred young men were rounded up and driven off to Rome to work as labourers in munition factories outside Rome. The mayor of San Pietro called an emergency meeting of the remaining 1,200 inhabitants. It was decided that the whole village should be evacuated, the able-bodied young men and women living rough on Monte Sammucro or trying to reach the Allies, whilst the rest of the inhabitants, who numbered around eight hundred and who were over fifty or under sixteen, took refuge in some caves in the ravine to the west of the village. They set about knocking down the rock separating the caves until all eight hundred villagers were together in one enormous cave. They stocked up with sacks of flour and figs, built bread ovens, then begun making the entrances to the caves proof against shell bursts. They did this by covering the entrances with two overlapping blocks of stone. The masons who thought of such an ingenious protection showed remarkable foresight. For water the cave dwellers relied on cisterns just outside the cave. The next German snatch squad who visited San Pietro found it deserted. They soon nosed out the inhabitants in the cave, searched it for able-bodied males and, finding none, they flung dead sheep into the cisterns. Anyone who went near the village fountain for water would be shot dead, the Germans said.[3] The village was now occupied by a unit of the 3rd Panzer Grenadier Division.

Twelve of the villagers camping out on Monte Sammucro found refuge in a large drain pipe about six hundred yards east of the village. On the night of 3 November a US patrol clashed with a detachment of the 3rd Panzer

---

* In Italy it would have been known as a paese, a cross between a village and a small town.

Grenadiers in the area of the drain pipe. Next day a platoon of Panzer Grenadiers searched the area. When they caught sight of the San Pietrans huddled in the pipe they opened fire with automatic weapons. Eleven villagers were killed outright. One mortally wounded girl lived long enough to tell the San Pietrans who found her that as the Germans kept on firing she thought, 'Why are they doing this to us?' It says a great deal for the humanity of the San Pietrans that they did not consider the killings a massacre. They put it down to trigger-happy troops who probably thought the villagers in the drain were US troops or spies.

The villagers in the caves sent out volunteers each night to get water from the fountain. The sentries guarding it usually turned a blind eye. But one night two young girls filling canteens were shot dead. For a few days the villagers in the caves sucked water from fissures in the rock but some of the elderly were unable to suck the fissures. More volunteers were called for. Two other young girls went to the fountain. The sentries held their fire. From the second half of November, when the II/15th Panzer Grenadier Regiment, 29th Panzer Division took over, a live-and-let-live approach to civilians using the fountain began.

Captain Meitzel was quick to realize that his hard-hit battalion – it had received no replacements* since the disastrous attack of 13 November – had acquired a superb defensive position – by courtesy of Hitler once again. San Pietro's western ravine had sheer cliffs. That ruled out any attack from the west. The northern and southern approaches to the village were overlooked by Forward Observers on Monte Sammucro and Monte Lungo. They could call on artillery and mortar DF whenever it was needed. If necessary Captain Meitzel could also call on Korps 170 mm guns and 220 mm mortars. And, provided they were not supporting their own infantry, the Hermann Göring Divisional artillery was at his disposal. They were lying up close to his own Divisional artillery. In San Pietro itself he had several Russian 76 mm SP guns as well as a section of anti-tank guns guarding the Venafro-San Pietro road. The section was commanded by a Lieutenant Heinemann. He placed his guns in some caves twenty yards from the entrance to the village. The terrain to the south of San Pietro consisted of a series of steep olive terraces as easy to defend as they'd be difficult to attack. The northern and eastern approaches to the village also consisted of terraces. An enemy attacking down them from the north would come under surveillance by Forward Observers on a low spur of Monte Sammucro overlooking San Pietro. (The 36th Forward Observers never picked up this vital enemy OP.)

---

* Its strength was around 200. Men who had been wounded were re-joining the battalion every day but others were deserting to the Allies.

Captain Meitzel thought it likely that the enemy might probe both the northern and southern approaches to the village but was confident that the main attack would come from the east, and that it would be made by infantry. (In case the US forces tried to use armour he had one culvert on the Venafro-San Pietro road mined and the largest bridge plugged with a charge of dynamite. An enterprising patrol from the US 180th Regiment, 45th Division, removed the dynamite.) He decided to use the eastern ravine as a second line of defence and organized his first some five hundred yards further to the east. After laying out an apron of barbed wire running from the Venafro-San Pietro road right up to the northern slopes of Monte Sammucro his pioneers built a dozen pillboxes big enough to take Spandau crews. The pioneers had no cement and had to learn the craft of dry stone walling – and capping – as they went along. The heavy rains caused several of the pillboxes to collapse on top of their occupants.[4]

Captain Meitzel chose a house with red walls for his CP. He was confident he had enough men to do the job. His main concern was supplies. These had to be brought in from San Vittore, the Regimental HQ. The San Pietro-San Vittore road was impassable. Supplies had to be brought up Highway Six and a mile-long road to San Pietro. From the first week in December onwards the road leading to the village was shelled day and night. The shelling and the rain reduced the consistency of the road to a morass. The German Transport Corps nicknamed the road 'The curve of death'. Some drivers kept going with punctures caused by shrapnel. Others took shelter in ditches until the shelling eased. If Meitzel's battalion was to hold San Pietro the Transport Corps would have to keep the supplies coming in.[5]

Clark decided that the 3rd Division needed a rest and refit more badly than his other US Division. They had been in the line for fifty-nine days. Their battle casualties totalled 3,265, their sick 12,959.* The sudden escalation of men becoming ill was a warning of things to come. The 5th Army was not equipped for mountain warfare and the weather they were encountering – bitter cold and almost continual rain – was causing havoc to the health of echelon troops as well as those who were in the line.

The relief of the 3rd Division by the 36th (Texas) Division, II Corps, took place on the night of 16/17 November in pouring rain and on roads clogged with mud. A British convoy in front of the 36th Division got stuck in it and

---

* The average proportion of battle casualties to sick in 5th Army divisions during October-November was 3 to 1. The US 3rd Division's very high sick rate was due to the fact that it had been rushed to Salerno without their bed-rolls, ground sheets, greatcoats, or shelter halves (bivouacs). They had to make do with a single blanket to keep out the cold and damp. In spite of Truscott's repeated requests to have the kit sent on, it only caught up with the Division in late November. After it had left the Line. See *Command Missions*, page 276.

had to start digging themselves out. If they failed to make it by first light the German artillery would have a turkey shoot. The British did managed to dig themselves out in time and the rest of the relief went smoothly. Lucas noted that US convoys never got stuck on muddy roads because, unlike British and German vehicles, US ones had four-wheel drive. Lucas believed that the four-wheel drive had a lot to do with winning the War. He was deeply concerned with the conditions II Corps were putting up with: 'It has rained for two days and is due to rain for two more, so say the meteorologists,' he wrote in his diary on 13 November. 'In addition it is as cold as hell. I think too often of my men out in the mountains. I am far too tender-hearted ever to be a success at my chosen profession.' A revealing statement.

During his first night in the line Private Lee Fletcher, 20, I Company, 3rd Battalion, 143rd Regiment, US 36th Division, who had come straight from a sunny orchard near Naples, was woken up by enemy shelling. It was pouring with rain. His foxhole was waterlogged. Standing close by was a mule with its bladder hanging out of its rectum. Behind it lay the bodies of two long dead GIs. The enemy's harassing fire kept Fletcher in his foxhole all day. His feet were soaked and he had no spare pair of socks.[6]

Aware of the danger of his men going down with trench feet, Major-General Fred Walker, Commanding Officer of the 36th Division, ordered his quartermaster to get as many pairs of socks as possible and on 18 November he noted in his diary. 'I have instituted action to procure 12,000 combat suits, 6,000 pairs of leather gloves and 2,000 gasoline heaters for the men in the front.' But such equipment was not to hand. The 50,000 Arctic combat suits and overshoes* Eisenhower had requested in September had not been given sufficient priority. Arctic suits and overshoes did not start arriving in Italy until mid-December. And they came in bits and pieces. The first consignment to reach 141st Regiment, 36th Division, whose fighting strength was by then around 1,200 men, consisted of 597 combat jackets, 1,017 combat trousers, 1,110 arctic overshoes and 350 stoves.[7] Most of the 36th Division who were in the line in December had to make do with heavy, cumbersome greatcoats which were not waterproof, and rubber raincoats which made the men sweat and did not keep out the cold. (British X Corps' overcoats and gas-capes posed similar problems.) The scarcity of socks was a cause of even more concern. Unlike the British Army, who always had its men carry a spare pair of socks with them, the US Army relied on a quick replacement service. This no longer existed. When the 45th Division put in for 45,000 pairs of socks they were told there were none available. The 36th QM did manage to get socks for everyone in the division but not until mid-December. Heavy wool socks for engineers wearing gumboots and working

* galoshes

86

up to their knees in mud did not arrive until March 1944. Forward Observers who had to spend hours absolutely still to avoid being spotted by their opposite numbers were never issued with combat suits. All they got were rabbit-skin hats with ear flaps.

Mud severely restricted the firing power of heavy US guns. Each time they fired a single round the recoil buried them deep in the mud and their crews had to dig them out before they could open fire again. When Lucas visited the 15th Evacuation Hospital he found doctors standing in six inches of mud operating on wounded men. He comments on how the war had forced medical research to find new life-saving drugs and how medical teams had established surgical units just behind the line for men too severely wounded to be moved. (The Afrika Korps had pioneered the system in North Africa.) Unit Medical officers in the 36th Division were under strict orders to send only severe cases of trench feet to hospital. Corporal William Gallagher, 23, E Company, 2nd Battalion, 143rd Regiment, had a buddy who went sick and was told, 'You don't have feet hanging off your legs. You just have slabs of meat.' He was sent back to his foxhole. Corporal Gallagher's feet were playing him up as well. But he found a way of catching them on the blink. 'At night I would put my hand in front of my eyes and if I couldn't see my hands, off would come my shoes.'* Corporal Gallagher discovered that an officer in the 143rd Regiment had come up with the same idea,[8] a remarkable bit of intuitive medicine from a remarkable division.

The 36th Division was the only National Guard unit to retain all its senior officers. Like the bulk of the division they were Texans. When Major-General Fred Walker took over the division in 1941 he found the standard of its training and the calibre of its officers so high he decided not to replace them with regular officers from other non-Texan divisions. The T-patchers – a nickname derived from the T on their divisional flash – loved Walker for that. When they were chosen to help spearhead the US landings at Salerno in preference to the experienced 34th Division they were very proud. They fought hard at Salerno,† apart from the unfortunate 2nd Battalion, 143rd Regiment. Discovering that a battalion from the US 45th Division had retreated, leaving his left flank open, the CO of the 2nd Battalion ordered his men to lie doggo, in the hope that the enemy wouldn't spot them. The Germans took the CO and most of his battalion prisoners. General Walker was furious. In his extraordinarily candid diary he lambasts the CO of the 2nd Battalion and then lashes out at National Guard officers in general: 'A

* For some reason all ranks in the US Army called boots shoes. The US issue boots had hard rubber soles, useful for a quiet approach on a road patrol. British Army boots had steel studs. A platoon trying to walk quietly up a road made a noise that could be heard a long way off.
† Their infantry companies suffered 40% battle casualties.

little learning is a dangerous thing. This fault applies to most National Guard officers. They will not learn their job, they will not discipline their troops, they will not carry out orders of higher headquarters. I have to do much of their work for them.' Walker blacklisted three National Guard lieutenant-colonels, and replaced two of them with regulars. He was bitter about Major-General Dawley being replaced as VI Corps Commander by Lucas during Salerno. Walker thought he should have had the job: 'This indicates to me that friendship is playing an important part in selection of good officers for positions of general command. . . . I am the senior general officer in Italy, that is I was, until my juniors, Eisenhower, Clark, Lucas, Gerow, Woodruff, Keyes, were promoted over me. Of course, I am not a graduate at West Point and have no friends at court to look out for me.'

Walker was equally scathing about British* X Corps having been directed to take Naples. 'I don't think they will ever do it.' They did, and Corporal Leonard Rice whose 143rd Regiment, 36th Division, was attached to the British 7th Armoured Division who took Naples, described them as 'Great troops. I will always remember them.' One wonders what Walker would have said if he had discovered that Lt-Colonel Charles Denholm, a West Pointer, and new Commander of 2nd Battalion, 143rd Regiment, was using British battle drill to re-train it. After the 36th Division's failure to cross the Rapido in January, 1944 – a forlorn hope foisted on them by Clark – all but one of Walker's senior National Guard officers were replaced by regulars, on Clark's instructions this time. Walker wrote, 'I do not understand how men can go into the National Guard, give their time to qualify as officers, when they know they are going to be discriminated against and mistreated if and when war comes. No wonder the National Guard officers dislike and distrust all regular officers.'[9]

Observed harassing fire by enemy artillery caused many casualties among the 36th Division's forward units. The T-patchers had been told the Germans were short of shells, but there didn't seem to be any shortage on their front. 5th Army intelligence had yet to discover that during the first battle for Mignano Gap the enemy artillery had increased their stock-piles of shells and were able to fire far more freely.

The enemy's harassing fire was usually carried out by light artillery. The 29th Division's heavy guns, commanded by Major Jürgen Wöbbeking,

---

* In January, 1944, British 46th Division failed to cross the Garigliano in an attack aimed at helping the US 36th Division cross the Rapido a few days later. General Hawksworth visited General Walker's headquarters to apologize for his division's failure, an act of rare courtesy. Walker's response to this was to note: 'The British are the world's greatest diplomats but you can't rely on them for anything else'. Lucas considered British X Corps 'A broken reed'. Clark agreed with him. The only US general in the 5th Army who appreciated the courage and tenacity of British troops was Truscott, whose division had worked closely with British 56th Division throughout the advance to the Winter Line.

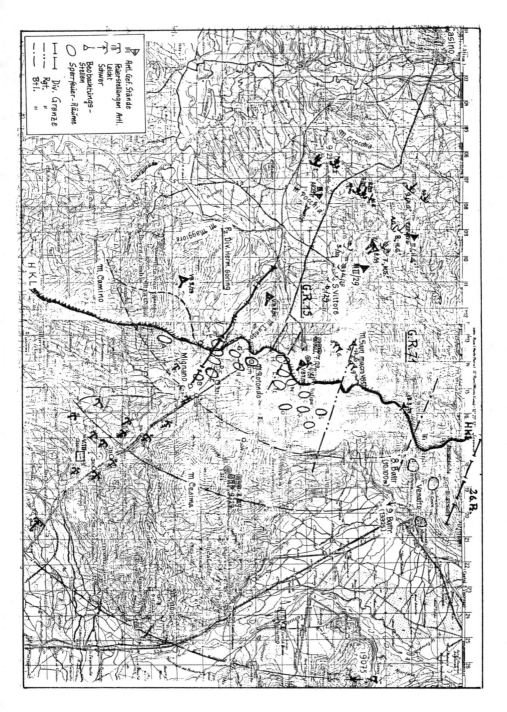

concentrated on counter-battery fire. With the aid of his Forward Observers Major Wöbbeking quickly worked out the whereabouts of nearly all the 36th Division's batteries.* They outnumbered his by about three to one. The US guns had a much greater muzzle flash than the German guns and could be more easily spotted. The calibre of divisional guns were very similar, the heaviest US gun being 155 mm, the heaviest German 150 mm. In counter-battery work the US guns had the enormous advantage of being able to send out reconnaissance planes – Piper Cubs† – whenever the weather permitted. The Pipers located the exact positions of the German batteries and wirelessed back their positions to their own guns. Soon after Major Wöbbeking's batteries moved into position Piper Cubs flew over them. In the shelling that followed several of Major Wöbbeking's guns were destroyed. Guns were still a precious commodity in the 10th Army, even though replacements‡ were reaching it, thanks to Kesselring's new powers as Supreme Commander. No replacements were sent to Major Wöbbeking's battalion and he had to work out some way of foxing the Pipers. The night after his guns were destroyed he moved all his batteries to fresh positions and installed dummy guns in some of the old positions. At the same time he had trucks drive out to the dummies, men trample the grass and let off high explosives to simulate the sight and sound of muzzle flash. US forward observers took them for the real thing and when Piper Cubs reported the tracks left by the trucks and the trodden grass round the dummies US battery commanders concluded that the enemy batteries had not been destroyed or forced out of their positions. They began shelling them again, and kept on shelling them until the front began changing.

Major Wöbbeking had another problem to solve. How to fire at the US batteries without giving his guns' new positions away. If his batteries opened fire in the usual way – all guns firing simultaneously – they would soon be spotted by Forward Observers or Pipers, and the numerically superior US guns would have another field day. Major Wöbbeking gave orders for all available guns – and mortars if the range was right – to fire a single round at one US battery. This meant between forty and sixty guns, including tanks and SP, concentrating their fire on four enemy guns. The US Forward

---

* See copy of Major Wöbbeking's firing map. This was examined at a 36th Divisional Artillery reunion in 1991 and found to be very accurate.
† These flimsy and vulnerable planes had to circle slowly over a target at an altitude of 500 feet to 600 feet to make sure of the exact location of the enemy guns. They were a relatively easy target for the 88 mm and lighter anti-aircraft guns that were positioned round the German field guns. Lucas noted that 'Piper Cubs were largely instrumental in making our artillery the terrible scourge it is. It results, however, in the losses among lieutenants of Field artillery having higher losses than any other branches.' 16.12.43
‡ These were mainly light Italian and Russian guns.

Observers would have very little chance of locating any of Major Wöbbeking's guns as they fired their single round. Forward observers got their best results from spotting batteries opening fire at regular intervals and the US battery on the receiving end of the barrage had a very unpleasant time, sometimes being forced out of their positions, and losing guns as well as men.[10]

All German gunners had a direction-finding technique for locating medium to large Allied wireless sets. It was nothing new; Allied gunners used the same technique, but, under pressure, German gunners had raised their game until they could locate enemy wireless sets within seconds of them being switched on. The German 170 mm gun outranged the US 'Long John' 155 mm and 240 mm guns by about ¾ of a mile. They could fire a good 18 miles and had been the scourge of US Divisional and Regimental Headquarters. The way the enemy always pinpointed them worried everyone from Clark downwards. 5th Army Intelligence suspected that the German batteries possessed a secret sensor device which 'locked on' to the Headquarters wireless sets. Back in October General Truscott's HQ had been heavily shelled whilst he was conferring with General Templar. 'We had just started discussions in our War Room tent when German artillery fire began screaming into the Command Post. Exploding shells shook the War Room tent, fragments whizzed about overhead, and several passed through the tent while we were talking. General Templar seemed to pay no attention and I was determined not to be outdone. When we finished our discussion, he asked me to see our Command set up. We sauntered about whilst I showed it to him with a nonchalance that I was far from feeling. Shrapnel whistled about – one bit even cut the side seam of the breeches I was wearing. Returning to the War Room tent, we found my staff standing about, with a British officer lying on his back under the shelter of a small bank about a foot in height. We thought at first he was wounded but he quickly reassured us. 'I say,' he said, as he scrambled to his feet, 'It's no good getting shot unless one jolly well has to.'[11]

Early in November both Clark's and Lucas's vehicles had been strafed by the Luftwaffe on the same day. Both had dived into the nearest ditch. That particular hit-and-run raid cost the Luftwaffe eleven planes, all shot down by US anti-aircraft fire. The XII Air Support Command also caused problems. VI Corps HQ was just outside Venafro. US planes kept on bombing the town in mistake for Cassino. On 1 December Lucas wrote, 'They do this too damned often . . . It must be poor briefing or else they can't read a map. They were not fired on till they dropped their bombs.' Most of these missed Venafro but they caused fifty civilian casualties. On 15 March, 1944, forty-three US heavy bombers once again mistook Venafro for Cassino. This time they bombed accurately. Venafro and other towns behind it were reduced to rubble. Ninety-six Allied soldiers and 140 civilians were killed, and many hundreds wounded.

On Monte Corno Colonel Darby's longest running show was in full swing. III/71st Regiment, 29th Panzer Grenadier Division had relieved the unit of the 3rd Panzer Grenadier Division who had been holding the mountain's main peak. On the afternoon of 19 November two companies of the 71st tried to rush the Rangers' positions. They moved so quickly that Colonel Darby had no time to call down DF from 4.2" mortars. Both sides pelted each other with grenades. The Rangers held and the enemy withdrew to the shelter of some large rocks below the main peak. German artillery opened up on the Rangers and the two companies of Panzer Grenadiers attacked again, overrunning part of the Rangers' positions. The Rangers drove them out. The enemy retreated to the rocks and reformed. At dusk they attacked again. They didn't get so close this time but as they retreated they left snipers behind. The Rangers had suffered such heavy losses in the fighting that Colonel Darby had to call up his reserve company to reinforce them. Although Colonel Darby dismissed all German soldiers as 'Krauts', and in his account of the action fails to mention what formation the Rangers were up against, he must have realized that this particular bunch of Krauts were much more formidable than the previous one.

During the morning of 20 November Rangers patrols eliminated all the enemy snipers but the main body of the enemy kept up harassing fire from the main peak all day long. At dawn on 21 November the 83rd Chemical battalion mortared the peak. As soon as the barrage lifted the sniping began again. That night Colonel Darby ordered 4th Rangers to replace the 1st. In two days' fighting the 1st had lost nearly 40% casualties. 4th Rangers at once counter-attacked. B Company's attack failed but E Company got round the rear of the enemy and destroyed two Spandau posts. Later the same day a fighting patrol from B Company dropped a Bangalore torpedo into an enemy dugout and spotted forty of the enemy digging positions below the peak. On 22 November Companies E and C launched an attack on the new enemy positions, but as they closed on the enemy two fresh enemy companies counter-attacked under cover of a creeping barrage. One of them outflanked E Company, and D Company of the 509th Parachute Battalion had to rush to their aid. US artillery and 4.2" mortars opened up on the enemy artillery, but the enemy continued to attack and enemy shelling forced the Rangers Cannon *Company out of their position. At midday Colonel Darby's CP reported that the Rangers were running out of grenades but that D Company paratroopers were pushing back the enemy. As the Panzer Grenadiers

---

* Heavy machine gun.

withdrew they were caught in a 4.2" barrage and suffered heavy casualties. An artillery OP officer reported 'dead Heinies all over the place'. But Darby told General Middleton that he was afraid that one more enemy counter-attack might overrun the Rangers positions. He asked for a company of the 180th Infantry as reinforcements and Middleton promised to send them up.

The enemy attacked again just as the 180th Battalion was arriving. In the resulting confusion the Rangers' lines were almost broken, but once again they held on until the enemy withdrew. Down at the base of the mountain enemy shellfire killed the Rangers' communication officer and two of his section. (Out of twenty-two members of the section all but three were killed or wounded during the fighting on and around Monte Corno.)

The enemy continued to press home their attacks. On 24 November they once again almost broke through the US lines. Colonel Darby, who was up front, sent an SOS to his CP asking for all possible DF fire available. The US artillery and 4.2" mortars gave it all they had – during the Monte Corno battles they fired over 40,000 rounds – and the counter-attack was broken up.

On 25 November the enemy went on the defensive. They had shot their bolt. III/71st Regiment's CO, Captain Spohr, had been killed by US artillery fire. His reports and those of his successor, Captain Breitschwert, convinced Colonel Kruger that the battalion had done all it had been asked to do, apart from recapturing Monte Corno's second peak. He reported the situation to General Fries, who agreed with him. The battalion had suffered 157 battle* casualties. Considering the fire power used against them these were light and show how skilfully the Panzer Grenadiers had used the terrain and how they had turned the accepted maxim – that attacks or counter-attacks should not be made unless the attackers outnumbered the enemy by at least three to one – on its head. On Monte Corno the US forces outnumbered the enemy by more than three to one. But the casualties made further full scale counter-attacks by the III battalion difficult to sustain. Captain Breitschwert was ordered to keep probing the enemy defences in the hope that his men would find a gap.[12]

On 26 November Colonel Darby decided to try blowing up the enemy on the main peak. The Rangers buried 800 tons of TNT beneath the peak, but the enemy guessed what they were up to and during the night they temporarily abandoned the peak. As the Rangers detonated the explosives the enemy charged them. Once again they dented the US lines. They then

* Between 11 November and 17 December, when the Rangers' action on Monte Corno finally ended, they lost 27 killed or died of wounds, 121 wounded and evacuated, and 200 sick. III/71st sick for the period 19 November – 17 December totalled 43. They were equipped with excellent winter combat kit. Kesselring had acted very quickly during the November lull in the battle and the whole of XIV Panzer Korps had received winter clothing.

took up residence on the peak again. Colonel Darby tried a 'softly, softly' approach. A Ranger patrol put a loudspeaker near the peak, surrounded it with anti-personnel mines and Colonel Darby played a mixture of propaganda and Vienna waltzes on a gramophone. 'No German tried to get through the mines to get to reach the loudspeaker,' writes Colonel Darby. Did he really think they would? The Panzer Grenadiers then tried a ploy of their own. One of their Italian girlfriends had the nerve to walk up Monte Corno and tell the first American she met that the Germans had pulled out of the village of Concasalle below Monte Corno. The news was received with scepticism by the Rangers' intelligence officer, but the girl's visit set off a spate of rumours. The enemy were dressing up as women. Colonel Darby writes, 'They were even dressing up as monks and nuns'. It reminds one of the scare stories of German partroopers dressed as nuns dropping on England in 1940.[13]

During the third week in November the 2nd Battalion, 143rd Regiment on Monte Rotondo was relieved. On their way back to their rest area, where they were constantly shelled, Colonel Gallagher's company passed a crowd of tank crews, artillery men, medics and engineers. They wandered up to have a word with 'the boys of the infantry', giving them cigarettes, candy and cups of coffee. Their quiet tribute to the lads at the 'sharp end' was, for Gallagher, 'the greatest compliment that was accorded us, the infantry . . . I went through Rome when it fell and I was in Times square, New York, when the war ended but those occasions . . . generated a different kind of emotion. On that dirt road you could feel the transmissions of care and concern. Who knows, maybe it was an experience of love.'[14]

From the rest area Colonel Gallagher was sent on a fighting patrol to probe the outlying defences of San Pietro. About seven hundred yards east of the village an Italian led them to the house occupied by the enemy. The Germans, taken by surprise, exchanged fire with the patrol for about quarter of an hour, and then the four occupying the house surrendered. Regimental HQ passed on their congratulations. They were the first prisoners to be taken from the area of San Pietro and might reveal vital information about how strongly the village was held. Clark was still hopeful that the countryside west of the village would be suitable for tanks. The ground he called 'flat' was full of ridges and low hills which enemy forward observers and infantry could make excellent use of. By 11 November he had realized that 'the hill mass running north of San Pietro', (i.e. Monte Sammucro) was 'critical terrain'.[15] He was learning. Now that Monte Rotondo was safely in Allied hands Clark could concentrate on plans for taking San Pietro and using his armour. Monte Lungo is not mentioned in any of 5th Army's Forward

Operations. To Clark Monte Lungo was a minor nuisance, an excellent observation post for the enemy, and that was all.

Another 36th Division patrol that must have caused alarm and confusion among the Germans was carried out by A Company, 1st Battalion, 143rd Regiment, and the battalion's pioneer platoon. US pioneers were trained to lay and lift mines. They also doubled up as litter-bearers (stretcher-bearers) and porters. This particular patrol had been planned by the Pioneer Platoon Commander, Lieutenant Fred 'Dynamite' Young, 21, who had won a Silver Star at Chiunzi Pass delivering ammunition up a road under direct observation from enemy artillery and mortars.* After an A Company officer had carried out a twelve-mile patrol behind Monte Rotondo, Lieutenant Young suggested to him that they carry out a joint patrol behind the enemy lines in the same area, leaving land mines at a point likely to worry the enemy and permission from the 1st Battalion's CO was obtained for the venture. Young had a note printed 'Courtesy of Young's Pioneers, we'll call again' which he rolled in wax paper. The object of the patrol was not to blow up Germans but to show them that US forces could plant mines when and where they fancied. The patrol – five pioneers and a covering force of infantry – set off one evening late in November. They penetrated the enemy lines and got as far as a large building three miles to the rear. Germans were walking in and out of it and it was clearly an HQ. Young's pioneers armed four mines, left them on the road near the HQ and headed for home. On the way they passed an enemy patrol returning to their own lines. The enemy didn't spot them.[16]

It was not unknown for German and Allied reconnaissance patrols to pass each other at night, both sides turning a blind eye. Corporal Ray Wells, 21, D Company, 141st Regiment, 36th Division, went one better. His squad arrived near the top of Monte Rotondo in the dark. His squad sergeant said they'd be moving on soon so not to dig in, and then disappeared. Corporal Wells felt uneasy. He was a heavy machine gunner, and his weapon had to be dug in before it could be fired. His rifle had been made in 1903. The other two members of his squad were armed with Colt revolvers. As the three of them huddled together they heard men moving towards them up the slope nearest to the enemy. In his anxiety Corporal Wells forgot the password. He shouted 'Give the password!' 'We don't know it!' someone answer with a rich American accent. 'Advance and be recognized!' shouted a relieved Coporal Wells. The men tramped up until they were within a few yards of the squad. By then Corporal Wells could see from their helmets

---

* The truck received a direct hit. Lieutenant Young was bady wounded in one leg but he kept on going.

that they were Germans. 'Mighty nasty weather,' said their leader. Corporal Wells, too dazed to be afraid, agreed that it was mighty nasty. He was staring at the Schmeisser the German was holding. 'Waal, we'll be off now,' said the German. 'Good luck!' At no time during the encounter did Corporal Wells feel afraid. But months later when he thought of it he broke out in a cold sweat.[17]

The 36th had arrived in the line without any mules. All portering had to be done by hand. The mountain terrain was so rugged that the men acting as porters wore out their shoes in three days. Thirty mules arrived at 143rd's Forward HQ early in December, to the relief of the men who'd been acting as porters. The relief quickly turned to dismay. The mules couldn't take it. They'd been used to mule tracks, not to trails with jagged rocks. They fell over precipices or became too exhausted to carry a load.

Three Ultra decrypts in November provided a particularly rich haul of information. The first, dated the 12th, reported Kesselring's concern at the loss of Monte Corno and the imminent relief of the 3rd Panzer Grenadier Division by the 29th. The second dealt with 10th Army's strength in tanks and anti-tank guns. A comparison with an October decrypt is interesting.

	October	November
Operational tanks	149	182 with 47 in reserve
Heavy anti-tank guns	85	320

The decrypt also showed that stocks of ammunition were rising steadily and fuel stocks were being maintained above danger level. The Allied strategic bombing of railway communications was effective but Kesselring had managed to keep up the flow of supplies by using merchant shipping. The third decrypt, 20 November, carried a general appreciation of the 10th Army's situation from Kesselring to OKW, in which he told them exactly what he intended to do with each division under his command.[18]

Those merchant ships brought luxuries as well as necessities. Unlike the US and British Armies the German armies always saw to it that all ranks were well fed when possible. The lull in hostilities enabled Panzer Korps' divisional messes to come up to peacetime standards. The officers got French Champagne – or rather the officers in all divisional messes except the 29th Panzer Grenadier Divisions did. General Fries ordered the mess cooks to serve the same food as the men in the front line were getting. What General Fries' staff officers thought of this is not on record but there's no doubt about how it would have gone down with the men in the line. Although General Fries' decision was certainly not intended as an exercise in public relations he could hardly have done anything more calculated to show his men the lengths to which he was prepared to go to share their hardships.[19]

General Walker was also keenly aware of the conditions his men were living under: 'My heart beats with sympathy for them . . . how they endure their hardships I do not understand.' But like most of the German generals he ate two good hot meals a day without worrying about what his men were eating: 'For dinner today we had stewed rice, salmon croquettes, diced carrots, bread, gravy, hot chocolate and bread pudding.' Not up to most German divisional messes but luxurious compared to the hard tack his men were getting.

Clark had begun planning his second attack on the Mignano Gap on 16 November. Alexander visited Clark at Caserta on 18 November and suggested he delay the attack until 12 December. 8th Army would be launching a major attack across the Sangro on 20 November. It would almost certainly force 10th Army to transfer divisions facing 5th Army on to 8th Army's front. It was a reasonable assumption and Clark welcomed any pressure on the enemy. But he suspected Alexander was giving Montgomery a head start in the 'Rome stakes'.* He told Alexander he would attack as soon as 5th Army was ready to resume the offensive. A likely date would be 2 December. 5th Army's meteorological section had forecast that 1 and 2 December would be clear and sunny. Clark needed two such days in which the XII Air Support Command could soften up the enemy defences and harry their supply lines and bases. Alexander agreed to let Clark choose his own date for the attack. The two generals discussed the need for a new landing near Rome, should the Gustav Line prove as tough as intelligence reports indicated. Clark was confident he could take Mignano Gap with another frontal assault. The only way of avoiding this would be to launch an amphibious landing near the mouth of the Garigliano, but this would mean the 5th Army having to mount two amphibious exercises in rapid succession, something no army would care to contemplate.[20] Clark arranged for 5th Army units to stage amphibious exercises near Mondragone and Naples in order to try and deceive the enemy into believing he was planning an amphibious landing. 5th Army's meteorological section warned Clark that the month of December 'provides the most unfavourable weather conditions of the year for military operations. It is the culmination of the rainy season.'[21] Up to 10.79 inches could be expected. Clark code-named his new attack 'Operation Raincoat'.

The line-up for the attack was very different from the first battle. The British 7th Armoured Division had left for Sicily to embark for Operation

* On 4 November Clark had had a conference with Lt-General Alec Richardson, Alexander's Chief of Staff. General Richardson told Clark that Alexander was going to order 8th Army to advance on Rome. Clark asked Richardson if Alexander intended that 8th Army should take Rome. Richardson said it would be first past the post. In his account of the conference in *Calculated Risk*, pages 223-4, Clark makes no mention of this part of the conference.

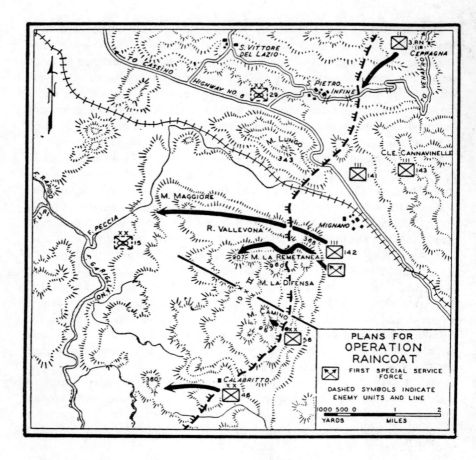

Overlord. Two out of the three regiments of US 88th Airborne Division would be accompanying the 7th Armoured Division to the UK. For the time being their third regiment, the 504th, would remain in 5th Army. In place of the two divisions Clark had already received two regiments – the US – Canadian First Special Service Force, and the 1st Italian Motorized Brigade, the first Italian army unit to fight for the Allies. In December the Free French 2nd Moroccan Division would also join 5th Army.

The First Special Service Force had been raised in the summer of 1942. It was to be parachuted into Norway to sabotage enemy installations. Colonel Robert Frederick, a staff officer of US GHQ, carried out a feasibility study of the operation and said it would be suicidal. The Norwegian government in exile also objected to the plan. It was dropped, but the raising of the 1st SSF went ahead, with Colonel Frederick as its commanding officer. Studebaker manufactured the armoured vehicle that had been intended for use on snow in Norway. It would become known as the Weasel, and would prove very effective on waterlogged ground as well as on snow. The 1st SSF was made up of three combat regiments, each around 600 men strong, and one service regiment. The latter carried out all administration jobs and fatigues. Each combat company had five officers and seventy-five other ranks, much the same as a Ranger company, but a 1st SSF company had 6 Browning heavy machine guns (all the Rangers heavy machine guns were in their Cannon company), six flame-throwers and six 60 mm mortars. Most platoon commanders were American and most company commanders Canadian. Senior officers and other ranks were 50% US, 50% Canadian. All officers were handpicked but some of the other ranks were made up of men other units couldn't handle. Private Bob Davis, 18, who came from North Carolina, had been in trouble with the police since he was 13 and was soon in trouble with the armoured regiment in which he'd enlisted. His skill as a tank driver resulted in his being made an instructor. A 'learner' officer proved so dumb that Davis kicked him. Davis was awaiting court martial when he read a 1st SSF announcement asking for volunteers: 'Single men ages between 21 and 25 who have completed three years or more of grammar school and are within occupational range of Lumberjacks, Forest Rangers, Hunters, Northwoodsmen, Game Wardens, Prospectors and Explorers.' Davis had never gone to school and his only steady job had been boot-legging. He volunteered just the same and was accepted.[22] Colonel Frederick had enough clout to have the court-martial quashed. When Davis arrived at 'Freddie's Freighters' training camp in Montana he discovered what he'd let himself in for. All ranks had to qualify as skiers, mountaineers, parachutists, saboteurs and first-class shots. They also had to become experts at unarmed combat – Colonel Frederick borrowed the finest instructor in the States from Fort Benning* and never returned him – and carry out all the usual infantry training, as well as forced marches of up to 60 miles. The distance was the same as forced marches in Commando and Rangers training, but the 1st SSFs marches were always made at night, putting even more strain on the men taking part in them. Anyone who fell out was returned to his original unit. Several times Davis came very close to falling out. He kept going because he was determined to stay with the Regiment. It had given him a sense of security and comradeship he'd never known before.[23]

In July, 1943, the 1st SSF took part in the attack on the Aleutian islands. The Japanese evacuated them twenty-four hours before the task force arrived. When the 1st SSF returned to the States it was earmarked for the Mediterranean sector. Clark at once asked them to be sent to 5th Army. The

* US Infantry Training Depot.

Regiment arrived in Naples on 19 November and immediately moved up to the front. It was attached to the 36th Division.

Montgomery had chosen 20 November to launch his attack across the Sangro because he knew from Ultra decrypts that the river was only held by one regiment of the untried 65th Infantry Division. The Division had been raised in Holland and consisted mainly of teenage Germans. But heavy rain and subsequent flooding forced Montgomery to postpone his attack until 27 November. By then the whole of the 65th Division was in the line – their Commander, Major-General von Zielberg remarked, 'The dug-outs will hold; whether the troops will remains to be seen' – and elements of the 26th Panzer Division were alongside them. An attack made by the 8th Indian Division was repelled. The 2nd New Zealand Division secured its initial objective but could make no progress against the 26th Panzers. On 28 November the North West African Tactical Bomber Force subjected 65th Division's echelons and communications to saturation bombing. Early on 29 November Montgomery sent in the 78th Division under cover of a barrage aimed specifically at the 65th dugouts. 6,000 – 7,000 rounds were used. The barrage killed many of the Germans in their dugouts. One battalion broke. They ran through the tunnels connecting the dugouts with the rear. As they emerged they were shot down by units of the 78th Division who had slipped round to the back entrances of the tunnels. The whole of the battalion was, in Wentzell's words, 'liquidated'. The 78th had broken through the 65th Division's centre and looked unstoppable. One might have expected Kesselring and General Lemelsen to have had sharp words for the battalion that had broken, but they both realized that the Division had received such a terrible pounding that no blame could be attached to it for breaking. They expressed particular concern for the battalion.[24] General Lemelsen noted that one regiment of the 78th had slipped through the boundaries between 65th Division and 26th Division. 'The Devil knows how he always finds out where the boundaries are,' he remarked to Kesselring.

General von Zielberg had lost an arm in the saturation bombing. On Kesselring's recommendation Lemelsen flew in Colonel Baade to take over the 65th Division. He arrived in the middle of another saturation raid and reported that it was worse than anything he'd experienced in North Africa. With 26th Panzers keeping the Allied armour at bay Colonel Baade managed to bind the 65th Division into a fighting force,* but by 1 December the 78th Division had turned the flank of the Bernhardt. Both German and Allied commanders believed that the Adriatic sector was wide open. If 8th

---

* For his handling of 65th Division Colonel Baade was promoted Major-General and given command of the 90th Panzer Grenadier Division. The Division had taken so long to get to the Sangro front that its Commanding Officer had been relieved.

Army reached Pescara they'd have an easy ride to Rome. But the weather became impossible for flying, a regiment of German paratroopers linked up with the 65th Division and 26th Panzers, and the 78th Division ran out of steam. While it was being relieved by the 1st Canadian Division the German forces, free at last from Allied bombing if not from pressure from 2nd New Zealand Division, regrouped. When the two Dominion Divisions attacked together they encountered much stiffer resistance. Once all the 44th Division had arrived at Mignano Gap Kesselring switched two more parachute regiments to the Adriatic front. The weather continued to make bombing an occasional business, the terrain favoured the defenders, and on 28 December Montgomery called off the offensive. For him his attack was a near miss. For Clark is was a bull's-eye. XIV Panzer Korps would receive no help from the Adriatic sector during 'Operation Raincoat'.

Clark had ordered seventy-five heavy bombers, twenty-four mediums and 178 fighter bombers to support 5th Army's attack. The planes would keep up a dawn-to-dusk assault on 1 and 2 December. The scale of the bombing was about par for the course but the attack's artillery support would be something special. 925 guns* would open up a simultaneous barrage at dusk on 2 December. 820 guns would concentrate their fire on the Monte Camino massif. The new US 8″ gun-howitzers would take part of the bombardment. They were capable of outranging all enemy guns by several miles when fired for interdiction purposes. When used as a howitzer they proved to be the only Allied gun capable of destroying the standard enemy dugout of rock and railway sleepers/ties.

A diversionary attack by US VI Corps on the enemy's left flank would begin on 28 November. In the centre 3rd Rangers would carry out a fighting patrol to San Pietro on 1 December. If the village was heavily defended elements of the 36th Division would take it. The 36th would also deal with Monte Sammucro. On 2 December the First Special Service Force (which, along with the 36th Division and the Italian Motorized Brigade, made up US II Corps† under the command of Major-General Geoffrey Keyes) would tackle Monte La Difensa. Clark allowed them three days to capture the mountain. They would then take Monte Rementea. Monte Maggiore would be taken by 142 Regiment, US 36th Division. Once Monte La Difensa had fallen and that flank of the Camino Massif had been cleared the 1st Italian Motorized Brigade would take Monte Lungo. Clark had told Walker he wanted the Italians to have an easy option, an objective they couldn't fail to take on their first time out, and had suggested Monte Lungo. Walker agreed that Monte Lungo was an appropriate objective for them. On 5th Army's

* XIV Panzer Korps had 16 170 mm guns, 32 210 mm mortars, 173 divisional field guns, 4 batteries of Nebelwerfers, and support from a substantial number of SP guns and tanks.
† With US 1st Armored Division in Reserve.

left flank British X Corps' two divisions, 46th and 56th, would attack Monte Camino and Calabritto. McCreery chose the 56th Division for Monte Camino, the 46th for Calabritto. The 46th Division would attack on 1 December so as to protect 56th Division's left flank.

Von Senger, whose handling of XIV Panzer Korps during the first battle had impressed Kesselring as well as General Lemelsen, was not taken in by the amphibious exercises off Naples and Mondragone. He believed that Clark would have to make another frontal assault on the Mignano Gap sector, and that this time the heaviest attack would fall on his men holding the Camino Massif, the 15th Panzer Grenadier Division, but had no idea when the attack would be made, or which units would make it. The patrols carried out by the Division had proved singularly ineffective, well below their usual standard. The only prisoners they had taken were two young Italian girls from a village near Calabritto. The girls were returned to their homes before the battle began.[25] The Division's failure to identify any enemy units worried Von Senger. He was well aware of the peculiar sense of isolation and loneliness that can affect men holding mountain positions: 'The mountains intensify all fear and demoralizes.' He paid a number of visits to the Camino Massif to check on the Division's morale. He found the old hands determined enough but the young polyglot replacements looking a bit lost, as well they might. At Calabritto I/129th Regiment had laid out a barbed wire apron whose size and depth was up to First World War standards. Thanks to Von Senger the Division would be able to call upon some first class reserves. Kesselring had agreed that the two battalions of the von Corvin battle group would form part of XIV Panzer Korps. No more shuttlecock war games for the Hermann Göring infantry.

5th Army Intelligence reported that Monte La Difensa and the saddle joining it to the Monte Rementea was held by III/104th Panzer Grenadier Regiment, some 250 men strong. Another 100 or so men from the III/129th Panzer Grenadier Regiment were occupying the saddle between Monte La Difensa and Monte Camino. Colonel Frederick chose Second Regiment, commanded by Colonel D. D. Williamson to make the attack on Monte La Difensa. Third Regiment, commanded by Lt-Colonel Edwin Walker, would be in reserve. First Regiment, commanded by Colonel Alfred Marshall, would act as reserve to 142nd Regiment in their assault on Monte Maggiore.

Colonel Williamson chose Lt-Colonel Tom MacWilliams's 1st Battalion to lead the assault. MacWilliams, a former history professor at New Brunswick University, knew what had happened to Colonel Sherman's 7th Regiment on Monte La Difensa, and sent out scouting parties – in pairs, an officer and a sergeant – to find a way up the cliffs. The scouts operated in daylight, passing along the lower slopes of the eastern side of the mountain, which were held by the 142nd Regiment, and climbing up to the mountains' cliffs. These began about eight hundred feet from the summit. Major Edward Thomas, 1st Battalion's Executive Officer, a regular from North Carolina, teamed up with Sergeant Howard van Ausdale, half Dutch half Red Indian. He had been a prospector and was the best scout in the battalion. On their first day on the mountain a guide from the 142nd Regiment led them to his company's positions. Major Thomas noted that the men were exhausted, the steepness of the mountainside making the simplest project difficult. 'The Forward Observer was gaunt, dirty and had the first case of combat shakes I had seen.'[26] Major Thomas and Sergeant Van Ausdale reconnoitred the mountain's north-facing cliffs. The lowest cliff was about two hundred feet high. Van Ausdale spotted a cleft that led right to the top. In places the rock was rotten and there were numerous overhangs. But the men's jump-boots helped them get a grip on the rock slabs, and the fact that they were not carrying heavy equipment made it relatively easy for them to get just below the top. They didn't look over in case the enemy spotted them and pinpointed the cleft as a likely line of attack. They had already had a sighter of the rest of the cliffs from lower down the mountain and knew they were not so high. Now they had climbed the main cliff they understood why Colonel Sherman's men had failed to climb it. With heavy equipment it could only be climbable with the aid of ropes.* Every single cliff would have to be roped up before the attack. This would be a tricky business. But getting the second Regiment to an LOD on time would be almost as difficult. To climb up the whole of Monte La Difensa in one night was out of the question. It would have to be a two-night job. The first would be spent getting the regiment to a base where it could lie up under cover during the day. It would start climbing the cliffs as soon as it was dark. The base would have to be well up the mountain. Colonel Williamson, Major Thomas and Lt-Colonel Robert Moore, CO 2nd Battalion, Second Regiment, eventually found an excellent spot in a pinewood about halfway up the mountain. Major Thomas had to ensure that the Second Regiment arrived at the base before first light. It would be marching across country from Presenzano, six miles from the foothills of Monte La Difensa as the crow flies, and at least twice as far on the ground, and would then have to climb 1,500 feet to the pinewood. Major Thomas had only done the Presenzano approach march once, in darkness. He had timed himself so he was able to work out a rough march schedule. 1st Battalion's attack would be led by Captain Rothlin's I Company. Captain Rothlin was very much aware that since the Force had left the States on 28 October it had had very little exercise. The men were like boxers who had stopped training a month before the fight. Knowing that the attack was

* The First Special Service Force carried climbing rope as part of their equipment.

imminent he worked his company from dawn to dusk. After a few days of routine marches and runs the men were in better shape and Captain Rothlin opened up the throttle. He force marched them until they cursed him.

On 12 November 169th Brigade had moved up to the foothills of Monte Camino to cover the withdrawal of 201 Guards Brigade. Whilst reconnoitring the Battalion's position Brigadier Lyne and Lt-Colonel J. B. H. Kealey of the 2/6th Queen's were both injured by an 'S' mine. Lt-Colonel J. Y. Whitfield, DSO, took over temporary command of the Brigade, Major F. A. H. Ling command of the 2/5th, and Major A. J. Renshaw command of the 2/6th.

The Battalion lived in caves and holes in the ground, sometimes sharing them with Italian peasants whose homes had been destroyed. The weather was terrible and life a struggle, with cold wind and rain. The whole Brigade was maintained and supplied over a most primitive jeep track that was two feet deep in mud. At one place this track went in at the front door of a cottage, out of a window, and then down some steep steps. But the jeeps managed it and the troops got their hot meal each night.

Major-General Templar visited the brigade and explained McCreery's plans and his own to all the Queens' officers. 46th Division would attack Calabritto and Pill-box Ridge on 1 December, securing the base of Bare Arse for 167th Brigade, who would assault it on 2 December, simultaneously with 169th Brigade's attack on Razorback. The ridge was held by about 150 men from II/104 Panzer Grenadier Regiment, the battalion which had attacked the Guards during their attack on Monte Camino. The Queen's could expect tough resistance. Once Razorback was captured 169th or 167th Brigade would tackle Monastery Hill. General Templar also told the Queen's that the First Special Service Force would carry out an attack on Monte La Difensa simultaneously with the assault on Razorback. He later talked with the officers of 2/5th Queen's, whose battalion would lead the assault. He emphasized that its success would depend a great deal on how much their patrols got to know about the enemy strong-points. He also told the officers about their artillery support. It had been planned by Brigadier Calvert Jones, Royal Horse Artillery, Commanding Officer of British 10th Corps Artillery. Owing to the extreme steepness of the target areas he had decided to dispense with the usual support barrage. Instead he planned a series of what he called 'terror crashes'. In much the same way as Major Wöbbeking had directed all guns and mortars under his command on to a single US battery so Brigadier Calvert Jones would direct all 303 guns at his disposal – as well as 4.2" mortars – on to each identified enemy strongpoint. Each 'crash' would last for approximately one minute. All known enemy strongpoints would be 'crashed' three times before the assault troops went in. US batteries using phosphorous shells would illuminate targets for the British guns, which included all available calibres from 25 pounders to 7.2".[27] (Stock-piling so many shells proved a terrible strain for some of the gunners. 113 Field Artillery Regiment, which would support 169th Brigade's attack, were dug in round Conca, a village three miles south east of Monte Camino. The rains had made all roads leading to the village impassable to vehicles. Shells weighing several hundred pounds had to be manhandled in the dark through deep mud for hundreds of yards.)

Major Ling established a special 2/5th patrol company under the command of Captain J. Fleming. Their main objectives were to deny the enemy patrols to the Queen's forward area, to find routes up Razorback, to avoid being taken prisoner – so as not to give identification – and to pinpoint as many enemy strongholds as possible. All patrols went out at night but those whose job it was to find out the lay of the land at the top of Razorback had to lie up all day under the noses of the enemy, with only gas capes and leather jerkins as protection against the cold. But under the leadership of Captain Fleming and Captain C. D. Griffiths, D Company Commander, the patrolling reached a very high standard. When a German left his Spandau for a few minutes Captain Griffiths picked it up and hid it. On another occasion he and his patrol occupied an enemy position while its occupants had gone to breakfast. Several times Queen's patrols on the way to the top spotted German patrols coming down. The enemy patrols failed to spot them. By 1 December all 2/5th company commanders, platoon commanders and most section leaders had been to the top of Razorback and to within at least 100 yards of their objectives. All German outposts had been located and the habits of their occupants studied. Such patrolling would prove invaluable when the attack went in.

Razorback, which ends at the bottom of Monastery Hill, has three distinctive pimples. Major Ling named them Pip, Squeak and Wilfred – in ascending order. Below Pip were two outcrops named Twin Breasts. The approach to Twin Breasts was marked by a large squat rock named the Stone Man. The 2/5th Queen's would attack Razorback via the Stone Man and Twin Breasts. Whilst the 2/5th were tackling Razorback a company of 2/6th Queen's would carry out a diversionary attack on the saddle between Monte Camino and Monte La Difensa. The remaining companies of the Brigade would be needed as porters. The proportion of combat troops to porters tells its own story.

2/5th Queen's established an advance base at Campo. The village was in full view of Razorback so all stores had to be brought up at night. The inhabitants of the village, who had stayed put, observed the daylight curfew with great care.

On 30 November Brigadier Lyne returned from hospital, and Lt-Colonel Whitfield resumed command of 2/5th Queen's. Colonel Whitfield had won his DSO at Salerno but he had stamped his personality on the battalion in Tunisia. During its first action he had insisted on acting as company runner between his two leading companies because he felt he was the right man for the job.

Chapter V

Camino Massif II. Monte Pantano. San Pietro. Monte Lungo. Monte Sammucro

The first of December was as sunny and clear as the Army's meteorologists had promised. From the top of the barracks in which they were billeted the First Special Service Force watched the constant streams of fighter-bombers attacking the Camino Massif. It was very reassuring. A private from 3rd Regiment chalked up the words 'Freddy's Freighters – Difensa or Bust' on a barrack-room wall.[1]

At 1400 hours Major-General Keyes arrived to talk to the Force. 'You have been preceded by a great reputation but you haven't been blooded yet,' he remarked. 'War isn't Hollywood and men do not die dramatically.' The last sentence did not go down at all well with the General's audience. Whatever else he said these were the words they remembered.*

At 1600 hours all three combat regiments began boarding their transport, with 1st Battalion, 2nd Regiment, in the lead. Private First Class Donald Mackinnon, 2 Section, III platoon, 1st Company, remembers the drive to the front: 'At the start it was still light, still possible to be spotted by German observers. We went at breakneck speed, the driver nervous and anxious to drop us off and get the hell out of there. As darkness fell guns seemed to be firing all round us. The sky lit up sporadically with great flashes of light enabling us to see the mountains and the lower clouds.'[2]

139th Brigade (16th Durhams, 2/5th Leicesters, 5th Sherwood Foresters) British 46th Division, had already moved off to attack Calabritto and Pillbox Ridge. The leading companies – Leicesters and Sherwood Foresters – ran into the barbed wire apron in front of the village. It proved impenetrable and after suffering heavy losses from mines and Spandaus they retreated to

---

* But many forgot who had said them. Clark, who made himself as unpopular with the 1st SSF as he had with other 5th Army units, attended a 1st SSF veteran reunion after the War. Believing it was Clark who'd told them 'War isn't Hollywood' they booed him as he entered the hall.[3]

the start line. A second attack was planned for the night of 2/3 December. This time the infantry would be supported by tanks and sappers.

In the meantime the First Special Service Force had debussed at Presenzano. Major Thomas and Captain Rothlin were met by a guide from 142nd Regiment. He led them a different way to the one Major Thomas had taken – up a long, winding stream. The men were ankle-deep in mud and water and could only plod through it. I Company soon fell behind the scheduled pace. Major Thomas knew that if it fell too far behind the men would never make up the ground and the rear company of 2nd Regiment would arrive at the pinewood in daylight, giving the game away. Captain Rothlin was equally aware of the danger. Once the guide had led them out of the stream and up a muddy trail Captain Rothlin forced the pace. I Platoon, which was immediately behind him, responded at once. But II and III Platoons, unaware of the change of pace, fell further and further behind. When they finally caught up with the lead platoon the men were just finishing a rest. Captain Rothlin took no excuses from the other two platoons. He said they'd been straggling, told them it was vital for them to keep the pace and that there was no time for them to have a rest. Even in daylight the rear platoon of a company has difficulty in keeping up with the others on a forced march. At night things are worse. II and III did their best to keep the pace but when they caught up with I Platoon it was just finishing another rest. An angry Captain Rothlin again ordered II and III Platoons to keep going without a rest. Private Mackinnon recalls that his platoon officer Lieutenant Larry Piette 'was furious and Herb Forrester threatened to tear off his sergeant's stripes. We were afraid we would be too exhausted to be worth much in battle.' The platoon thought they were going straight into action. They had not been told that they were to rest up in the pinewoods. As they pushed on in the dark their stamina took a beating. They had cursed Captain Rothlin when he'd force marched them during training and they cursed him again. Later they would realize he'd been right both times. Behind them, in various degrees of order and disorder, the rest of the Regiment followed on.

As the head of the column passed through the 142nd Regiment's outposts Major Thomas's anxieties increased. He had only once taken the path to the pinewoods and that had been in daylight. There were forks ahead. In the darkness it would be easy to take the wrong one and get lost. In spite of Captain Rothlin's forcing the pace the company was still behind schedule. Plodding along the stream had done the damage. Major Thomas wished he had reconnoitred the route himself. He soon had something else to worry about. Colonel Williamson and his combat group were right behind him. 'Colonel Williamson was like a man gone mad. He cursed, complained, and criticized as we made our way up to what if I made no mistakes would be a

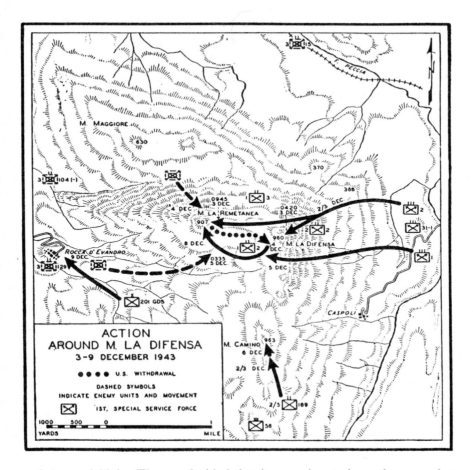

ACTION
AROUND M. LA DIFENSA
3-9 DECEMBER 1943

● ● ● ● U.S. WITHDRAWAL

DASHED SYMBOLS
INDICATE ENEMY UNITS AND MOVEMENT

🗵 1ST. SPECIAL SERVICE FORCE

1000   500   0   1
YARDS   MILE

safe haven.' Major Thomas decided that it was wiser to keep the news that
the whole regiment was behind schedule to himself.[4]

As Mackinnon's platoon passed through 142nd Regiment Lines one of the
T-patchers asked what Regiment they were. 'First Special Service Force,'
someone answered. 'Never heard of you!' jeered the T-patcher.

During rest breaks Major Thomas went ahead to try and make sure he
took the right turning. The Regiment arrived in the pinewood on schedule.
The 1st and 2nd Battalion made it in darkness. First light was breaking as
the 3rd Battalion arrived. Major Thomas shouted at them to hurry up. When
the last of the exhausted men were safely in the shelter of the trees Major
Thomas relaxed for the first time that night. 'I can't remember in my life
such a joyous relief I had as they came under cover.'[5]

While most of the 2nd Regiment erected pup tents and slept, Captain
Rothlin, Sergeant van Ausdale, Sergeant Fenton, III Platoon's second scout

and two other privates from the same platoon – it would be leading the assault – set out to rope up the main northern cliff, a taxing job at the best of times; coming on top of the approach march, a very demanding job indeed. They didn't return until around 1500 hours. Bob Davis, II Platoon, alongside his Canadian buddy, Private Bill Frazier, watched them walk into the pinewoods. 'I still don't know how they did it – how they went up and came down, then went up again. It was an ordeal doing it just once,' he recalls.[6]

Once the main cliff had been scaled the same body of men would rope up the smaller cliffs as they came to them, working in the dark, under the noses of the Germans; as nerve-wracking a job as there could be.

At 1615 hours Colonel MacWilliams passed word round for the 2nd Battalion to get ready to head up the trail. Men dressed for action, checked their weapons, and got into single file. They hit the trail almost exactly as the great barrage opened up on the Camino Massif. Of the 820 guns firing 346 were aiming at the higher slopes of Monte La Difensa and the two saddles on either side of it. In the first hour they fired 22,000 shells; eleven tons a minute on some targets. German batteries were quick to answer. 'Shells roared overhead in both directions like fast freight trains,' Mackinnon recalls. Von Senger, who was visiting troops on Monte Sammucro saw the Allied barrage begin: 'What I saw astonished and dismayed me. The northern slopes of the Camino Massif . . . were under a bombardment of an intensity I had not witnessed since the big battles of the First World War.'*

Up on Monte La Difensa Mackinnon noticed the bloated bodies of some of Colonel Sherman's men. Who would be next, he wondered. The whip-like crack of a Spandau switched his thoughts. Like all Allied troops he was impressed by the sheer power of the sound it made. The Spandau, which was somewhere further up the mountain, was firing a lot of tracer. Mackinnon thought they might be pin-pointing targets for their artillery.

I Company reached the base of the northern cliffs at 2300 hours, right on schedule. They and the remainder of the Regiment were to rest there whilst the artillery support put in another two hours of saturation shelling on Monte La Difensa's peak and its forward slopes.

Davis had a ringside view of the barrage. 'I shall never forget it. The

---

* The barrage on the Camino Massif was one of the most concentrated of the Second World War. In four areas 500 yards square 1329 tons of shells were laid down in 75 minutes. Some wag in the 36th Division watching the stream of shells landing on Monte La Difensa christened it 'Million Dollar Hill'. During the first twenty-four hours of the battle 89,833 rounds were fired by British guns, 64,000 rounds by US guns. During the second twenty-four hours a further 53,096 rounds were fired.

shells were bursting on that slope all over the place, and continued to do so over and over again. It lit the slope right up. It seemed like the mountain was on fire. I never saw a barrage like it during our whole time. You wouldn't think an ant could crawl out of it alive.'[8]

At 0130 hours the barrage lifted and I Company began climbing the main cliff. In addition to carrying their sixty pound rucksacks, weapons and extra ammunition the men were lumbered with platoon weapons. Davis and Frazier were sharing a 60 mm mortar. They were lucky. The man behind them was carrying a five gallon drum of water weighing nearly fifty pounds. As men slowly pulled themselves up the cliff their equipment banged on the rock. 'Echoing off the side of the rock, it was much louder to us than anybody else,' Davis reckoned. He and the rest of the company were too busy climbing to be afraid the enemy might hear them. Getting to the top of the cliff was the only thing that concerned them.

Once the whole company had made it van Ausdale led the men wide of some enemy outposts. One of them opened up with a Spandau. 'They couldn't get an angle on us,' Davis recalls. 'We were too far round the curvature of the mountain for them to be any concern to us. They kept firing tracer at us to try and direct the attention of their artillery on us. But we didn't worry about that.'

Van Ausdale found a reasonably easy passage up the next cliff, only about thirty foot high but steep, and he and the rest of the roping party roped it up. The route van Ausdale had chosen had taken the company to an area of the cliffs not covered by the enemy. The next cliff was not so steep – luckily for Davis, who lost his footing and fell several feet on to a small saddle of rock. His helmet fell off and he spent a long time trying to find it. It took him nearly an hour to catch up Bill Frazier, who must have been glad to hand him the 60 mm mortar.

The urgency and physical strain of the climb occupied Mackinnon's mind to such an extent that he was unaware until later that his knuckles, knees and shins were rubbed raw. Major Thomas, who was coming up with II Company, was glad that 'The dark masked the drop. The climb under combat load was incredibly difficult. Scrambling up cliffs with every foot and hand-hold doubtful required superhuman effort by soldiers weighed down with equipment. Every loose rock clattered with a sound magnified a thousand times to our ears. There were many pauses in the movement upward and those of us behind the point of the column never knew why. As fatigue took hold there was a constant concern that a dozy and exhausted soldier might not move off after one of the stops, leaving the battalion split asunder across the face of the mountain.'[9]

Colonel Williamson and his combat team – Major Grey, Captain Eino Olney, his S2, Staff Sergeant Meiklejohn, Intelligence Staff Sergeant Bill

Story and a wireless operator – were bringing up the rear of the Regiment. The continued halts had played havoc with Colonel Williamson's nerves and when his team's wireless failed he became, in Story's words 'extremely agitated'.[10] He was convinced that something had gone seriously wrong with the plan of attack. He told Major Grey that he believed I Company would be detected before they got to the summit and the secrecy of the attack compromised. The only thing to do was for him to report back to Colonel Frederick, whose advanced CP was on a ledge of the main cliff. Major Grey volunteered to go forward to find out what was happening. There would then be no need for Colonel Williamson to see Colonel Frederick. Williamson agreed that Major Grey should climb up to the head of the column but insisted that he was going down to consult Colonel Frederick. There was no arguing with him, although both Major Grey and Staff Sergeant Story guessed the likely outcome of such a move. Story accompanied Colonel Williamson down to Colonel Frederick's CP. Frederick took one appalled look at Williamson and said 'Colonel! What are you doing here?' then hustled him out of earshot.

At the head of the column I Company had climbed the last of the cliffs. Van Ausdale and Fenton found a trail that appeared to lead right up to the peak and set out to make sure it did. I Company's historian described the trail as 'wet and slippery and at times almost vertical'.[11] The rest of I Company dumped their heavy equipment and sleeping bags and prepared for action. At around 0430 hours on 3 December van Ausdale returned to say that the peak was only a hundred yards away and that the trail led straight to it. I Company's platoons adopted open formation and with III Platoon in the lead headed for the summit. Mackinnon could see the rocks of the peak silhouetted against the skyline. 'We tried to make as little noise as possbile. II and I Platoons were close behind us.' The whole Company reached the edge of the summit without being detected. But as Captain Waters' II Company climbed up the last cliff they dislodged some rocks. A German sentry on the peak yelled a challenge. Flares exploded, bathing everyone in their sepulchral light. Automatic fire raked III Platoon. Both sections went to ground. Mackinnon's landed behind some rocks. Sergeant Maginty's were caught in the open. Within less than a minute three of them had been shot dead and others wounded. A German ran towards Mackinnon's section with his hands up. Mackinnon's buddy, Syd Gath, raised himself above his rock to take the German prisoner, then rolled back on to Mackinnon 'For God's sake, Syd, you're on top of me!' he shouted, and pushed him off. Gath rolled over and lay still. The left side of his head had been blown open. The bullet had been fired from behind the surrendering German, who had disappeared into the darkness. Mackinnon automatically faced his front, trying not to let the shock of Gath's death affect him.[12]

Van Ausdale and Fenton had gone to ground behind a rock in front of Sergeant Maginty's section. Realizing it was in trouble, they worked their way round their left flank and gave them covering fire while the section removed their wounded. II Platoon had now joined the battle. Davis caught a glimpse of Captain Rothlin standing behind a rock. A few moments later Davis heard a burst of Schmeisser and saw what he thought was Captain Rothlin's body sliding down the rock, 'I think that's the Captain!' he said to Frazier. It was. Lieutenant Piette took over command of the company, who were now concentrating on the job of eliminating Spandau posts and snipers. While van Ausdale took eight men to bomb snipers in a cave, Davis's section were pinned down by the sniper who had killed Gath. He was holed up in a tunnel of rocks, using a Schmeisser. Davis and the rest of the section found it difficult to spot the entrance to the tunnel. They fired in its direction, but the sniper didn't return fire. The section reckoned he was waiting for another target. While the section gave him covering fire, Davis crawled round to the left of the tunnel and spotted its entrance. It was only a few inches wide. To get a grenade in it Davis would have to run straight at the tunnel – and provide the sniper with another victim. As he rejoined the section he was struck on the head. He slumped down, thinking he'd been shot, and cursing himself for losing his helmet. Frazier examined his head. It was cut and bruised. He had been hit by a rock. The Germans were throwing rocks like grenades. One hit a sergeant in I Platoon in the face and temporarily blinded him.

Word about the sniper in the tunnel got round. A private called Dennis George came up with a rifle grenade launcher. This was intended to be fired lying down because of its kick. Davis pointed out the entrance to the tunnel. George stood up and fired the grenade launcher from the shoulder. The grenade went straight into the tunnel and exploded inside it.

Fighting was still going on all round the peak, I Company bearing the brunt. III Company got stuck on the last cliff. Their company commander had just reached the top when the enemy opened fire. Although the bullets were passing yards overhead the officer 'froze'. Lt-Colonel Moore, who was coming up behind III Company with his 2nd Battalion, was exasperated by yet another unexplained halt at a time when everything should have been moving quickly. He climbed up the cliff and asked III Company's commander why he wasn't advancing. 'We're pinned down by enemy fire!' he said. 'Get off the rope!' Moore said, 'I'm bringing my battalion through!' And he did.[13]

Davis's section had another deadly game of hide-and-seek with a second sniper. They got him quite easily. They saw a private called Soutaila charge an enemy bunker. A sniper in another bunker shot him in the stomach. Soutaila fell on the ground, writhing in agony and gasping for breath. He sounded as if he was choking. Ignoring point blank fire from both bunkers Soutaila's buddy ran up to him, bent down, removed his dentures, then dragged him to safety. How Soutaila's rescuer wasn't hit and how he had the wit and courage to bend down and remove the dentures is something Davis has never figured out. By now it was first light. The battle, which had lasted an hour, was nearly over. Only isolated Spandau posts and snipers were still holding out. One German who tried to surrender to Davis was shot in the back. Davis reckoned that 'by the way he was dressed up in his best uniform' he'd been waiting his first opportunity to surrender and one of his comrades had been waiting for him to try. Davis was still pondering about the irony of this when he was hit in the mouth by shrapnel. Whether from a grenade or a small mortar he wasn't sure. His mouth and tongue swelled up until he couldn't talk. 'But it wasn't bothering me at all.' The exhilaration of knowing I Company had licked the enemy had seen to that. The awareness of just what they and the rest of the First Special Service Force had achieved would come later.

Shortly after dawn the clouds which enveloped the peak lifted. Davis saw the summit was a round saucer about a hundred yards across and surrounded by a dense *chevaux de frise* of rocks that had served its defenders so well. In the distance bunches of enemy troops were retreating towards Monte Rementea. 4.2" mortars were directed on to them but as the first rounds were in the air the clouds came down again. And out of the clouds came an enemy mortar barrage that had everyone on the summit going to ground. The only enemy now left on Monte La Difensa were snipers on the reverse slope of the mountain. They were waiting for targets.

Lieutenant Piette ordered I Company to move into the saucer and dig in. The ground was soft. As the men dug, Lieutenant Piette made out a casualty list. I Company had started out five officers and 67 ranks strong. Captain Rothlin and eight men had been killed – five Americans and four Canadians Mackinnon noted – and sixteen wounded. The more seriously wounded were put in a German rest hut in the middle of the saucer to await evacuation. The walking wounded made their way down the eastern trail, which was already coming under enemy mortar fire. II Company had lost only two men killed. It had been a I Company show. They had killed thirty-five Germans and taken thirty-seven prisoners out of a total of forth-three. 1st Battalion's Commander, Lt-Colonel MacWilliams, came up and congratulated them and said they were going into Battalion reserve. That sounded good. In reality it meant they were stuck in the saucer for the rest of the battle, and enemy mortars and artillery hardly ever stopped firing at it. During the next four

16. General Clark with his senior Air Support commanders. Photo taken late November.

17. Field Marshal Kesselring.

18. General von Vietinghoff.

19. General Lucas.

20. General Walker.

21. General von Senger.

22. Northern face of Monte Sammucro. San Pietro is on right at base
of mountain.

23. Eastern face of Monte Sammucro. Points 570, 630 and 670 are to
the left, Point 957 on the right.

24. Monte Camino. Second time up.

25. Monte Camino. Monastery Hill.

days I Company would lose another eleven men from wounds and twenty-four from trench foot and pneumonia, leaving them with the strength of one officer and twenty-two men.

Although Captain Waters's II Company was low on ammunition – dangerously low in Major Thomas's opinion – Lt-Colonel MacWilliams was determined to attack Monte Rementea straight away. As the company began moving down the saddle linking the two mountains a mortar shell killed Lt-Colonel MacWilliams and one of his sergeants. Major Thomas took over command of the battalion and ordered Major Waters to bring all of his men back to the peak. As III Company regrouped Colonel Frederick and Colonel Williamson arrived on the summit. Major Thomas told them that he thought the attack on Monte Rementea should be postponed until II Company had its full quota of ammunition. The two senior officers agreed with him. II and III Companies dug in on the summit, while the 2nd and 3rd Battalions found cover in the rocks below it.[14]

A body count of dead Germans totalled seventy-five. About half the men had been killed in the barrage of the previous night. Of the forty-three prisoners, twenty-nine were from the 115th Reconnaissance Regiment, thirteen from the III/104th Panzer Grenadier Regiment. Two companies of the 115th, who had only recently moved into the Line, had been holding the summit. These prisoners had been too well dug in to be affected by their barrage but said that men in their company on the forward slope, who had been in more rudimentary dugouts, had been blown to bits. Mackinnon had the job of escorting three prisoners down the eastern trail. Two of them were 'young as boy scouts, happy to be out of it.' The rest of the prisoners varied from Germans who had served with their regiment from Sicily onwards, and whose bearing showed it, to more 'boy scouts' and 'Eastern Europeans pressed into action by the Germans and very willing to surrender.'

During the afternoon 3rd Regiment brought up food, water and ammunition up the Eastern trail and helped a service battalion search for wounded among the rocks. The more seriously wounded were evacuated by litter. Anti-sniper patrols were sent out, but the snipers appeared to have withdrawn. Outposts were established to give warning of the expected enemy counter-attack.

At dusk on 2 December 2/5th Queen's and the company of the 2/6th who were attacking the saddle between Monte Camino and Monte La Difensa moved off on their separate attacks. D Company, who were leading the 2/5th – their objective was Squeak – were allowed to leave their rucksacks* at Campo. The rest of the battalion had to carry them as far as the Stone

---

* They would be portered up the mountain by a company from 2/7th Queen's.

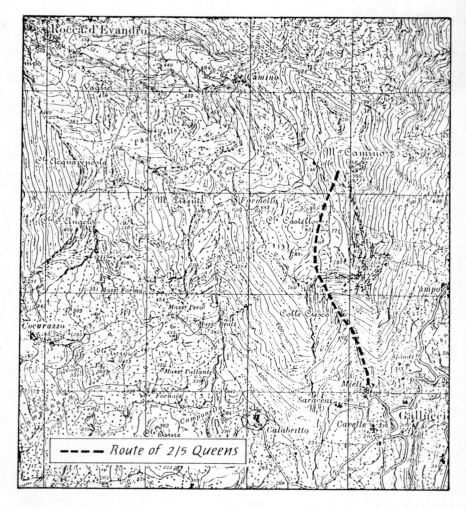

---- Route of 2/5 Queens

Man. They had been going for half-an-hour when X Corps barrage opened up. Landslips caused by the 'terror-crashes' brought the advance to a temporary halt. Men took what cover they could find from the falling rock. Once the 'terror crashes' had lifted from their axis of advance they toiled on up the steep and trackless mountainside. It took them four hours to reach the Stone Man.

Captain Griffiths knew that Squeak had two lines of defences – dugouts blown out of solid rock and a series of caves behind the dugouts. He planned to send 18 Platoon round the enemy's left flank while Lieutenant J. D. Allison's 16 Platoon went for the dugouts. 18 Platoon reached the entrance

116

to the caves before being spotted. As Spandaus opened up 16 Platoon attacked the dugouts. In the hand-to-hand fighting that followed Lieutenant Allison was mortally wounded and the attack repulsed. But 18 Platoon bombed the enemy out of several caves and hung on, exchanging fire with the enemy in the dugouts.

By midnight C Company (Captain P. M. Bramwell) had established themselves on Pip but the enemy was still holding out on Squeak. Lieutenant Allison died on his way down the mountain but not before meeting up with Lt-Colonel Whitfield. What Lieutenant Allison told him persuaded the CO to go forward and take command of 16 Platoon himself. At first light on 3 December he led the platoon in a charge that took the enemy by surprise. Those who weren't killed or wounded surrendered. At 0900 hours another thirty Germans gave themselves up without a fight.

The enemy on Wilfred beat off a fighting patrol from B Company. The 2/5th forward observer, Captain Acheson, brought down a heavy barrage on the pimple. When it lifted B Company took Wilfred quite easily.

It had been a great night for Allied infantry. The First Special Service had captured Monte La Difensa. US 142 Regiment was driving the enemy back towards the summit of Monte Maggiore, 2/5th Queen's had taken Razorback, and 167 Brigade, 7th Ox and Bucks leading, had taken Pts 727 and 819. A small enemy force had put up a token resistance. (The Ox and Bucks had found four of the enemy asleep.) The only units out of luck had been C Company, 2/6th Queen's – they had been pinned down on the Monte Camino – La Difensa saddle by enemy fire from Monastery Hill and positions on the saddle itself – and the Leicesters and Sherwood Foresters. Their second attack on Calabritto and Pill-box Ridge had gone in with the tanks and sappers. While the tanks shot up the Spandau crews in and around Calabritto the sappers blew gaps in the barbed wire. The Leicesters and Sherwood Foresters charged through it at dawn and got to the outskirts of the village before their attacks were broken up by very heavy mortaring and shelling. Although forced to withdraw two hundred yards they succeeded in taking out the Spandaus on Pill-box Ridge.

Lt-Colonel Whitfield had not been ordered to attack Monastery Hill but as his battalion was now right below it it seemed only logical that they should attack it. A reconnaissance patrol from A Company was pinned down by heavy automatic fire from the base of the hill which was covered with low cloud. A second patrol from B Company climbed halfway up the hill before being heavily mortared. Only the patrol leader, Lieutenant Lilley, and his runner reached the chapel. It was unoccupied. The enemy were in their watchtower next to the summit.

Colonel Whitfield ordered Captain Bramwell to make a reconnaissance of the hill that afternoon with a view to C Company attacking it the following morning. The CO considered the company too tired to make an attack that night.

Low cloud blanketed Monastery Hill on 4 December. C Company reached the chapel around noon without losing a man but as they prepared to attack the tower it began hailing. The hailstones were as big as mothballs. They struck the men's faces and numbed their hands on their weapons. Number 13 and 15 Platoons tried to work their way round the tower only to find that its blind side was built over a precipice. The Regimental historian writes: '14 Platoon tried to crawl up the open rock face in the centre, and their platoon commander, platoon sergeant and two section commanders were killed.'[15] It is surprising that such brave men should remain unnamed. Bren gunners giving covering fire for the assault had to stop firing because the hail had numbed their fingers so badly they could no longer pull their triggers. Captain Bramwell ordered the company to take up temporary positions behind the chapel while he covered their withdrawal with a Bren. Later that afternoon he met Colonel Whitfield and a company commander of the 1st London Irish whose men were to assist C Company making another attack on the tower that night. Officers went forward, taking cover behind a large rock a few yards from the base of the tower, and had a close look at it. The enemy showered them with grenades but none scored a hit. Once the officers had withdrawn Colonel Whitfield told Captain Bramwell he would reinforce C Company with a platoon from B Company. The platoon were heavily shelled on their way up the hill. Only seven men made it back to their start line.

At about the same time B Company's platoon was being shelled, C Company, 2/6th Queen's, made another attack on the enemy blockhouses on the saddle between Monte Camino and Monte La Difensa. US forward observers mistook them for the enemy, and their artillery opened up on the company, killing Major Ridings and one of his platoon commanders, Lieutenant A. F. N. Irish, and wounding fourteen other men. This was an inexcusable mistake because II Corps and X Corps Artillery commanders had made the saddle a fire-free zone to avoid such incidents. When Colonel Whitfield got back to his CP on Pip he was startled to find it crowded with white-faced Russian officers. One of them, a general, was walking around muttering 'Blood and mud! Blood and mud!'[16] Major Renwick, a British officer attached to Clark's HQ, introduced the General to Whitfield and explained how the Russian officers came to be there. They had arrived at Clark's headquarters at Caserta the previous day. At dinner the General had told Clark that Russia was doing most of the fighting against the Germans and that he and his officers would like to see what the Allies were up to in Italy – what sort of effort their infantry was making. The General gave the impression that he already knew the answer: not much. So Clark had ordered Major Renwick, who spoke Russian, to take them up Monte Camino on mule-back. The party had got shelled on the way. They had also seen a long line of stretcher bearers struggling through the mud with wounded men. By the time they reached Pip the Russian delegation no longer thought the Allies were shirking.

The company of London Irish due to rendezvous with C Company at Monastery Hill lost themselves in the dark, so Colonel Whitfield ordered D Company to take their place. In the meantime he replaced C Company with the remaining two platoons of B Company. This understrength company would simply occupy the ground. In the dark B Company moved into the Monastery, out of a bitter wind and with a roof over their heads. A welcome change from gas-caped dugouts.

Private C. F. Cranville, a signaller with Tac HQ, had caught glimpses of C Company's attack on the tower from his slit trench near the base of Monastery Hill. He'd spent most of the previous forty-eight hours laying and maintaining wire up and down the mountainside. 'I never found anything to laugh at on Monte Camino,' he recalls,[17] and speaks for most men who fought there. For once the infantryman's ability to laugh at just about everything was in very short supply.

On 4 December Lieutenant Toby Sewell commanding 16 Platoon, 2/7th Queen's, led his men up Monte Camino. They were carrying sandbags full of grenades and ammunition. As they neared the summit of Monastery Hill the mist covering the chapel and the enemy's tower lifted. Before it came down again Lieutenant Sewell caught a glimpse of the tower and some of its defenders. 'They were just out of grenade range,' Lieutenant Sewell recalls. 'Unfortunately at this stage of the war the British Army had given up the Ely grenade launcher. If we had had them we'd have been able to lob grenades into the tower.'[18] The German and US Armies used grenade launchers and placed a very high value on them. The British Army put a new grenade launcher into service in 1944.

Lieutenant Sewell and five of his men picked up a badly wounded man in a blanket – there were no stretchers available – and began carrying him down the mountainside. Heavy rain alternated with hail and snow showers. The weather looked set to stay that way, but at dawn on 5 December the sun came up. For the first time since the attack on Monte Camino began there were no clouds or mist covering Monastery Hill. The enemy in the tower directed their heavy mortars on to the chapel. Italian farmhouses have slates thick enough to keep out mortar bombs but the chapel's slates proved as vulnerable as its rafters. With a sudden crash the whole roof collapsed on top of B Company, killing or injuring many men. As the survivors crawled out of the ruins the enemy in the tower counter-attacked, taking two prisoners and inflicting more casualties. B Company had lost two platoon commanders and its CSM killed, and their company commander severely wounded. It was now led by its surviving platoon commander, Lieutenant Hill, who was also wounded. He and two other walking wounded Queensmen began making their way down Monastery Hill. They met Colonel Whitfield climbing up the hill to find out what had happened to B Company. As Lieutenant Hill was describing how the roof of the chapel had collapsed he was wounded again by a stick-bomb. The enemy began singing. They had plenty to sing about. But as it grew dark their two prisoners jumped out of the tower and made their way back to their company.

On the night of 5/6 December B Company, 2/7th Queen's, under the command of Major Alan 'Sandy' Sanders, DSO, arrived to reinforce 2/5th Queen's. Colonel Whitfield ordered Major Sanders to send patrols up Monastery Hill, prior to carrying out an attack on it early on 6 December. The patrols reported that the remains of the chapel and the tower were both occupied by the enemy.

During the night Private Cranville heard the Queen's wounded lying on Monastery Hill crying out in agony. He reported their plight to Regimental Tac HQ. At first light the Regimental medical officer, Captain Aiello, arrived at the base of Monastery Hill with medical orderlies, stretchers, and a Red Cross flag. As he began leading the party up the hill the enemy fired over their heads. Captain Aiello backed off, waving the Red Cross flag, then advanced again. The enemy fired a second volley. Captain Aiello told his party to withdraw. Private Cranville heard him say 'Its no good'. Hard men, those Panzer Grenadiers.

As B Company, 2/7th Queen's, were preparing to attack Monastery Hill Brigadier Lyne phoned Colonel Whitfield and told him he was sending up the rest of 2/7th Queen's to take part in the attack. While Whitfield was awaiting their arrival the enemy on Monastery Hill put up the white flag. Whitfield ordered Major Sanders to take his company up the hill and accept the surrender, while he himself came along to be in at the death. When they were about two-thirds of the way up the hill the party was mortared. Major Sanders and his leading platoon took cover. When Sanders started to lead his men up the hill he saw Whitfield 'standing on a col below the chapel quite in the open. He called me over to him. "Get a move on!" he hissed. He quite put the wind up me.'[19] But before Major Sanders could get a move on a heavy 4.2" mortar barrage forced even Whitfield to take cover. The enemy on Monastery Hill dropped their white flag and made a run for it straight into a company from 167th Brigade, who shot them all dead. The company may well have thought the enemy were charging them instead of trying to escape.

That night, 6/7 December, the rest of 2/7th Queen's relieved the 2/5th, who made their way back to Campo. They had lost twenty-six killed, fifty-three wounded and nineteen missing (few of these were ever accounted for). 2/5th's action on Razorback and on Monastery Hill was the hardest they fought in the Italian campaign.* 2/7th Queen's remained on Razorback and Monastery Hill until the whole of the Camino massif had fallen.

During the afternoon of 3 December General Wilbur, Executive Commander of US 36th Division, contacted Colonel Frederick at his CP and told him that the US 142nd Regiment was coming under heavy fire from Monte Rementea. When did he intend to attack it? Colonel Frederick contacted Colonel Williamson, who said he was planning a dawn attack on 4 December. He also told Frederick that he believed the enemy would counter-attack Monte La Difensa. Their conversation – by wireless. The wire had been cut by enemy fire – was cut short by a flurry of mortar shells landing close to Frederick's CP. He switched off, waited a few minutes, then switched on again – and immediately received more mortar shells. Being an artilleryman Frederick realized that the enemy had zeroed in on his wireless. He switched off again and made little use of his wireless for the rest of the battle.

As darkness fell it brought a cold mist with it. Later it began raining heavily. The water brought up the mountains had been nothing like enough to go round and men caught the rain in their shelter halves or licked if off the moss on the rocks. But as the rain kept on it soaked the men to the skin. The temperature was close to freezing. As the men shivered with cold the enemy bombarded the summit with 'screaming meanies'. The appalling sounds of the missiles rattled everybody. When the first salvo landed Sergeant Story was checking wire near Colonel Frederick's CP. It wasn't his job but nobody else seemed to be doing it. Story, 19, had been a chorister before he joined the Force and had to put up with a lot of good natured ribbing. He was out to prove he could do a lot more than sing. When he heard another batch of 'screaming meanies' apparently heading for the summit he felt sorry for the men occupying it. Then there was a howling roar. As Story flung himself to the ground he glimpsed several flame-coloured projectiles. They exploded all round him. A large piece of shrapnel landed next to his shoulder. 'Could have had my fucking arm cut off!' he whispered to himself. Then he got angry. 'I wish the bloody Colonel would check the wire himself!' But it was no longer a case of checking the wire. Nebelwerfer projectiles had blown whole sections of it to bits. He would have to report this to Colonel Frederick. He'd have to find a team to mend the wire. Story suddenly felt an acute sense of loneliness. Combat wasn't so

---

* Lt-Colonel Whitfield was awarded a bar to his DSO, and the Russian Order of the Red Star. Within six months he had been promoted Major-General and given command of British 56th Division.

bad when you had your buddies around you. When you were on your jack in the dark, liable to get plastered by another dose of 'screaming meanies', it was grim. 'I could bleed to death,' he thought. 'No place to hide, no way to defend myself. Knowing there will be no one to say what really happened if you catch it, and they find what's left of you.'[20]

Sergeant Story reported the destruction of the wire to Colonel Frederick, who told him to find a wire repairing team. He climbed back up the mountain, reported Colonel Frederick's orders to Colonel Williamson, rounded up a wire repairing team and took them back down the mountain checking the wire as they went. They mended the breaks in it near Colonel Frederick's CP. On their way back up the mountain they came under fire from a variety of missiles and found more breaks in the wire. It was a rough night for Sergeant Story but worth it. Next morning Colonel Williamson awarded him a battlefield commission.[21]

Colonel Frederick asked General Wilbur if he could spare a battalion from Colonel Marshall's 1st Regiment to replace the 1st Battalion, 2nd Regiment, when it moved off to attack Monte Rementea. Like Colonel Williamson, Colonel Frederick believed that the enemy was bound to counter-attack Monte La Difensa. As the 142nd Regiment had now taken the summit of Monte Maggiore, General Wilbur agreed to Colonel Frederick's request. Colonel Marshall chose Lt-Colonel R. W. Becket's 1st Battalion for the job.

Lt-Colonel Becket's scouts quickly found a trail leading in the direction of Monte La Difensa. Apart from enemy harassing fire on Monte Maggiore it was a quiet night. Becket led his men up the trail in single file. They'd been going about half an hour when a Schmeisser opened fire with tracer. The bullets passed in front of the column. A second Schmeisser opened up. The bullets passed behind the rear of the column. The next instant German artillery and mortars opened up on the area indicated by the Schmeissers. Their fire swamped the column. After their initial shock the uninjured men rallied well, in spite of there being no cover. A patrol led by Major Ojola went after the snipers. The remaining men clung to the ground. The barrage lasted twenty minutes. When it lifted the 1st Battalion had lost three officers and twenty-three other ranks killed, and around sixty wounded. Many of the wounded had been tended to during the shelling but Colonel Becket had managed to get a message through to Colonel Marshall, who sent up part of the 2nd Battalion, 1st Regiment, to look after the wounded, leaving Becket free to march the remainder of his battalion towards Monte La Difensa. 'Towards' is the word. The 1st Battalion got lost in the dark. Just after Becket got through to Marshall the wireless he'd been using was destroyed. All the other wireless sets in the battalion had been knocked out as well. There was no way of letting Colonel Williamson know that the battalion was lost and getting guides sent out to find them.

Colonel Williamson heard about the shelling from Colonel Marshall, who also told him that the remainder of the 1st Battalion was 'on their way'. Major Thomas had his battalion stand-to an hour before dawn on 4 December, prior to the attack on Monte Rementea. But when Colonel Becket's battalion failed to appear Colonel Williamson told Major Thomas he was cancelling the attack. If Monte La Difensa was counter-attacked he would need Major Thomas's battalion to help repel the enemy. It was an unpopular decision. Both Lt-Colonel Moore and Major Thomas considered it the wrong one. But Williamson had a point. Becket's 1st Battalion had been earmarked to take Major Thomas's 1st Battalion's place when they moved off to attack Monte Rementea and Becket's Battalion had not arrived. By temperament Colonel Williamson was not a man to take risks. If the wire had been in working order he could have consulted Colonel Frederick but the wire was not in working order.

Instead of mounting an attack on Monte Rementea Colonel Williamson ordered Major Thomas to send a fighting patrol to it. The patrol reported the mountain undefended, but the sounds of many of the enemy moving in the valley below the rear slopes of the mountain. Another patrol captured two prisoners from the III/104th Panzer Grenadier Regiment. At first they were reluctant to answer questions but after they were given something to eat they said their battalion would be attacking Monte La Difensa at dawn the following day – 5 December. They also spoke of the havoc caused to their supply lines by the US artillery and mortars. Most of the battalion's mules had been killed and men badly needed in the fighting had to take their place.

Soon after the two prisoners had been interrogated the clouds lifted. A forward observer on La Difensa spotted about four hundred of the enemy in the area where the prisoners had been taken and brought down a heavy concentration of artillery fire on them. When the barrage lifted the forward observer reported that the battalion had suffered heavy casualties. The enemy counter-attack never materialized. But direct observation of the summit put the enemy snipers on their mettle. They had been lying up on the western slopes for forty-eight hours, soaked to the skin, with whatever food they'd had on them long since eaten. But they shot to kill and kill they did. As Colonel Williamson was organizing anti-sniper patrols the clouds came down. The patrols failed to find any trace of the snipers, who had quickly withdrawn – and not just for safety. These men for whom killing was a form of sport had gone back for more ammunition, food and water.

Major Thomas, caught in a mortar barrage on the summit, jumped into the nearest fox-hole. The private occupying it had parked his rifle with the bayonet still on. The bayonet went straight through Major Thomas's calf. When the barrage lifted two men helped him over to the German rest hut.

'The wounded were placed in a hole in the ground and evacuated in order of wound seriousness. Since mine was far from life threatening I soon achieved seniority in the hole. It was an unpleasant few days. The cover over the dugout was light timber, too light to stop a mortar shell and the mortaring was constant, leading to a continuing apprehension as to whether the next round was coming through the top. Mortaring is unpleasant when one is about and active but in an immobilized state the nerves do get jangled.'[22]

Major Jim Grey took over command of the 1st Battalion. The rain became as constant as the mortaring. By nightfall Colonel Frederick became worried about the effect of it on the condition of his men. There was no external cover available, but, after some prodding, 5th Army HQ allowed the Force's Supply Officer, Colonel Orne Baldwin, to draw six cases of Bourbon for medicinal uses. The Service Battalion brought up two cases to the 2nd Regiment's HQ during the night, which was mercifully free of rain. Colonel Williamson gave a bottle to Lieutenant Story and told him to give it to Major Grey. Major Grey, like everybody else, had been making do with rainwater to drink, and was so dry he could only croak this thanks. Each member of the Regiment received two ounces of whisky. Teetotallers passed their rations on.

The fifth of December was warm and sunny. There were no longer any snipers round the peak and mist in the valleys on the eastern slopes of Monte La Difensa gave cover from view. Colonel Williamson ordered 2nd Regiment to dry out in the sun. The men took their clothes off, sunbathed, and read mail from home, which had come up with the whisky. During the morning Colonel Becket's Battalion arrived and 1st Battalion, 2nd Regiment, were ordered to prepare to attack Monte Rementea that afternoon. Colonel Frederick decided the time had come to deal with the enemy holding the saddle between Monte La Difensa and Monte Camino. Most of the mortaring – but not the 'screaming meanies' – had been coming from the saddle. Colonel Frederick had delayed attacking it before because of reports that Monastery Hill had fallen, and he'd expected the enemy on the saddle to withdraw. But Monastery Hill had not yet fallen. The attack on the saddle, where the enemy's two blockhouses had a number of Spandaus covering them, would have to go in without a support barrage, owing to the agreement between II Corps and X Corps artillery. The fact that it was a sunny day would make the attack even more hazardous. Lt-Colonel Moore's 2nd Battalion, 2nd Regiment, supported by a company from 3rd Regiment, were briefed for attack on the saddle during the afternoon.

The 1st Battalion, led by Major Grey and with another company of 3rd Regiment replacing 1 Company, moved off towards Monte Rementea around 1400 hours. They soon came under observed fire from Rocca d'Evandro. Casualties were so high that Major Grey ordered his battalion to dig in. But he sent out fighting patrols to Rocca with orders to deal with the mortars and Spandaus which had caused the casualties.

Lt-Colonel Moore's attack started off in mid-afternoon. Captain Hubbard's 5th Company were in the lead. After smoke had been laid down by light mortars 5th Company advanced in open formation. As the smoke cleared the enemy Spandaus opened up. But 1st Platoon, led by Lieutenant Wayne Boyce, went in so quickly that they dealt with the Spandau crews – who made no attempt to surrender – and the first blockhouse quite easily. The platoon regrouped. The second blockhouse was two hundred yards away. Apart from a few rocks the ground was bare. The company mortars didn't have the range to lay on smoke. The platoon would have to go in cold, dodging from one clump of rock to the next. This they did, losing men every time they showed themselves. When they reached the last clump of rocks the platoon had suffered 50% casualties. As he led his remaining men in their final charge on the blockhouse Lieutenant Boyce was hit by three bullets. He kept going, shouting orders to his men, and telling them to close in on the blockhouse from three sides. This they did. They slipped grenades through its loopholes and killed all its defenders. Only then did Lieutenant Boyce collapse. He died of his wounds, almost at once. His courage makes words like gallantry seem superfluous.[23]

On 6 December Major Grey's 2nd Battalion advanced on Monte Rementea. There was no fire from Rocca, and they found the mountain unoccupied. Colonel Frederick knew the battle was nearly over but he was more concerned than ever about the condition of his men. He'd been right to worry about the effect of the rain. The First Special Service Force was the only Allied unit to be fully equipped with Arctic combat suits. But by some oversight none of them had Arctic overshoes. The result was an outbreak of trench foot, particularly severe among the men who had spent long periods without activity. Colonel Frederick sent a message to General Walker asking for his unit to be relieved as soon as possible. His men were 'willing and eager but are becoming exhausted'. He also mentioned that snipers 'are giving us hell'* and that if the British failed to take Monte Camino that night 'it should be promptly attacked by us from the north'. General Walker did not answer Colonel Frederick's message. Walker had no reserves to put in the First Special Service Force's place. He was also deeply involved in preparing attacks on Monte Sammucro and San Pietro.

The 3rd Coldstream, who followed up 167th Brigade on the night of 3 December, had an approach march up Bare Arse that none who survived it

---

* They had infiltrated through the 1st SSF lines during the night. Some of them had hidden among rocks close to the eastern trail, and were shooting up anything that moved on it.

would forget. Because there was no moon men could not see the giant boulders until they were on top of them. Those behind cannoned into those in front. In the end each man had to hold on to the pack of the man in front of him. As the men stumbled along like a battalion of the blind leading the blind some well-hidden German forward observer reported the whereabouts of the column to his guns. In the ensuing shelling the MO, Captain David Fazan, and the padre, Captain G. A. Levens,* were both killed and a number of guardsmen wounded. As the 3" mortar crews dived for cover they lost the baseplates of their mortars. When the shelling ceased the men continued their nightmare ascent. Once clear of the boulders it became a forced march. The battalion was now well behind schedule and in danger of being caught on the track in daylight. And their objectives, Pts 683 and 615, were well beyond Pt 727 and Pt 819. Their leading company commander, Captain J. M. G. Griffith Jones, saw to it that his men kept up a killing pace but realized that they were becoming completely exhausted and doubted very much if they would be up to attacking their objectives. Luckily Pts 683 and 615 were unoccupied. Three of the companies found shelter among the rocks but 4 and HQ had to dig-in in the open. Enemy snipers and mortar crews, who had reoccupied the village of Formelli during the night, slipped round the flanks of the battalion and opened fire. The signals officer, Captain J. C. C. Clark, was killed by a mortar bomb. The Coldstream mortar crews could not use their mortars because of the loss of the baseplates. All the wirelesses had failed and no wire had been laid to Tac HQ, which was back near the summit of Bare Arse. The Battalion had no way of raising any sort of support fire (runners would have been picked off by the snipers). Porters sent up with food, water and ammunitions that night were scattered by shell-fire. The men had to make do with emergency rations† and a few drops of rum. But a line was laid to Tac HQ and support fire guaranteed for the following day.[24]

The third of December saw no gains by 139th Brigade at Calabritto. On 4 December Lt-Colonel John Preston, the 16th Durhams' CO,[25] suggested to his brigadier that one way of ending the stalemate would be to let the Durhams attack the Germans' left flank at Cocoruzzo. The village was on the rear slope of Monte Camino, in the 56th Division zone of combat. The offer was turned down. But John Preston was not a man to give up easily. On 4 December the 2nd Battalion, Scots Guards, took Acquapendola Ridge under heavy shell-fire – three of their officers were killed by it. Acquapendola Ridge overlooked Cocoruzzo Spur. Once again Colonel Preston put forward his plan. This time his brigadier consulted Major-General Hawksworth, who

* Captain Levens was the second 3rd Coldstream padre to be killed within two months.
† Tins of concentrated chocolate.

approved of the plan, and obtained Major-General Templer's permission to pass through 56th Division's zone. In daylight on 5 December the Durhams, reinforced by a company of Yorks and Lancs, climbed Bare Arse and spent the night with the Coldstream on Pt 615. At first light the Durhams set off for Cocoruzzo and its spur, the Coldstream giving them covering fire. One Coldstream Officer, Lieutenant J. E. Hamilton, went forward carrying two Brens to make sure their right flank was covered. Five German snipers slipped in between him and the rest of the Coldstream and began firing at the Durhams' backs. Lieutenant Hamilton ran back to find out what was happening. One of the snipers shot him dead.* His Platoon Sergeant, Sergeant Lovelace, spent the rest of the day stalking the five snipers. He killed three of them.

The enemy on Cocoruzzo Spur were occupying two small hillocks at platoon strength. But they had enough covering fire from other enemy units to force the Durhams to wait till nightfall before launching an attack. On one hillock the Durhams had to use the bayonet before the enemy gave in. On the other peak nineteen of the enemy ran for it – straight into another company of Durhams who took them prisoner. 15th Panzer Grenadier Divison's left flank was in the air.[26] They could no longer hope to put up any more organized resistance or retreat at their own pace.† But a large party of Panzer Grenadiers fought their way past a detachment of 2nd Scots Guards, and the enemy in front of Rocca D'Evandro gave the 6th Grenadiers, now down to three understrength companies, a lot of trouble. One of the Grenadiers' outstanding platoon officers, Lieutenant T. W. Huntingdon, killed a Spandau gunner and invited the remainder of the crew to surrender. They shot him dead. It didn't pay to be chivalrous to the 15th Panzer Grenadier Division. Rocca D'Evandro turned out to be on the far side of a three-hundred-foot ravine. Not only was the village's large castle intact but the nearside of the ravine consisted of a series of precipitous terraces defended by about thirty Spandaus. The prospect of dealing with the castle as well as the terraces must have dismayed the Grenadiers. The terraces proved very hard to take. During 7 and 8 December Major C. Earle's III Company made two unsuccessful attacks on them. Divisional HQ, who had no idea of the difficulties involved, kept urging the Battalion to get a move on. On 9 December Major Earle led his company down the ravine again. They mopped up four Spandau posts and outflanked the rest of the enemy on the near side of the ravine.[27] At the same time the Scots Guards cut the road to Rocca D'Evandro.

The fall of Monastery Hill and Cocoruzzo left the First Special Service

---

* Between 2 and 5 December the Coldstream lost four officers and fifteen ranks killed.

† An Ultra decrypt of 7 December disclosed that the Division's situation on 6 December was critical, and was causing grave anxiety to Kesselring and von Senger.

Force free to mop up the snipers infesting Monte La Difensa and to deal with a strong pocket of enemy bumped by a patrol near Rocca. The snipers were all killed or captured by nightfall, 7 December, at small cost to the patrols. Major Grey's 1st Battalion, 2nd Regiment, attacked the enemy pocket early on 8 December. The weather was clear, and the US artillery fired a creeping barrage in front of the troops, as well as targeting the enemy positions. When the lead company of the 1st Battalion arrived at their objective seven men from the von Corvin Hermann Göring battle group surrendered without a fight. They were all that were left of fifty men. Twenty-five of them had been killed in the shelling, nineteen others had run for it. Proof that the best of troops could not stand up to Allied shelling unless they were well dug in.

Later that day 2/7th Queen's sent out a patrol to contact the First Special Service Force and were given a great welcome. They were introduced to every single officer in the unit and were surprised to find two Regimental Commanders in the line. 'We lead from the front,' Colonel Williamson remarked, unaware of the exploits of Colonel Whitfield.

During the night of 8/9 December the Force was relieved by US 142nd Regiment. Those who could still walk made their way wearily down the Eastern trail. Their casualties totalled 511, nearly 50%. Seventy-three officers and men had been killed, nine were missing, 313 wounded or injured and 116 sick, mainly from pneumonia exposure and trench foot. As the Regiment's historian relates, 'No one felt particularly triumphant'. But a triumph it had certainly been. The ascent and storming of Monte La Difensa was a most audacious feat. Both Clark and Major General Keyes sent Colonel Frederick their personal congratulations. And the Regiment went on to make itself a reputation as the toughest Allied unit in the field, as sure in defence as they were in attack.

During the night of 9/10 December all the enemy remaining on the Camino Massif retreated across the Garigliano. Or to put it bluntly they swam it. Floods had destroyed the bridges across the river as well as those leading to the western slopes of Monte Camino. Later senior officers of the 15th Panzer Grenadier Division would have to face a court of enquiry for leaving all the Division's heavy equipment behind on the Camino Massif. The Division suffered a further 974 casualties. Its monthly report for December no longer exists but from 1–10 December XIV Panzer Korps lost 352 killed, 1,051 wounded, 343 missing and 680 sick. British X Corps battle casualties during the same period totalled 941, US 11 and VI Corps 2,291 – 383 killed, 1,863 wounded, forty-five missing.

On 10 December 2/6th Queen's relieved US 142nd Regiment on Monte La Difensa. From the peak Lieutenant Toby Sewell spotted 'a great white building on another grey mountain and this we understood was another monastery'. It was the abbey on Monte Cassino.

In April, 1944, the Moroccan Goums, the most formidable mountain troops in the Italian Campaign, carried out a training exercise on Monte Camino. Inside the German watchtower they found the skeletons of two Queensmen – an officer and a lance corporal, two of the unnamed* dead from 14 Platoon, C Company, 2/5th Queen's. Deeply impressed by the bravery of the men who had scaled such an obstacle under fire they decided to put up a memorial plaque in honour of all British troops killed on Monte Camino.[28] The plaque was unveiled on 2 May, 1944, in the presence of McCreery and Brigadier A. Guillaume, commanding officer of the Goums' brigade. On every Good Friday since 1945 4,000 peasants from the villages around Monte Camino climb up the mule track in their bare feet, on a pilgrimage to the chapel. As they pass the plaque they give it an 'Eyes left!'

Clark, by now almost as obsessed by San Pietro as Hitler, told General Keyes he wanted a reconnaissance in force sent to the village to find out if the enemy were still holding it and, if they were, in what strength. General Keyes passed on the message to Walker, who disapproved of reconnaissance in strength. He believed San Pietro should be reconnoitred by small patrols. Walker picked 3rd Rangers for the job. The Battalion was commanded by Lt-Colonel Herman Dammer, a very experienced commander who had belonged to the original Ranger Battalion raised in Scotland.

The patrol was scheduled to go in early on 31 November. On 30 November one of the Ranger's company commanders, Captain James J. Larkin, another original Ranger, was wandering around Venafro. He had a chat with the driver of a jeep containing a very big wireless. The driver told him the Germans had some sort of sensor device that could locate medium to big wireless sets as soon, as they were turned on. A useful invention, Larkin thought.[29] Later he ran into an old friend of his who was now flying a Piper Cub. When Larkin told him his battalion were making a reconnaissance to San Pietro his friend suggested taking him on an aerial reconnaissance that afternoon. Larkin accepted, wondering what Lt-Colonel Dammer would have to say. It proved a rather unsettling trip. They weren't fired on by anti-aircraft guns but Larkin kept on hearing shells passing over and under the plane. It was in the flight path of Allied and enemy barrages. Once he'd got used to the sounds he spied out the land around San Pietro. When he reported back to Colonel Dammer the CO was pleased with his information, much to Larkin's relief.

---

* They remain 'known only to God' because the War Graves Commission's men failed to find or collect their identity discs. The tower would have made a splendid memorial to the Unknown Soldier but it was knocked down at the same time as the chapel was rebuilt (1946).

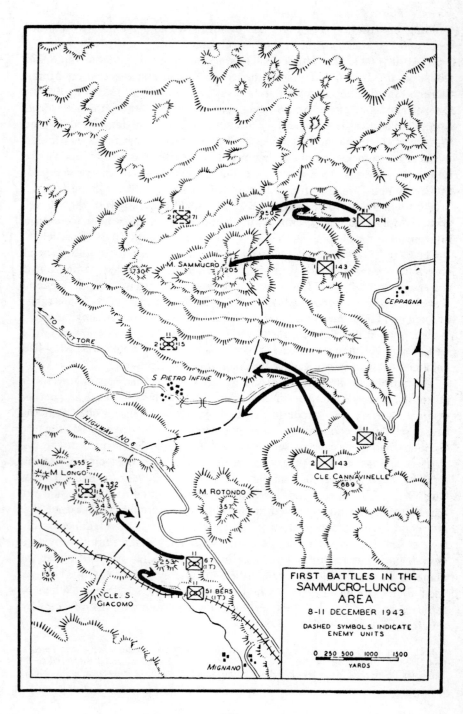

FIRST BATTLES IN THE
SAMMUCRO-LUNGO
AREA
8-11 DECEMBER 1943
DASHED SYMBOLS INDICATE
ENEMY UNITS

0 250 500   1000   1500
YARDS

The 3rd Rangers left their base at Ceppagna at dusk on 30 November and moved round the lower spurs of Monte Sammucro until they reached the outposts of the 18th Regiment, 45th Division, on a ridge overlooking San Pietro. The time was 2200 hours. The Rangers were on schedule. But darkness, rain and mist had reduced visibility to a few yards and made the steep slopes leading to the village very difficult to negotiate. Paths kept on petering out. In no way could the pace be forced. The Rangers were due to arrive on the outskirts of the village at 0100 hours. On a clear night this would have been fair reckoning. On the sort of night the Rangers had it was wildly optimistic. Their leading company finally made it to one mile east of San Pietro by 0530 hours.

The imminent approach of first light necessitated a complete change of plan. Instead of approaching the village from the east as well as the north and moving into it in darkness, Colonel Dammer decided to stay put until daybreak and then send out patrols to reconnoitre routes to the village. His men were in olive groves and well covered from view. Or so he thought. He was not to know that the enemy had forward observers on top of the 600-foot spur of Monte Sammucro directly overlooking the area of San Pietro. At first light two patrols from B Company set out for the village. Both patrols were spotted about half a mile from it and came under heavy automatic fire. As they did so enemy artillery opened up on the battalion. Colonel Dammer, an artilleryman, realized from the way the shells were landing among his companies that the enemy gunners knew exactly where they were. He ordered his men to disperse and dig in. It was still raining heavily. No chance of a spotter plane taking off to locate the enemy guns. By making calculations from incoming shells Dammer was able to work out roughly where the enemy were, and the battalion's Forward Observer reported the positions back to his guns. Heavy support fire from them in no way decreased the enemy guns rate of fire and Dammer realized that they were probably hull down behind a hill and impossible to hit with artillery. He ordered more patrols to reconnoitre the village, and warned his men that they would have to stick it out until it was dark.

Sergeant Carl Lehmann, 24, another original Ranger, was in charge of a squad of seven men, four of whom had just joined the battalion. He had warned them not to dig in near the terrace wall or under an olive tree. A direct hit on a wall would mix shrapnel with slivers of rock, as lethal as the steel. A direct hit on a tree would create an airburst. The shrapnel would explode in all directions. Foxholes could be peppered by it. But a shell landing in the middle of the squad's terrace carried more authority than Sergeant Lehmann. The four rookies rushed over to the terrace wall and began digging in beneath it. Sergeant Lehmann was too busy digging himself in to repeat his warning. He had almost finished his foxhole when a shell landed on top of the terrace wall. All four rookies were seriously wounded. Sergeant Lehmann ran over and gave them morphine.* The men's screams had been heard by the battalion's Medical Officer, Captain Gordon Keeble, who walked through the shelling with a coolness that Sergeant Lehmann envied, and did what he could for the wounded men.[30]

One Ranger patrol raided the outskirts of the northern approaches to San Pietro before being forced to withdraw. Four enemy fighting patrols that attempted to infiltrate the Rangers were quickly seen off.

At dusk the battalions reformed. Captain Larkin noticed 'an ambulance darting up the road to evacuate our more seriously wounded. We started to pull back under heavy harassing fire and were surprised to find we *could* withdraw'.

The Rangers had lost thirteen men killed and eighteen wounded, all by shell fire.[31] Walker, who received a report that the Rangers had attacked the village in daylight in close formation was very critical of 3rd Rangers and Colonel Dammer. Henceforth only patrols from the 36th Division would be used to reconnoitre the village.

The Rangers marched back to Venafro by the San Pietro-Ceppagna road. The old hands in the battalion felt that good men had been killed in a futile operation. Morale needed a lift. Once the battalion had been allotted a tenting area outside Venafro Sergeant Lehmann and his remaining men fastened two pup tents together – it was still raining – and then went into town to buy wine. They returned with a five gallon demi-john, into which Sergeant Lehmann dropped his remaining morphine and the squad 'sought and found oblivion'.[32]

In the morning Sergant Lehmann helped load wounded Rangers on to transport. He was interested to see that a Lieutenant who had recently joined the battalion and had boasted about what he was going to do to the Germans was on a stretcher 'limbs ashake, mouth agape, eyes astare. His bare feet bore a tag reading haemorrhoids – proof that only ranks suffered battle fatigue'.

Over on the right flank General Lucas's VI Corps had been making their diversionary attack. It had begun on 29 November in the hope that quick successes would lead to some of the forces defending the Mignano Gap itself being switched over to VI Corps front. But there were no early successes. Just one 'might have been'. At 0300 hours on 29 November II Battalion, 168th Regiment, 34th Division, attacked the summit of the 1,600 foot Monte Pantano. The mountain was held by II Battalion, 577th Grenadier Regiment,

* All Ranger Officers, NCOs and medics carried morphine. In other US units only medics carried it.

305th Division. Earlier in the month the 34th had knocked the 305th Division about and it's likely that Colonel Frederick Butler, commanding 168th Regiment, was hoping his 2nd Battalion would repeat the performance. But the 2nd Battalion came up against the fiercest resistance they had ever encountered. Their leading company had its central platoon's position overrun and the Grenadiers occupied them, enfilading the company's two wing platoons. Captain Benjamin Butler ran down the mountain, collected his reserve platoon and put in a bayonet charge that drove out the enemy. This set the pattern for the rest of the battle, positions continuously changing hands in a series of attacks and counter-attacks, savage hand-to-hand fighting and more men killed or wounded by bayonet than in the rest of the battle for Mignano Gap put together; friendly artillery fire that killed US stretcher cases placed ready for evacuation in positions safe from enemy fire, an enemy that refused to give up their part of the mountain no matter how often they were dislodged from it. They kept on coming. So did the 2nd. One of their soldiers who had his foot blown off was seen sliding down the mountain on his backside, determined to get to an Aid Post under his own steam. When the 2nd Battalion's casualty figures had reached 50%, and the 577th Grenadiers had been reinforced, Colonel Butler passed his 3rd Battalion through the 2nd. But the 3rd Battalion's CO and his leading company commander were both severely wounded on a reconnaissance, and the third attack, at first successful, was once again driven back to the start line by a reinforced 577th Grenadier Battalion. 168th's 1st Battalion had already been committed round the flanks of the mountain. All three battalion commanders had been severely wounded. On 4 December Colonel Butler informed General Ryder he believed his Regiment was no longer capable of taking Monte Pantano. The 168th was withdrawn. During the battle they had fired 400,000 rounds of ammunition and thrown 4,800 grenades. The 2nd Battalion accounted for most of these. It was later awarded the Presidential Unit Citation for gallantry.[33]

A few days later the 34th Divison was pulled out of the Line for a rest. They were replaced by the 2nd Moroccan Division, made up of mainly French officers and Moroccan other ranks. In their first attack – made in daylight and watched by General Lucas – they suffered over 200 casualties without closing on their objective. But something about their bearing during and after the battle convinced Lucas that they would quickly become first class troops. He was right. Always carefree about casualties – all ranks really did feel it an honour to die for France – the Division became the one the Germans least liked to encounter, partly because of the way the Moroccans fought but also because of the way their irregular troops, the Goums, behaved. They used to bring back ears to prove they got that close to the enemy.

General Keyes had a word with Walker, telling him that Clark thought a simultaneous attack on San Pietro, Monte Sammucro and Monte Lungo could result in the German centre collapsing. The way would then be clear for the drive to Cassino. Monte Sammucro and San Pietro were likely to be strongly defended but 5th Army Intelligence had reported Monte Lungo lightly defended. (It was in fact held by I/15th Panzer Grenadier Regiment, about 400 men strong, and very well dug in.) Clark told General Keyes he wanted Walker to blood the 1st Italian Motorized Brigade on it. As inexperienced troops the Italians needed an objective they couldn't fail to take. General Keyes passed on Clark's request to Walker, who grumbled about it – he'd met the Italian Commander, Brigadier Vincente Dapino, and hadn't thought much of him – but agreed that Monte Lungo was the right objective for Italian troops.

Walker planned the simultaneous attacks on San Pietro, Monte Sammucro and Monte Lungo to go in at first light on 8 December. 1st Battalion, 143rd Regiment, would attack Monte Sammucro's summit while 3rd Rangers tackled the montain's solitary peak, Pt 957. The 2nd Battalion, 143rd Regiment would attack San Pietro. The 3rd Battalion, 143rd Regiment, would be in reserve to the 2nd Battalion. General Dapino's 1st Italian Motorized would deal with Monte Lungo. Walker ordered Colonel W. F. Martin, 143rd Regiment's Commander, to have both the 2nd and 3rd Battalions send patrols to San Pietro.

The 1st Battalion, 143rd Regiment, was commanded by Lt-Colonel W. J. Burgess. Under the command of one of General Walker's sons, Lt-Colonel Fred Walker Jun., the Battalion had distinguished itself at Salerno and in the latter stages of the fight for Chiunzi Pass. In October Walker made his son his G3. Lt-Colonel Burgess, a Staff Officer at II Corps, was recommended as his successor. Nobody told Walker or Colonel Martin that Lt-Colonel Burgess was alcoholic and that Lucas had given orders for him to be 'dumped'. He should have been sent to hospital and dried out. Instead he was given one of the most taxing jobs in the army. Lieutenant Young remembered him in Texas where he was an outstanding training officer. Instead of the ramrod straight, up-to-the-minute officer Lieutenant Young saw a man who seemed to have aged ten years in eighteen months, who walked with a stoop, and who was liable to bite people's heads off for no reason. Lieutenant Young spotted his C.O. staggering up a mountain path to visit one of his forward companies and concluded that he was not physically fit enough for the job.

Lt-Colonel Charles Denholm, who had won the Silver Star as a battalion commander in North Africa, had retrained the 2nd Battalion, 143rd Regiment, to his own liking. He considered it to be in 'peak condition, highly motivated and ready to take on all comers'.[34]

The assault on Monte Sammucro would begin at last light on 7 December. The 1st Battalion, 143rd, would attack from the south-east, the Rangers from the east. 2nd Battalion, 143rd, would attack San Pietro from the east. They were occupying Cannavinelle Hill and would begin their descent at midnight and be on the LOD by 0500 hours. The attack would go in at 0620 hours.

The 143rd Regiment's patrols to San Pietro brought back plenty of information: 'Enemy strength estimated as one battalion, with perhaps another in reserve. Has plenty of artillery support and has available in San Pietro mines not yet laid. Morale fair to poor.' This estimate of the II/15th Panzer Grenadier Regiment's morale must have been based on a steady trickle of deserters from the battalion – eleven in one day – who had crossed into US lines in late November, shivering in soaked summer kit. The 143rd Intelligence Section had established that most of the deserters were veterans who had served with the Divisions since it had first gone into action in Sicily. But they did not attempt to find out what II/15th Panzer Grenadier Regiment's recent battle record was like. If they had 4th Rangers could have given them a warning. The Intelligence section might also have considered the fact that the battalion had whipped the 3rd Battalion, 143rd Regiment at Salerno in a very hard fight.

During the week that followed the 2nd and 3rd Battalions, 143rd Regiment, carried out day and night patrols to San Pietro. From the information they and forward observers gathered 143rd senior officers were able to compile an accurate picture of the village's defences and its supply lines. The patrols confirmed that it was held by the II/15th Panzer Grenadier Regiment. 'Enemy can defend San Pietro from south, north-east and will probably do so. Owing to the ravine to the west of the village they have no need to defend that side of it'. A later estimate – 6 December – reads 'Enemy likely to defend San Pietro from the east, delaying actions S and N of Venafro road with detached posts probably using booby traps and mines'. On the night of 3/4 December patrols spotted eight enemy pillboxes protected by barbed wire. The following night a patrol from the 2nd Battalion cut their way through the wire, destroyed one of the pillboxes and captured three prisoners. It was a brilliant bit of offensive patrolling. And the fact that the wire had not been booby trapped delighted Lt-Colonel Denholm. His battalion could cut their way through any amount of barbed wire provided it wasn't booby-trapped.[35]

One line in 143rd Unit Report dated 6 December reads: 'URGENT NEED AMMUNITION SHOELACES'. The men's original shoelaces had rotted in the rain. One can understand Colonel Martin's anxiety. Men can fight with inadequate equipment but not without shoelaces.

The 1st Battalion, 143rd Regiment, moved up to their LOD during the night of 5 December, 3rd Rangers were close enough to their LOD near Venafro. Captain Larkin, who was fed up with sleeping in a pup tent, moved his belongings, which included a much treasured sleeping bag – he always carried it into action with him to prevent it being stolen – into a 'beautiful little chapel' and bedded down on one of the pews. 'Next morning I woke up to find Italian women kneeling at the foot of my bed, praying.'

An hour or so before dusk on 7 December the officers of A Company, 1st Battalion, 143rd, were briefed on their part in the attack by their new Company Commander, Lieutenant Rufus Kleghorn. As A Company would be leading the attack Lieutenant Young was also present. Lieutenant Kleghorn opened proceedings by saying, 'I don't think there are any Krauts up there'. Lieutenant Young had the impression that the Company Commander didn't *want* there to be any Krauts up there. Young also hoped there wouldn't be any because Lt-Colonel Burgess had only committed A Company to the attack. The remaining companies would remain in reserve at the base of the mountain. This was breaking the rule that at least one company followed the lead company into an assault. If Lieutenant Kleghorn knew about the 3rd Rangers attacking Pt 957 he did not pass on the information.[36]

A Company moved up the trail in single file as soon as it was dark, Lieutenant Wiggins's platoon in the lead. Abreast of them came Lieutenant Young and his pioneer platoon, ready to check for mines. Apart from his Colt 45, Lieutenant Young was carrying an 8 mm movie camera, a copy of Clausewitz's *Das Krieg* and the remains of a home-made fruit cake.

It was not a particularly dark night. Looking back, Lieutenant Young could see the rest of A Company 'strung out like a giant caterpillar, expanding and contracting, moving slowly up the rocky, muddy slope, moving very quietly, then stopping to rest. We had all night to reach the summit. We just had to arrive before dawn.' At around 2230 hours Lieutenant Wiggins's lead scouts reported 'possible mines'. Lieutenant Young and his platoons went forward to investigate. It was German signal wire. The further they moved up the mountain the more wire they found. To Lieutenant Young that meant one thing: Krauts-a-plenty. But why hadn't they mined the trail and set up outposts? Could Lieutenant Kleghorn be right after all? Lieutenant Young doubted it. Monte Sammucro was too dominant a feature not to be defended. Young recalled that Clausewitz put great emphasis on defending dominant mountains.

At around 0230 hours a fire fight broke out on A Company's right. Lieutenant Young could distinguish the slow 'dut-dut-dut' of Bars as well as Spandaus. So the Krauts were on the mountain. But who the hell were firing the Bars? Soon afterward the trail petered out. The men had to haul themselves over rocks. Lieutenant Young's shrapnel-filled knee began paining him. He told it to shut up.

It was still dark when both the leading platoons saw the darker outline of the summit against the sky. They only had a few hundred feet to go. Lieutenant Wiggins, his two leading scouts, and Lieutenant Young crawled to within fifteen yards of the crest. Then Lieutenant Wiggins began crawling up to the peak by himself. Lieutenant Young watched him go 'very slowly, very quietly, grenade in hand, up to the top of the crest. Then he wriggled back down, holding up two fingers, indicating two sentries or two outposts. He then gave his grenade to me and moved off to the right and disappeared . . . I presumed he was going to deploy his platoon strung out below'. From way down the mountain there was a crash. Spandaus and Schmeissers opened up from the crest. But luckily they were firing from a gully to the left of A Company – the easiest route up the mountain. The enemy were obviously expecting an attack from there. The firing went on for a long time, a dozen or so automatic weapons firing at nothing. 'Waste of ammo', Young thought. None of A Company fired back. But the Germans on the peak suddenly 'picked up' Young's platoon and began throwing egg bombs at them. Easter bunnies, Young called them, useless things. But one landed right next to his head and he wasn't wearing a helmet. He couldn't hear properly with one on. He felt a searing pain. Blood poured down his face and neck. For a moment he wondered if he'd had it. Then one of the sentries on the crest stood up and yelled, *'Die kommen hier nach oben!'* and began firing his Schmeisser at Young's platoon. Young pulled out his Colt and fired back. Young was the battalion's champion shot with a 45. He admired the way the sentry ducked and weaved to avoid the bullets, and still kept firing his Schmeisser. When he had no bullets left Young put back the revolver in its holster, stood up and threw the grenade Lieutenant Wiggins had given him. Before the grenade exploded the sentry fired another burst of Schmeisser. A bullet struck Young's left hand 'smashing bones, zipping open the palm, opening it up like a hot dog sausage is opened up to spread mustard'. The force of the impact almost knocked Young off his feet. But immediately after his grenade had exploded he heard a cry of pain. Young wondered if he'd killed the sentry or just wounded him. There was a clattering of boots on the crest. More Germans opened fire with automatic weapons. They also began rolling down boulders in the direction of Young's platoon. Both Sergeant Wilson, Young's Platoon Sergeant, and Private First Class Owisanick were badly crushed by them. But they could still walk.

Young decided it was time to leave the fighting to the unwounded members of the platoon. After appointing Corporal Leonard Rice acting platoon sergeant he told Sergeant Wilson and Private First Class Owisanick to follow him down the mountain. There was no sign of Lieutenant Wiggins. Young wondered if he'd been wounded. And where the hell was Lieutenant Kleghorn? As Young made his way down the mountain he kept on repeating

'Lieutenant Kleghorn?' to the men he passed. At the tail of the column someone answered, 'Here'. Young told the Company Commander what was happening up front and warned him that if the enemy caught the column strung out on the mountain they'd have 'a real turkey shoot'. Lieutenant Kleghorn didn't say a word.

Young and his wounded walked on down the mountain. The shrapnel in Young's knee was 'screaming at me'. He reached the battalion's LOD at first light. 'Dynamite, you look terrible!' said Captain Richard Burrage, the Battalion's Adjutant. After telling Captain Burrage and the Battalion's S3 everything he knew he tried to interest them in his movie camera. Neither of them wanted it so Dynamite went off to hospital with it still in his haversack.*

Young had been right to worry about Wiggins. He too had been trying to find Kleghorn when he was severely wounded by automatic fire.† Kleghorn finally rose to the occasion, took over command of Wiggins's platoon and, with two sergeants in the lead, the platoon stormed the crest, killing or wounding all the Germans defending it.

Private First Class Joe Gallagher, 19, was in the platoon behind. He heard a lot of yelling, cursing and screaming. By the time his platoon reached the crest everything was quiet. The platoon went on to attack Pt 1142, about fifty yards away from the main peak. The Germans defending it didn't put up much of a fight. 'We took quite a few prisoners when we captured it. Basically they were very much like us – and scared of what we might do to them after we'd taken them prisoner. We never mistreated prisoners.'[37]

A Company did their best to dig in on the two peaks. Private First Class Gallagher recalls. 'It was solid rock with a light formation of earth. We scratched the earth off it and piled rocks round it, or took shelter between boulders.'

Enemy artillery and mortars were zeroing in on the peaks. At 0700 hours, under cover of a heavy barrage, the first counter-attack came in. Making skilled use of cover – the approaches to the peaks were covered in rocks – the enemy got to within grenade range of A Company. Each side used up all the grenades they had. Runners brought up more grenades for the enemy. A Company had to make do with Bars and rifle fire. The company had lost a third of its strength in the attack and the enemy barrage. Kleghorn contacted the Battalion CP and reported 'situation critical'. A Company needed more grenades, more men and more annumition – in that order.

---

* His left hand was permanently crippled. A medical board down-graded him, and said they would post him out of the infantry. Young somehow got himself upgraded to A.1. again and returned to 1st Battalion, 143rd Regiment, in time to take part in the 36th Division's breakthrough at Anzio.

† On leaving hospital Lt Wiggins was invalided out of the infantry.

Whilst Lt-Colonel Burgess was dispatching two platoons – one from C Company, one from D – up the mountain the pioneer platoon brought up grenades and ammunition. But it was far from a straightforward delivery. Lieutenant Young pieced together what happened when he returned from hospital. 'We had a rolling munitions dump with the 23rd British Armoured Brigade. When the situation for A Company became critical we drew the lot. It wasn't enough. One of my squads went racing round in a truck to other units who could share some powder and ball. The two other squads were busy carrying the stuff up the mountain. A very busy day but happy customers. "You call, we deliver. No order too small. Special Foxhole deliveries. No extra charge on Sundays".'

The steady re-supply of ammunition and grenades enabled A Company to hang on until the two fresh platoons arrived at the summit. When the enemy below Pts 1205 and 1142 received an extra volume of fire and grenades they broke off the battle. For the time being the reinforced A Company were subject only to intense harassing fire.

The 3rd Rangers had left their LOD at Ceppagna at the same time as A Company began their attack. But Walker had failed to take into account that the ascent to Pt 957 was a shorter haul than the way up to Pt 1205. It was also less steep. The simultaneous attacks that Walker was hoping for were a dead duck from the word go. The Rangers ran into enemy outposts half way to Pt 957. It was this exchange of fire that Lieutenant Young had heard. The Rangers quickly dealt with the outposts and by 0400 hours on 7 December E and F Companies were only a quarter of a mile from Pt 957. As they moved into the saddle between Pt 957 and Pts 1205 and 1142 they came under Spandau and mortar fire from the rear. The Rangers took some casualties, including Captain Larkin's radio operator, but the bulk of them made it to Pt 957.

'The enemy were close and directly above,' Captain Larkin writes. 'We engaged in a lively exchange of hand guns, very close in.' E Company, led by Captain Larkin, began climbing the peak, which was about seven hundred feet high. Captain Larkin and several of his men reached a ledge twelve feet from the top of the peak. That last twelve feet was sheer, and there was a pillbox on top of it. The enemy showered the Rangers with stick grenades. One exploded on top of Larkin's pack. 'I felt warm liquid when I reached back. I thought it was blood, but it turned out to be water from my canteen, which was full of shrapnel.'

By now it was first light. Captain Larkin's party began coming under fire from the enemy on Pt 1205 and Pt 1142. Reluctantly Captain Larkin gave the order to withdraw. 'I hated to do it. We had never had to do it before.' When they reached the base of the peak Captain Larkin helped some other Rangers carry an officer, Lieutenant Parrish, who'd been badly wounded in the buttocks by a grenade. They came under a murderous fire from the main peaks. 'It became clear we weren't going to make it. Then, out of the blue, came a tiny cloud. Whether anyone believes it or not we simply walked out under the small cloud, which consistently moved in the right direction, at just the right speed. I'm not a religious man but by then I knew that Sister Annette's rosary was working.'[38]

Sergeant Lehmann had been watching the assault on Pt 957 from the cover of some rocks about 200 yards away. After he had helped carry Sergeant Parrish to safety Captain Larkin went back to look for a missing Ranger. Coming under heavy fire he had to run for it. Suddenly he went up in feathers. Sergeant Lehmann and his squad burst out laughing. 'They've hit the fart-sack!' one of them yelled. The squads elation was short-lived. Two Rangers leading a close friend of Lehmann's called Joe Phillips passed through the squad. 'Joe was shaking and crying out of his mind. He was one of the original Rangers and had distinguished himself in North Africa, Sicily and Italy.' Lehmann was afraid Phillips had broken down completely. 'But as soon as he got to the Aid station he recovered his wits and checked out to come back to us, carrying a box of rations all the way, and apologizing to anyone who listened for having bugged out.'[39]

Captain Kettle did all he could to save Lieutenant Parrish's life. He failed. Both he and Captain Larkin felt personally responsible for his death.

Captain Larkin climbed into an empty foxhole to have some sleep. When he woke up he realized the foxhole wasn't empty. The previous occupant had taken a direct hit. 'He was scattered all over the place in very small pieces. I was still in shock, still trying to adjust, when 2nd Lieutenant Scotty Monro came down the path with another Ranger. As he came up to the grotesque scene he casually observed, 'Some of these new guys will never learn to take care of their equipment.'

The 2nd Battalion began the descent of Cannavinelle Hill at 2100 hours on 7 December, with Lieutenant John Kline's pioneer platoon in the lead. Their job was to make a forward ammunition dump in no-man's land. They would be covered by a platoon from E Company. Private First Class Clover, shoving a box of ammunition downhill, described it as a 'backside' descent.[40] The weight of the ammunition and the muddy paths had the platoon slipping and sliding and grasping at trees for support. Once they reached the bottom physical discomfort was replaced by fear. Stock-piling ammunition in no-man's-land is a dangerous job, even if you are covered by a rifle platoon – which happened to Corporal William Gallagher's. They were under orders to stay put after the pioneers had completed the dump and to await the rest of the battalion, who would pass through them at dawn. Corporal Gallagher, much addicted to working out the odds of life and death, was wondering whether his platoon would get shot up by the rest of the battalion in mistake for Germans. In no-man's-land Private First Class Clover kept on 'seeing' figures watching him, a phenomenon common to men working on patrolling no-man's-land. Suddenly Corporal Gallagher heard someone walking along the San Pietro-Ceppagna road, a little to his left. A shot rang out. A voice screamed, 'I'm an American Officer!' It was Lieutenant Kline. He had been shot in the stomach by one of Corporal Gallagher's platoon. He died within minutes of receiving first aid.

At 0500 hours the 131st Artillery Battalion began firing a preliminary barrage to cover the San Pietro attack. Forty-eight 155 howitzers were used instead of the usual thirty-two. Lieutenant Harold Owens, Forward Observer on Monte Rotondo, was excited. It was the first time he had ever directed so many guns. But he also knew that when dawn broke enemy forward observers would be trying to pinpoint his position.[41] An enemy counter-barrage opened up soon after the US barrage began.

The main body of the 2nd Battalion moved into attack at 0620 hours. From the safety of Battalion headquarters Private First Class Clover watched the leading companies – E and F – scramble over olive terraces and then come under fire. 'The skirmish lines sagged and changed to "bump and run" tactics, charging from tree to tree, firing, then hitting the ground – British battle drill lives!' Two hundred yards from the LOD the US troops ran into the barbed wire protecting the enemy pillboxes. As men began cutting the wire they triggered anti-personnel mines and were killed or severely wounded. Those behind the wire were shot up by Spandaus firing from the pillboxes. The fact that the wire was booby-trapped came as a shock to the 2nd Battalion. they had been told it was not booby-trapped. As some men surged along its perimeter, trying to find a gap, Lieutenant Richard Stewart and several of his platoon were shot dead trying to jump over the wire. Others succeeded in crawling underneath it but were shot dead by the Spandaus in the pillboxes.

Captain Andrews, Battalion Adjutant, was up with E Company. Their commander, Captain Eben C. Bergstrom, suggested both companies should withdraw and let their artillery soften up the defences. The idea was not taken up. Enemy mortars and artillery were zeroing in beyond the wire. G Company, who were following up the other two companies ran into the worst of the mortaring and shelling,* and withdrew to the LOD. Sergeant Nick Bozic, a Forward Observer with G Company, radioed Captain Jim Skinner at 131st Battalion CP on Monte Rotondo for support fire. He had only just got the message off when shells landed all round him and he was

* Along with the 3rd Battalion, back in reserve. Private Bob Bunker, carrying 52lbs of mortar shells, took evasive action and fell into a ravine. His injuries put him in hospital for six weeks. Serious accidents were commonplace at Mignano Gap.

wounded in one leg. It was almost as if the Germans had picked up his message and were giving him the treatment.[42] They hadn't picked up the message, just Sergeant Bozic's radio. Captain Skinner ordered support fire for G Company. It was effective enough for them to reform and make a second advance. Captain Skinner was critical about the way his battalion artillery was being handled. 'There wasn't a concentrated barrage on the enemy's front line. Only San Pietro got shelled. My unit depended mainly on Forward Observers with 2nd Battalion's companies for firing opportunities and their casualty rates were so high that there was little continuity in the shelling.'

Captain Skinner had the job of escorting forward observer replacements to the companies. When he guided a close friend, Captain Brownyard, into the battle zone he wondered if he'd ever see him again. Later that day Captain Brownyard was brought back on a litter. He was riddled with shrapnel – forty pieces were removed from his body – but made a complete recovery.[43]

131st Battalion's guns did all they could to neutralize the enemy guns, who were firing from behind Monte Porchia, but with little success. By midday all infantry and forward observers' radios had been knocked out by enemy fire. Lieutenant Wendell Phillippi, the 2nd Battalion's Communications Officer, established telephone links with all the companies. He then organized his platoon in a round-the-clock checking of the wire. Although badly wounded in one foot he refused to be evacuated. One of his men 'was blown to bits just a few feet from me. I corresponded with his parents. They wanted details but I never had the heart to give them.'[44] By nightfall all twenty-three of the wiring party were dead or wounded.*

Corporal Gallagher's platoon, which had not been involved in the attack, had watched F Company pass through them. They said E Company was somewhere on their left. Corporal Gallagher's squad sergeant sent him to find out exactly where. He ran through an enemy artillery barrage, saw three US soldiers attacking a pillbox then bumped into a G Company sergeant who had just seen one of his men cut in two by a burst of Spandau, and was badly shaken. He told Gallagher that E Company had taken up defensive positions fifty yards from the barbed wire. Gallagher returned to his platoon and guided them over to E Company's positions. His squad was reinforced by a Sergeant Whitey, who had one of his toes blown off and his back peppered with shrapnel. The Battalion Medical Officer, who was under orders to send all men still capable of fighting back into the battle, had patched him up and sent him back.

By noon Colonel Martin realized that the attack had stalled. The 2nd

---

* Lieutenant Phillipi was awarded the Silver Star.

Battalion had only penetrated the barbed wire in a couple of places and these gaps were covered by Spandaus. He ordered the 3rd Battalion to try to work their way clear of the barbed wire, two companies attacking from the north, the other company crossing the Ceppagna-San Pietro road and attacking from the South. Colonel Martin believed the enemy would not have protected these approaches as thoroughly as the eastern one. He was right. But the company of the 3rd Battalion who attacked from the south were confronted with booby-trapped terraces. As they tried to climb them they were shot down by Spandaus firing from below the walls of the village.

The two companies attacking from the north had to climb down terraces. They weren't booby-trapped. But as the companies reached a clearing in front of the northern walls of the village they were caught in a cross fire. Captain Meitzel had seen to it that a dozen or so snipers were in positions beneath the northern walls, which had Spandaus firing from them. The two companies of the 3rd Battalion had to make a quick withdrawal. They tried attacking under cover of terraces north-east of the village. They had no trouble from snipers and no crossfire, just Spandaus.

Private Schwenn, 8 Company, II/15 PGR, who was firing one from on top of the northern wall of the village, described what happened to some of the 3rd Battalion. 'Our section had the luck to be able to traverse nearly all the terraces in front of us. So we were able to help a group of men out in the open on our right. The Americans had spotted their positions. We shot down the first section who charged them. And others who followed. None of the Americans realized they were being shot at from the flank. The appalling din of battle drowned the sound of our gun'.[45]

The men shot down by Private Schwenn belonged to Private First Class Lee Fletcher's I Company. His own platoon was a little further up Monte Sammucro and suffered heavily from snipers, mortars and automatic fire. They were commanded by a sergeant, their officer having been killed by enemy shelling before the attack began. Within one hour of launching the attack I Company's commander had been killed, his successor seriously wounded and the company reduced to two understrength platoons. Realizing that the 3rd Battalion's attack had also failed Colonel Martin ordered them to dig defensive positions. I Company occupied part of the area where 3rd Rangers had dug in and suffered the same steady drain of casualties from artillery and mortar fire.

As darkness fell the exhausted men of the 2nd and 3rd Battalions were ordered back to within two hundred yards of the LOD. Lt-Colonel Denholm told Colonel Martin that his men had been shot to bits trying to fight their way through booby-trapped barbed wire. It was simply not a viable route for an attack on the village. He was also angry with his patrols for failing to spot that the barbed wire had been booby-trapped. This seems a bit hard on the patrols. They had got through it twice – once when they reached the village itself and spotted the cache of mines, and again when they had destroyed the enemy pillbox. It was surely not their fault if the enemy had been a bit casual about where they'd attached the mines to the wire. And the destruction of the pillbox may well have resulted in the wire being more heavily booby trapped.

Colonel Martin reported the failure of the attack to Divisonal HQ, emphasizing how the booby-trapped barbed wire had held up the 2nd Battalion's attack, and would hold it up again. In spite of this General Walker ordered the attack to be renewed on 9 December. The 36th Division had a rigid attack procedure. If one failed it was to be renewed as soon as possible, no matter what the obstacles were. The news that the attack was to be renewed came as a shock to Lt-Colonel Denholm. He still believes that the order to renew the attack was the result of 'pressure from higher than division as neither Martin nor Walker by nature were incautious of the lives or well-being of their men'.[46]

The attack on San Pietro was renewed at 0845 hours, 9 December. There was no pretence about a dawn attack. It was almost as if Colonel Martin, who may have shared Lt-Colonel Denholm's feelings about the renewal of the attack, had put it off for as long as possible, restricting the number of hours in which it could be made. The ranks of the 2nd Battalion went into action with a sense of numb resignation, wondering how on earth those in charge thought that their infantry could breach the enemy lines. The leading scout in Corporal Gallagher's squad was shot as he leapt down a terrace near the barbed wire. In the squad behind Gallagher's a man was severely wounded. 'His screams went on for hours.' All the medics in E Company had been killed and wounded, and there was no morphine to ease the pain of that severely wounded man. The enemy defence barrage of artillery, mortars and rifle grenades was heavier than ever.

For Corporal Gallagher, who'd fought at Salerno and would go on to fight at Anzio, it was the most terrible concentration of fire he ever experienced. 'It was constant, never-ending.' Several newcomers to the platoon broke down under it and had to be led to the rear. Attacks all along the line came to nothing. All the 2nd and 3rd Battalions gained was a longer casualty list. At dusk both battalions were ordered to withdraw two hundred yards. Corporal Gallagher's platoon built themselves sangars in a ravine. Gallagher was lying down, checking his sangar for length, when a shell landed next to it. The blast blew down one side of the sangar on top of him. A sergeant picked the stones off him. He was unhurt but his rifle had been blown apart. He 'felt naked without it.' The first thing he did next morning was to look for another. He found one next to a dead private who'd belonged to the Battalion's wiring party. Two of his buddies were lying dead beside him.

Gallagher's own squad, which had begun the battle with eleven men had been reduced to five. In thirty-six hours the 2nd and 3rd Battalion, 143rd Regiment, had suffered 61% casualties.

Captain Meitzel described his Battalion's losses as 'light'. The only crisis during the fighting had occurred during the afternoon of 9 December. The Battalion had begun running short of rifle grenades. They formed a vital part of the defensive screen. Captain Meitzel contacted Regimental HQ at San Vittore and asked for a substantial number of grenades to be sent to San Pietro as soon as possible. Under the eyes of the US Forward Observers a small truck filled with grenades sped up the 'mad mile' to the village. The US gunners missed it. They missed it on the way back, and continued to miss it as the same driver and sergeant delivered two more loads of grenades. What courage!

Captain Meitzel had a different sort of escape. One of his staff, following the conversation between a US Forward Observer and his gunnery officer, heard them remarking about the number of men visiting the house with the red walls. The house had clearly been pinpointed as a possible CP. Captain Meitzel ordered the house to be evacuated at once. Three hours later it was destroyed by US shell fire. Captain Meitzel chose a cave in the ravine where the San Pietrans were living for his new CP. The San Pietrans were dying off, some from exposure, some from lung and chest diseases, some from wounds. One night a US fighter bomber had spotted a light coming from their cave – the San Pietrans were making their bread – and presuming it was an enemy outpost had aimed a bomb at it. The bomb exploded just outside the entrance to the cave. The stone panels built to withstand shell blast were blown inwards. Ten San Pietrans were killed and many wounded. The seriously wounded died because their wounds became septic or gangrenous. The San Pietrans had no doctor and no medicine. Every morning those who had died in the night were taken out and left unburied in the ravine. Nobody had the strength to dig the graves. Later the ravine became known as *La Valle Della Morte*. US troops of a like mind named the valley running below San Pietro Death Valley.

On 10 December Walker visited his battered battalion. He brought back a badly wounded man in his jeep and took him straight to hospital. On 12 December Lucas met Walker and found him, 'low in his mind. I don't see why as his division hadn't been in action very long'. Walker had clearly been keeping those 61% casualties to himself.

The 1st Italian Motorized Brigade took over the US toe-hold on Monte Lungo from 141st Regiment, 36th Division, on 7 December. A reconnaissance patrol sent out to Pt 343 did not return. Brigadier Dapino planned to use a battalion of the 67th Regiment to assault Pt 343 in a frontal attack from the east whilst a battalion of the 51st Bersaglieri worked their way up the railway running alongside Monte Lungo and then took the enemy in the flank. Each battalion had a fighting strength of around five hundred men keen to show that given the right cause they could fight as well as anybody else. After a preliminary barrage at 0530 hours the attack began at 0620 hours on 8 December.

A thick mist cut down visibility to fifteen yards. This was a mixed blessing. It would give the leading companies every chance of taking the enemy by surprise but would make it impossible for them to ask for artillery support if they needed it.

The two leading companies of 1st Battalion, 67th Regiment, dealt with two enemy outposts, then nosed around in the mist until they found a gap between two German companies on Pt 264. The Italians overran a platoon of the enemy and plunged on up the mountain. Meeting no opposition they guessed they had broken through the enemy lines and began yelling with triumph. In the words of the I/15th Panzer Grenadier Regiment's CO, Captain von Heyking, 'There was nothing to stop them reaching the summit except that man Scherling!' Corporal Ewald Scherling was convalescing from a wound in a hut near the summit of Pt 343. Hearing firing, he rushed out from the hut with his Spandau. Mist prevented him from seeing the Italians, but their yelling gave their positions away. Certain of victory, they had abandoned all pretence of attack discipline and were bunched together like students celebrating newly awarded degrees. When Scherling opened fire* the Italians went down 'like corn cut by a scythe'. Within a few minutes the two companies had virtually ceased to exist. All ten officers had been killed or wounded and they had taken between 70 and 80% casualties.[47]

Realizing from the screams of the wounded that he'd been on target, Corporal Scherling ran down to join his company. By the time he reached it the remnants of the two Italian companies had withdrawn. But his Company Commander told him that more Italian troops were approaching the positions. Corporal Scherling led his company in a counter-attack, firing a Schmeisser. The fresh Italian troops, already shaken by the screams from their leading companies, were in no mood to withstand such a charge. They turned tail and fled back to the LOD.[48]

The Bersaglieri attack up the railway was out of luck as well. The enemy spotted them through gaps in the mist and when they advanced up the southern slopes of Monte Lungo they were quickly halted by heavy automatic fire and mortaring. According to the Italian Official History they also came under fire from caves on Monte Maggiore. Monte Maggiore had been cleared of the enemy by US 142nd Regiment, but it seems quite

* Scherling had a number 2 'feeding' the Spandau.

26. Monte Camino. British stretcher bearers on the last leg of their four-hour journey down the mountain.

27. Monte Camino. Goums' plaque to British dead.

AUX COMBATTANTS BRITANNIQUES
TOMBES GLORIEUSEMENT AU MONTE CAMINO
NOVEMBRE DECEMBRE 1943
LES GOUMS MAROCAINS

28. Monte la Difensa.

29. Medic from First Special Service Force with back-pack.

30. Major-General J.Y. Whitfield. His remarkable agility earned him the nickname Squirrel Nutkin.

31. Italian infantryman from 67th Regiment advancing up Monte Lungo on 8 December.

32. German dugout on Monte Lungo.

possible – and in character – that the Germans had slipped back into the cave under cover of darkness. The Bersaglieri reformed and tried a second attack. Without the artillery support they could not call on because of the mist the attack was as unsuccessful as the first.[49]

By 10 o'clock Brigadier Dapino realized his attack had failed. He recalled the Bersaglieri and the 2nd Battalion, 67th Regiment, who were preparing for another direct assault on Pt 343. At first he reported many hundreds of casualties but by the end of the day these had been reduced to forty-seven dead, 102 wounded and 131 missing.

Clark, always jumpy about possible counter-attacks, thought that the enemy might be headstrong enough to try and break through the Italian brigade and had eight 8″ gun-howitzers lay down DF on Monte Lungo.

That night Captain von Heyking pieced together the part Corporal Scherling had played in the battle. After congratulating him for his exceptional initiative and courage Major von Heyking took off his own Iron Cross and placed it round Corporal Scherling's neck. The CO told him he was recommending him for the Knight's Cross. Corporal Scherling seemed surprised at what all the fuss was about. He was killed at the battle of the Garigliano in January, 1944. Later that month he was awarded the Knight's Cross posthumously.[50]

The US Official History writes off the attack as a disaster from the word go. The Italian Official History is nearly as disparaging. They make no mention of the 1st Battalion, 67th Regiment's remarkable breakthrough. Clearly Brigadier Dapino, who must have heard about it from the surviving officers of the leading companies, did not see fit to make it part of official records.

Up on Monte Sammucro the reinforced A Company of 1st Battalion, 143rd were coming under intense pressure from the enemy. On 8 December Colonel Kruger reinforced I/71st Regiment with his second battalion. Pts 1205 and 1142 were to be retaken 'at all costs'. Early on 9 December two companies of the I/71st Panzer Grenadiers worked their way into the saddle between Pts 1205 and 1142. Making good use of the cover given by the rocks, they began sniping A Company from close range. They then crawled to within grenade range of the T-patchers. Both sides used up all their grenades before the enemy withdrew. As they withdrew a fighting patrol from A Company went after them, taking a company commander and twenty of his men prisoner. No sooner had the patrol returned when the enemy made a second counter-attack, supported by a heavy artillery and mortar barrage. This time the Panzer Grenadiers charged towards the peak in open formation. A Company's forward observers brought down a heavy artillery barrage on the advancing enemy and the attack was quickly broken up. The enemy went to ground until dark, then moved on to the saddle. Patrols from

A Company reported a large body of them lying up there. They were dispersed by the US artillery during the night of 9/10 December.

Further down the mountain the 3rd Rangers were still trying to take Pt 957. Captain Larkin's Report on E and F Companies failure to take the peak convinced Lt-Colonel Dammer that further daylight attacks were not feasible. On 9 December he ordered Lieutenant Palumbo's B Company to attack it at dusk. B Company took the enemy by surprise and the Rangers quickly captured the peak. The company then took up positions among the rocks on the slope of Pt 957 facing the enemy, expecting a counter-attack. None developed. At dawn the enemy began shelling the Rangers. The rocks offered limited protection from the shrapnel. Two young Rangers cracked under the strain and, as the number of men killed and wounded rose sharply, Lieutenant Palumbo realized the position was untenable, and gave the order to retreat. 1st Sergeant Donald McCollum yelled at his men to run zig-zag down the rear slope of Pt 957. 'If you fall over keep rolling!' he shouted. Sound advice.[51]

Lt-Colonel Dammer made a fresh plan of attack for the night of 10 December. If the enemy had reoccupied the peak they were to be dislodged, the pillbox occupied by one section of the company – A – making the attack, while a second section was to lie in the rear of the peak, out of sight of the enemy. The rest of the company were to withdraw to the LOD. The attack went in under a particularly heavy barrage from the two artillery battalions supporting the Rangers. The enemy had reoccupied the peak. They were quickly dislodged from it, and two sections of A Company took over its defences. Their artillery support kept up DF round the peak all night long.

As a rule German infantry attacked in daylight*, relying on speed, fieldcraft and the objective being clearly visible to compensate for the fact that they were also visible to the enemy and would be likely to suffer higher casualties than if they had attacked at night. For an army whose infantry was at a premium this was a costly way of going about things. Colonel Kruger, who had planned the 71st Panzer Grenadier Regiment's daylight attack at Salerno, which had come close to defeating 5th Army, had the good sense to realize that further daylight attacks on Pts 1205 and 1142 would be broken up by US artillery. He ordered the CO of his II Battalion, Captain Schneider, to make a night attack. Apart from a likely saving of casualties the element of surprise might do the trick. At 0045 on 11 December two companies of II Batallion attacked Pts 1205 and 1142. They overran A Company's outposts and scrambled up the rocks towards the two summits. A Company could

* So did the French.

hear them coming but couldn't see them. They had no flares left. All they could do was fire blindly at the enemy. A forward observer asked for DF, reporting that the enemy were closing in but that it was too dark to see them. The officer in charge of 133rd Battalion, who were on call for a support barrage, had the brilliant idea of mixing phosphorus shells with HE. The phosphorous shells lit up the sky like giant flares, and silhouetted the advancing enemy. A Company had something close to a turkey shoot before the enemy broke off the attack. Between 0400 and 0600 the enemy turned their attention to Pt 957, putting in a number of counter-attacks. They were all broken up by artillery DF.[52]

During the next two days the fighting on Monte Sammucro reverted to long-range artillery duels, harassing fire and patrols. The enemy harassing fire on Pts 1205 and 1142 never let up. Major Wöbbeking was making full use of the windfall of shells he'd inherited from 3rd Panzer Grenadier Division. Private First Class Bill Ebberle, a forward observer for 133rd Battalion, never slept at all during his six days and nights on Pt 1205. But lack of sleep wasn't his main concern. It was lack of water. Ebberle was always thirsty. There was never enough water to go round. Ebberle licked moss and kept an eye open for the pioneer platoon and their five gallon cans of water.[53] The cans were brought to within a thousand feet of the summit by mules. (The 36th Division had got hold of some hardy specimens who were handled by Italian Army muleteers.) From that point onwards there was a 45% incline which the mules couldn't manage. Everything had to be humped up to the summit by the pioneers and by B Company. Colonel Martin, who could ill afford to use B Company as porters, suggested to Walker that the Italian Motorized Brigade should act as porters. Walker sounded out Brigadier Dapino, who said his men were at Mignano Gap to fight not to act as porters to other units.

Corporal Rice made one trip up to the summit, carrying a five gallon can of water on his back. 'It was hard to carry because the can could not be filled enough to keep the water from sloshing around in the can. The sloshing action seemed to work against your forward motion. That made it extra hard and tiresome to carry compared to the hard items.'

As he reached the summit he saw men 'stretching out their shelter halves and raincoats to catch rain and condensation . . . and Captain Birkhead lathering up for a shave'. Corporal Rice had once attended a lecture given by Captain Birkhead on how important it was to keep yourself neat and tidy. Captain Birkhead clearly believed in what he preached. Rice's other memory of the summit was the constant shelling, and the way the medics never flinched under fire. While other men could keep their heads down the medics had to run the gauntlet of the shelling, attending to each man as he was hit, and arranging for the severely wounded to be evacuated. Corporal

Rice did his share of litter-bearing. Each litter required six men to carry it. 'The two litter bearers downhill would have to hold their end of the litter above their heads and the two bearers uphill would have to hold the litter at ankle height to try and keep the litters as level as possible. It was hard not to drop a litter when you slipped. Sometimes during a barrage we would hit the ground and shake up the wounded. It was impossible to keep from jarring them because of the steep terrain. We learned that the more seriously wounded would not cry out or complain. Those not so seriously wounded would let you know if you jarred them.'[54]

When it had started up the mountain A Company had been one hundred and ten strong. By 12 December it was down to fifty. Most of the casualties had been caused by harassing fire. Morale among the survivors remained high. 'We never once did think the Germans would take the peaks,' Joe Gallagher recalls. 'Our biggest concern was how to evacuate our wounded and get our rations. Everyone I knew in A Company had one thought only – to survive. If you had a pain you lived with it. If you were freezing cold you endured it. When the mortars and 88s came in you scratched at the rock like a dog trying to bury a bone. We became part animal in certain situations, the instinct to survive sharpened all the senses. The nights were the worst – long, cold and wet. You felt it more if you were on an outpost – you had to stay still, and no smoking. At night when I was asleep one small sound and I was totally awake and my weapon pointed to where the sound came from . . . We were all scared shitless most of the time but never wanted to show that part of yourself to your buddies. No matter how bad things were my buddies always found something to laugh at. I'm sure a combat soldier's sense of humour is quite different from the rest of the Army's.'[55]

Gallagher's platoon had been the object of one of the oldest ploys in history. They had spotted a herd of sheep heading their way. Behind them a posse of German 'shepherds'. 'Six grenades later the sheep and Fritz took off for other parts.' Gallagher noticed that one of the Germans was wearing a camouflage jacket the same colour as the US army raincoats. He reported this to his section commander, who passed the message on. Lieutenant Kleghorn ordered everyone to remove their raincoats. As it was raining hard at the time one would have thought this an unpopular order, but US army raincoats, made of thick rubber, made everyone sweat and didn't keep out the cold. (At nights the temperature hovered around zero.) Most men were glad to get rid of them and wear their greatcoats instead. Better warm and wet than cold and sweaty.

The German dead scattered around the slopes of Pts 1205 and 1142 were comforting, if smelly, objects. Don Whitehead, as Associated Press war correspondent, visited Pt 1205 on 12 December and reported, 'The slopes of Monte Sammucro were strewn with dead'. (The after-action body count totalled exactly one hundred.) It showed just how effective the defenders all-round fire-power was.

Ernie Pyle was on the mountain too but did not visit Pts 1205 or 1142. Captain Burrage noticed that Pyle spent most of his time hanging around Battalion HQ trying to cadge liquor from Lt-Colonel Burgess's servant. But Pyle did make it to the Battalion's Aid Post, which was alongside B Company at the mule head. Gallagher, who had been badly concussed by a shell landing on rock that formed part of his foxhole, was evacuated to the Aid Post, and given injections which made him sleep. He woke up to see a strange face looking into his.

'I'm Ernie Pyle, son,' the journalist said. 'Have you any message you'd like sent to your folks?' Gallagher gave him his name but asked him not to use it. 'Most folks back home read his stories and I didn't want my folks to worry any more than they were. He promised not to mention my name. Then someone came into the tent and said they were bringing down the captain.'

The captain was B Company's Commander, Captain Harry Waskow. Waskow and his 2ic had gone up to Pt 1205 an hour or so previously to reconnoitre it (B Company were standing by to relieve A Company). As they reached the summit a sniper shot them both. Captain Waskow had been a much loved officer. Ernie Pyle described how B Company paid their last respects to him:

'It was hard to tell officers from men in the half light, for all were bearded and grimy dirty. The man looked down at the dead captain's face. He spoke directly to him as though he was still alive. He said, "I'm sorry, old man". Then a soldier came . . . and bent over and he too spoke to his captain, not in a whisper but awfully tenderly, and said "I sure am sorry, sir". Then the first man squatted down and he reached down and took the dead officer's hand, and he sat there for a full five minutes, holding the dead man's hand and looking intently into the dead face, and he never uttered a sound all the time he was there. And then finally he put the hand down, and then reached up and gently straightened the points of the captain's shirt collar, and then he sort of re-arranged the tattered edges of his uniform around the wound. And then he got up and walked away in the moonlight.'

Ernie Pyle was already well known for his dispatches in the States, but this one made him a household name. Don Whitehead, who had risked his life on Pt 1205, must have thought it a hard world.

Ernie Pyle summed up the fighting at Mignano Gap in one short paragraph. 'Thousands of men have not been dry for weeks. Other thousands lay at night in the high mountains with the temperatures below freezing and thin snow shuffling over them. They dug into the stones and slept in little chasms . . . They lived like men in prehistoric times, and a club would have become them more than a machine gun'.[56]

151

If Pyle had heard about the Germans tumbling down boulders on top of attacking troops and that they were about to introduce an anti-personnel mine the size and shape of a cannon ball it would not have surprised him.

Most of the dead brought down the mountain were covered in blankets. An officer in the 36th Division's Engineers noticed just how important those blankets were. 'The blanket-covered dead lay stiffly lashed to their litters, with only their feet and their frayed muddy leggings protruding forlornly from under the blankets. Soldiers built up an immunity to such scenes . . . as long as the identity of the dead or the mark of a gaping wound were covered, the living could almost ignore the dead.'[57]

The same day that Gallagher talked with Ernie Pyle he was found fit for combat duties and sent back to Pt 1205. His platoon commander told him they were having a lot of trouble from the sniper who had killed Captain Waskow and his 2ic, and that he was to join a 'get that sniper' patrol led by Corporal Ryecroft, his Section Commander, and assisted by Private Red Alcott. The sniper was holed up in some rocks about one hundred and fifty yards from Pt 1205. The three men raced across the open ground between the two points, whilst the rest of the platoon gave them covering fire. As they reached the shelter of the rocks the sniper threw a grenade at them. It wounded Corporal Ryecroft and Private Alcott in the legs. Gallagher threw all the grenades he had in the direction of the sniper – somewhere up above them – then helped himself to Corporal Ryecroft's grenades. As he began throwing them the sniper landed a grenade between the two men. Neither was hurt. Gallagher told Corporal Ryecroft he was going to throw his last grenade at the sniper, then run round the side of the rocks and try and spot the sniper's exact position. If he saw him he'd shoot him. 'After I'd thrown the last grenade I threw rocks as well to keep his head down, then raced round the big rocks. I couldn't see the sniper but some of his pals further down the slope could see me. I dove into a trench to avoid their fire. The trench was a latrine. I was waist deep in shit. God, did it stink! Considering a rifle slug a better option than being pinned down in shit I took off and made it back to Pt 1205 without being hit. But when I reached my own area my buddy Leo Hese threatened to shoot me if I tried to get into our foxhole. I had to crawl off by myself, no one would come near me. I had to wait for the weather to freeze the stuff and scrape it off with my trench knife as best I could.' Corporal Ryecroft and Private Alcott were not seriously wounded, and were picked up by medics as soon as it was dark.

Gallagher wasn't bothered about the water shortage on Pt 1205. Providing he could get enough to make himself a pint of coffee he was happy. But he found the C and K hard-tack rations disgusting. K rations were made up of 4oz cans of ham and dried egg, cheese and bits of bacon, spam, a small bar of dried fruit, hard biscuits and instant coffee. C rations, a later introduction, were a bit more substantial: 'One Veg. beef stew, 90% vegetable. Beans in tomato sauce, one can hash – only identifiable contents, diced potatoes and a few bits of onion. Four hard biscuits. One can instant coffee, one can powdered milk, three sugar cubes, one can lemon powder, one can chocolate powder. Four pieces of hard candy. Four wormy cigarettes. Two sheets toilet paper.' An English officer described C rations as being 'more suitable for a school picnic than the battlefield'. Gallagher wished the inventors of both ration packs had been made to climb Monte Sammucro and sample them there. So many complaints were made about K and C rations that early in 1944 they underwent a scientific study. Both packs were deficient in protein and vitamins.[58] (They were replaced by a new pack, B rations, which had adequate protein and vitamin, and proved more popular with the troops.) British X Corps hard tack was bully beef, and ship's biscuits. The protein and fat content in corned beef is high. No ration study was needed in X Corps.

The expected relief of 1st Battalion's A Company by B Company did not take place, probably because Lt-Colonel Burgess, who was organizing it, was severely wounded while visiting Pt 1205. He had been moving freely among the men, congratulating them on a job well done, and showing something of his old form as an officer, when a shell had got him. Walker recommended him for the Silver Star, which he received, and he went on to become a very successful staff officer. Major David Frazier, a first class officer, took over the battalion. Captain Burrage considered the change 'the best thing that could possibly have happened to the Battalion'.[59]

A few arctic combat suits and shoe overlays arrived at 143rd Forward HQ on 12 December. They were forwarded on to the 1st Battalion's CP. Captain Burrage noted, 'they had a placket with a zipper on the right side at the groin where we could relieve ourselves without undressing'. No combat suits reached Pt 1205.

Around Pt 957 3rd Rangers and the enemy infantry were engaged in the usual niceties of static warfare – sniping, observing, patrolling and getting shelled. Rangers' D Company, whose positions were close to Pt 957, had suffered particularly heavy casualties from shelling. On 8 December they lost their company commander, Captain Cannon, comatosed from shell shock, and had ten other men wounded. Ranger Richard Stealey, 19, had been lying in a foxhole with his buddy Tom Peretrich when it had received a direct hit. Stealey was blown fifteen feet. Blood poured from his ears and nose. He called for a medic. 'You're lucky, Stealey', the medic said, plugging his ears with bandages. 'Lucky?' muttered Stealey. 'Yeah,' said the medic, and led him over to his foxhole. Stealey saw a leg lying in a pool of blood. That was all that was left of Peretrich. Stealey began to shake all over. He continued to shake for three days and three nights but he never went sick.[60] D Company, down to twenty-five men, was still the strongest company in the Battalion. (Their new commander, Lieutenant Jensen, was one of the original Rangers.)

Sergeant Lehmann had been made a sniper and spent many hours trying his luck without ever being sure he'd actually hit someone. He did overhear a Forward Observer bringing down fire on what he described as 'heavy concentrations of enemy'. Lehmann could see that the 'enemy' was only a farmer and his goats. He reported the matter to Lt-Colonel Dammer, who complained to the Forward Observer's CO about it.

D Company brought up two heavy machine guns to try and knock out an enemy forward observer on Monte Corno, who was directing artillery fire on to a bridge linking Ceppagna with Venafro. The bridge was a vital supply link. German guns destroyed it by day, US engineers repaired it by night. When the Rangers opened up with their Brownings the enemy replied with 20 mm cannon, forcing the Rangers machine gunners to back off.

Most of the Rangers were living off K rations. Others were tucking into German rations found in caves near Pt 957. These included fresh beef, fresh eggs and cheese, potatoes and bread. As the front stabilized Lt-Colonel Dammer organized a rota system whereby the Ranger companies took it in turn to go down to Ceppagna for a hot meal. They brought back water, rations and ammunition.

On a reconnaissance patrol the Rangers captured a German sergeant. He spoke English and was unwise enough to sneer at the time it had taken the Rangers to capture Pt 957. 'I thought you Rangers were tough,' he said. The Ranger sergeant in charge of the patrol smashed his teeth in with the butt of his Tommy-gun. He also relieved him of his poncho. This was part of the winter equipment being issued to the 10th Army. It was very warm and absorbed a lot of rain without letting the wearer get wet. The Ranger sergeant was threatened with a court martial, not for maltreatment of a prisoner, but for rendering a prisoner incapable of giving information. When the German sergeant was interrogated by the Rangers Intelligence Officer he could only spit blood.[61]

D Company's 1st Sergeant Anders Arnbal, 25, another old hand from Scottish days, had the melancholy task of making a daily roster of the company's casualties. He was getting fed up with the company always being on the receiving end. Early on the morning of 11 December he heard a German patrol approaching the company's position. He had time to arrange a reception committee of massed Bars and ordered them not to fire until he gave the word. Sergeant Arnbal waited until the enemy were just below the company's position before telling his men to open fire. Sergeant Arnbal dropped a pound of TNT on them for good measure. He figured that there would be no live Germans left and he was right. D Company had wiped out a corporal and eleven men.[62]

It was a cloudy day. There was very little shelling. Sergeant Arnbal was just thinking that for once everything had gone D Company's way when the clouds lifted and the Luftwaffe went into action. D Company watched several planes bomb the Ceppagna-Venafro bridge and fly on to bomb Venafro. The planes then flew back and circled the Rangers' positions, firing 20 mm cannon shells and dropping anti-personnel bombs. One of them scored a direct hit on one of D Company's Rangers, Private First Class McTeague, who was lying on his stomach reading a *Reader's Digest*. The impact almost separated his upper torso from his legs. Another D Company Ranger was seriously wounded and evacuated, along with a dozen more from other companies. It happened to be D Company's turn to go down to Ceppagna for a hot meal. The battalion cooks had moved themselves and their cookers into a large church. Whilst D Company queued up for a hot meal just inside the entrance Sergeant Arnbal noticed a priest holding a service at the altar. One of the cooks told him it was for the dead killed in the Luftwaffe raid.

The 3rd Rangers were now about one hundred strong. Walker ordered 504th Independent Parachute Regiment to relieve them the following night. But 504th Parachute Regiment jumped the gun. They began climbing up from Ceppagna in daylight on 12 December. Sergeant Arnbal noted that, whereas it had taken 3rd Rangers two hours to climb up to the ridge below Pt 957, it took the paratroopers four hours. They were all carrying bedrolls and other unlikely gear.

A paratroop major took over D Company's CP. When Lieutenant Jensen offered to show him round the company positions the major shook his head. 'That won't be necessary,' he said. 'We'll make our own assessments'. Lieutenant Jensen warned him that the enemy shelled the positions at first light every morning. The paratroop major just grunted.[63]

While the rest of the battalion marched down to Ceppagna D Company took up reserve positions just below their old ones. It was known to be shell-proof. From there they heard the paratroopers calling out to one another as if they were in a rest and recreation camp. The Rangers then saw them light up the cooking stoves in the open. They made no attempt to conceal the flames. This flagrant breaking of one of the basic rules of war – don't give away your position to the enemy – shocked the Rangers. They tensed, waiting for the German forward observers to direct their guns onto Colonel Tucker's men. But the German guns remained silent. The Rangers turned to talking about 504th Parachute Regiment. Paratroopers were supposed to be crack troops. 504's men were behaving like rookies. The Rangers had no way of knowing that 504th Regiment had spent their time in Italy operating independently from the rest of the 5th Army. After raiding the enemy's lines they'd return to their mountain hide-outs. These were never under observation by the enemy and they had got set in their ways. It had clearly not occurred to Colonel Tucker that his battalion was no longer in a 'rest and recreation' position. When his paratroopers lit up their stoves at first light on 13 December enemy artillery opened up at them. The horrified Rangers saw paratroopers clustering round their stoves blown to bits, heard the screaming of the wounded, and the sickening sound of bodies crunching into rocks. The barrage lasted for three-quarters of an hour. It was the heaviest barrage any of the Rangers had ever known. By the time it ended D Company were already making their way down the hill. From Ceppagna they watched wounded paratroopers being evacuated. This went on all day. The grapevine had it that 504th Paratroop Regiment had lost 176 killed or wounded in the barrage. This is unlikely because their total casualties during the time they spent at Monte Sammucro totalled fifty killed and 202 wounded. But they may have suffered 176 casualties in the first twenty-four hours on the mountain. As the early morning barrage died down the II/71st Regiment, convinced that whoever had relieved the Rangers were inexperienced troops, pressed home a series of counter-attacks in which both sides suffered heavy casualties. 504th Paratroop Regiment beat off the attacks with great skill. It was the II/71st Regiment's turn for a surprise. Down at Ceppagna 3rd Rangers were counting their own casualties: thirty-five killed and over 200 wounded and sick. Battle casualties of around 60%. 3rd Rangers would in due course receive a 5th Army unit commendation for their action at San Pietro and for taking Pt 957.

In six days fighting the 71st Panzer Grenadier Regiment had suffered another 314 casualties. Their dead included II Battalion's CO, Captain Spohr. General Fries flew to Frascati to see Kesselring. He told the Commander-in-Chief that his division was being asked to do too much – to retake the summit of Monte Sammucro as well as Monte Corno, to defend Monte Lungo as well as San Pietro. His battalions in the village could look after themselves but he warned Kesselring that the 115th Reconnaissance Battalion on Monte Lungo could well suffer another surprise attack under cover of mist, and could not be expected to hold the mountain indefinitely. The terrain favoured attacking troops. Kesselring, who rated Fries highly as a general, listened to what he describes as 'a tirade', then grinned at Fries and said, 'You're a Prussian. I'm just a Bavarian. Prussians don't ask how strong the enemy is, but where he is!' He went on to tell General Fries that if the 29th Panzer Grenadier Division was being asked to shoulder the lion's share of the fighting it was a compliment to the Division and to its commander.'[64]

General Fries returned to his headquarters with the satisfaction of knowing that he'd done all he could for his men. The news of his trip spread rapidly. It gave his hard-pressed Panzer Grenadiers a tremendous fillip. Their general was a man worth dying for.

Chapter VI

General Walker Tries Again

The bloody stalemate of Monte Sammucro, and the failure of the Allies to take San Pietro and Monte Lungo forced Clark and his generals to think again. Monte Lungo was clearly a much more difficult proposition than they had realized. Clark and General Keyes decided that 36th Division would attack Pt 358 while the 1st Italian Motorized Brigade, now reinforced, tackled Pt 343. The enemy holding the western peaks of Monte Sammucro would have to be dealt with by the 1st Battalion, 143rd Regiment, now at half strength, and 504th Parachute Regiment. Clark had no fresh units with which he could reinforce them. His main concern was still San Pietro. For Clark it had become a military Everest. It must be taken because it was there. He proposed that the infantry attacks on San Pietro should be supported by tanks. General Keyes was a tank man. He must have known that the chances of a successful tank attack on San Pietro were slight. But the chances of a successful infantry attack on the village seemed equally slight. He backed Clark's use of armour. Clark sent Colonel Brann to persuade General Walker that it was a good idea. Walker didn't think it a good idea. The terrain round San Pietro wasn't suitable for tanks, and if they tried to attack up the road leading to the village they would almost certainly be blown up by mines. But Walker accepted the support of the tanks. The way Clark handled things, he had no option.

Walker planned his attack very thoroughly. On the night of 14/15 December 1st Battalion, 143rd Regiment and 504th Parachute Regiment would assault the enemy on the western slopes of Monte Sammucro. If the attack was successful San Pietro would be outflanked and its defenders forced to retreat. The Germans on Monte Lungo would have to follow suit. There would be no need for frontal attacks on the mountain or the village. If the attack was not successful there would be simultaneous attacks on San Pietro by 2nd and 3rd Battalions, 143rd Regiment, the tanks, and 2nd Battalion 141st Regiment. The 2nd and 3rd Battalions, 143rd, would attack the village from the northern slope of Monte Sammucro, with tank support if the terrain permitted, whilst the 2nd Battalion 141st would attack from the south. All attacks would commence at midday on 15 December. If the attack was successful the enemy defending Monte Lungo would be out-flanked and would have to retreat. If the attack was not successful Monte Lungo would be attacked by 142nd Regiment on the night of 15/16 December. The 1st Italian Motorized Brigade would put in its attack in daylight on 16 December. Here Walker would have an advantage of six battalions to one. In numbers of men more like eight to one.

General Walker and his G3, Lt-Colonel Fred Walker Jun, began preparing for the assault on San Pietro by reinforcing the divisional artillery with three more regiments of 155 mm, and a regiment of Corps 240 mm. Both men were concerned about San Pietro's towers. They offered the enemy excep-tional observation points, and needed destroying. General Walker and his son hoped the 240 mm would do the job, but they discovered that they lacked sufficient velocity and the guns only knocked chunks off the towers. General Walker decided to call for a series of air strikes instead. Fighter-bombers from XII Air Support Command carried out several sorties against the village on or around 12 December. Colonel Walker watched the planes carry out the attacks. 'All the bombs landed well to the north-east or north-west of the town.'[1] The best one can say about the strikes is that the planes didn't drop their bombs south-east or south-west of San Pietro. The 36th Division still had one more option. To call on the new 8″ gun-howitzers. These[2] could certainly have breached the walls of San Pietro – Lt-Colonel Fred Walker doesn't believe this would have made any difference to the outcome of the battle,[3] an opinion that Colonel Milton Landry, who managed to get his battalions right up under San Pietro's walls does not share[4] – and would probably have destroyed the towers as well.

General Walker spent many hours coordinating the infantry and tank attacks on San Pietro. Lt-Colonel Joseph Felber, CO/753rd tank battalion, whose A Company would provide the tanks for the attack, ordered intensive ground and aerial reconnaissance of the San Pietro area. When he studied the reports and photos he was dismayed. To send his tanks across country, as Walker was hoping he would do, was to expose them to innumerable gullies and ravines which they might or might not be able to negotiate. Some of these natural defences were bound to contain enemy armed with anti-tank weapons. The only feasible cross-country route was a narrow trail off the northern side of the road. This led up to two terraces and then broadened out into a wider track. The trail had been spotted from the air. Just how practicable the route was would only be discovered by driving a tank up it, and as it was under observation by the enemy this could only be done during the actual attack. The alternative was to advance up the Venafro-San Pietro road. This had two culverts and two bridges, all four of which were likely to be mined. Walker called in the 36th Divisional engineers to see if they could help. When they learned that Walker planned to use 2nd and 3rd Battalions to attack San Pietro from the north and wanted the tanks to support them the engineers suggested blowing up a number of terraces so that the tanks had an easy ride on to the open and relatively flat terrain which would be the infantry's LOD. Both Walker and Lt-Colonel Felber were enthusiastic about the idea. On the night of 10/11 December the engineers blew up five terraces and made a trail leading to the 3rd Battalion's CP. In dry weather the tanks could have made it in top gear. But rain had turned the terrace earth into layers of slime. The lead tank got bogged down on the second terrace. As it tried to work its way out of the mud it threw a track, effectively blocking the route for all the other fifteen tanks. The scheme was abandoned. 2nd and 3rd Battalions, 143rd Regiment, would make their attack on San Pietro without tank support. The tanks would have to try their luck on the Venafro-San Pietro road.

On the ground the 2nd and 3rd Battalion patrols were making their presence felt. On the night of 13/14 December a combined fighting patrol from both battalions found a break in II/15th Panzer Grenadier Regiment's barbed wire apron, crossed the ravine below San Pietro's eastern walls, clambered through a partial breach in the walls and shot up an enemy platoon near the village church. They killed four and took seven prisoners. All eleven men belonged to 5 Company, II/15 Panzer Grenadier Regiment. This splendid foray was a great boost to morale. If a fighting patrol could penetrate to the heart of the enemy defences the chances of a 3-battalion attack backed by tanks being successful looked good.

Clark had decided that the second attack on San Pietro should be filmed by the 5th Army's Photographic unit so he could show what the Army was up against. The Army's Photographic Unit happened to be commanded by Major John Huston, who'd left his career in Hollywood because he wanted to see what war was really like and to record it on film. He and his cameramen arrived at Walker's HQ on 14 December. Huston wanted to film both the infantry and tank attacks but Walker refused to let him film the infantry attacks on the grounds that his cameramen were liable to end up dead. Instead he suggested that some of the infantry who would be taking part in the battle would re-stage it afterwards, and Huston could film that instead. Walker made no objection to the tank attack being filmed and Huston sent two of his cameramen up to Captain Jim Skinner's OP on Monte Rotondo. From there they would have an excellent view of the tank attack. Not to be outdone, Ernie Pyle climbed up to the OP as well.[5]

On 13 December Walker held a conference to coordinate the infantry and tank attacks. The 2nd and 3rd Battalions would attack San Pietro from the north. The tanks would attack up the Venafro-San Pietro road, the 2nd Battalion, 141st Regiment, from the south. All the attacks were scheduled

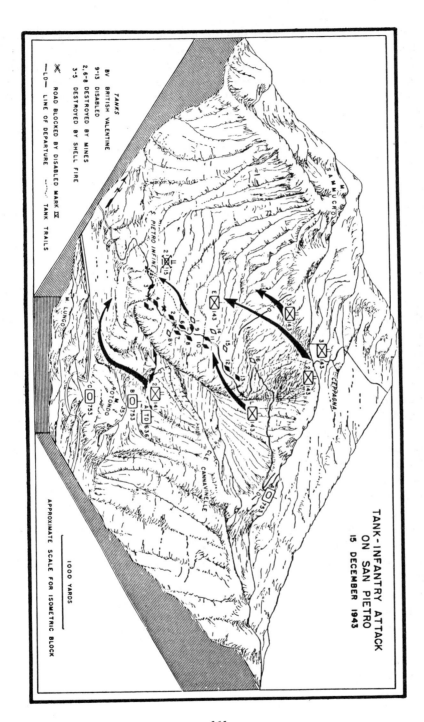

TANK-INFANTRY ATTACK
ON SAN PIETRO
15 DECEMBER 1943

TANKS

BV   BRITISH VALENTINE
9-13 DISABLED
2,6-8 DESTROYED BY MINES
3-5   DESTROYED BY SHELL FIRE

✕   ROAD BLOCKED BY DISABLED MARK ⅠⅤ
—LD— LINE OF DEPARTURE   ┄┄┄ TANK TRAILS

1000 YARDS

APPROXIMATE SCALE FOR ISOMETRIC BLOCK

161

to start at noon. Walker hoped that the tanks and some of the infantry would attack the village simultaneously. Lt-Colonel Felber asked for smoke to be laid down on Monte Lungo so that the German forward observers would not spot the tanks. He also pointed out that if any of the bridges and culverts were blown up before the attack he would need bridging tanks so that the attack could continue. Walker got hold of two British Valentine bridging tanks but only one of them was operational. He promised that Monte Lungo would be well 'smoked' and that the tank attack would be supported by the guns of two other companies of the 753rd.

At dusk on 14 December the 1st Battalion, 143rd Regiment, now reduced to half its original strength, set off to attack Pt 730, the highest of the three western peaks the enemy were defending. They were soon lit up by brilliant moonlight. The higher slopes of Monte Sammucro had no trees or bushes, no cover of any sort except a few rocks. The enemy on Pt 730 spotted the T-patchers when they were still a hundred yards away and opened up with Spandaus and mortars. The 1st Battalion lead company charged the enemy, only to discover that the peak was protected by a deep ravine. The company climbed into the ravine and took up defensive positions. The enemy, firing directly at the US troops, prevented them from making any attempt to scale the peak. The rest of the Battalion joined the lead company in the ravine. The Battalion spent the night exchanging fire with an enemy they could not see. By daylight the Battalion's fighting strength was down to 155 and they had run out of ammunition. Later that day a mule train moved up the mountain in a ravine running close to the one where the 1st Battalion was stranded. They delivered food, water and ammunition, and returned with some of the wounded. The 1st Battalion* was ordered to stay put and to continue to engage the enemy with small arms fire. 504th Parachute Regiment's attack on Pts 587 and 540 had been even less successful. They had been ambushed by the enemy five hundred yards short of their objective and had to fight their way back to their own lines.

A Company's, 743rd Battalion, column of tanks began moving up the road to San Pietro at 1100 hours on 15 December. 36th Divisional artillery were shelling Monte Lungo with smoke shells. A Company's Commander, Major George Fowler, had decided that his tanks should proceed up the road until it reached the trail junction. Tank number one of the leading platoon of four tanks would reconnoitre the trail whilst the remaining three tanks headed up the road for San Pietro, crossing a fifteen-foot culvert on the way. If the trail proved negotiable the second platoon of tanks would

* For their action on Monte Sammucro the Battalion was awarded a 5th Army Commendation.

follow tank number one across country. If it didn't they would follow the other three tanks into San Pietro.

The column crossed the first bridge and the main culvert without incident. When they reached the trail junction tank number one squeezed up it but reported the wider track impassable. Major Fowler ordered the tank commander to try and climb the terrace and make his way towards San Pietro across country. The tank broke down part of the terrace wall, climbed on top of it and headed for San Pietro.

As tank number two passed over the second culvert it struck a mine. A British bridging Valentine crossed safely and pulled to one side of the stranded tank. Tanks three, four and five crossed the culvert in the tracks of the Valentine and headed for San Pietro. Having crossed the culvert safely, the crews felt confident of making San Pietro. They only had three-quarters of a mile of open road to go. It was unlikely to be mined. It wasn't. The three tanks crossed through San Pietro's eastern gateway. Within seconds number three and number five tanks were knocked out by anti-tank shells. Both tanks caught fire. As tank number four slithered to a halt it, too, was knocked out. The crew of one of Lieutenant Heinemann's anti-tank guns, firing from a cave close to the road, had knocked out all three tanks. The US crews scrambled out of their burning vehicles and surrendered.[6] 141st forward observers recorded the tanks entering the village at 1511 hours.

Back at the culvert tank number six had struck another mine. Tank number seven struck one as well. The culvert was now blocked. Tank number eight began pushing tank number seven out of the way but in the process it, too, struck a mine. Tank number nine tried to push seven and eight out of the way but failed to shift them. It then tried to climb the road's retaining wall so as to get on to a terrace. It didn't make it.

By now the period of smoke shelling Major Fowler had asked for was over. Enemy observers on Monte Lungo directed their artillery onto the culvert, turning an exasperating situation into a dangerous one. The commander of tank number one had been reporting a most successful foray to Major Fowler, who was in tank number ten. Tank number one had knocked out several Spandau posts, shot up a group of enemy officers, and was now nearing San Pietro. Major Fowler decided that his remaining tanks should follow tank number one. Tank number twelve led the way. Half-way up the second terrace it turned over on its side, blocking the trail. Tank number thirteen tried to climb the terrace behind tank number twelve but threw a track. Major Fowler ordered the other two tanks on the trail to reverse so that he could lead them up an alternative route. As tank number eleven reversed into the road it slipped off it, landing on its side five feet below. Major Fowler found a path leading up a terrace and using his tank as a battering ram forced his way past the road's retaining wall and up on to the top of the terrace. The remaining three tanks followed on. Numbers fourteen and fifteen both threw tracks. Major Fowler's tank and tank number sixteen kept going until they came to a ravine. It was now growing dark and Lt-Colonel Felber ordered Major Fowler to pull back tank number one, which was shooting up enemy positions outside San Pietro, and return to base. By the only stroke of luck A Company had that day tank number one bumped straight into tank number twelve, and the impact righted the tank. Both were able to withdraw down the trail and join tanks numbers ten and sixteen. The tanks caught in the shelling at the culvert had lost six men killed and eight wounded (one died of wounds). The unwounded men walked back to base. Medics evacuated the wounded and tank recovery crews brought back the stranded tanks during the night.

Up on Monte Rotondo Captain Jim Skinner watched the tank snarl-up with dismay. Huston's cameramen filmed every moment of it. Ernie Pyle just watched. He never said a word. His silence impressed Captain Skinner. He sensed the journalist was storing every moment of the advance in his mind.

The 2nd and 3rd Battalions, 143rd Regiment, had gone into the attack at 1200 hours. The new axis of advance did not help them. The 2nd Battalion no longer had barbed wire to contend with but the undetected enemy observer overlooking the village directed artillery fire at the companies. Mortars, Spandaus and rifle grenades added to the 2nd Battalion's discomfiture. Lt-Colonel Denholm ordered two of his companies to dig in about a hundred yards from the northern wall of the village. He sent Captain Bergstrom's E Company, now about fifty men strong, across the Venafro-San Pietro road with orders to attack the village from the south-east.

The 2nd Battalion was clearly doing all it possibly could to close with the enemy. But the 3rd Battalion was lagging behind. Communication between their HQ and the Regimental CP had broken down and Colonel Martin went forward to see what was wrong. He found the CO of the 3rd Battalion and his staff sheltering from incoming fire in a large drain pipe – almost certainly the same one in which the Germans had shot dead the twelve San Pietrans. Colonel Martin ordered the CO to leave the drain pipe. The CO, who was in tears, refused to do so. One of his staff told Colonel Martin that the Operations Officer, Major Parks Bowden, was up front rallying the leading companies. Colonel Martin sent a runner informing Major Bowden that he was now in command of the Battalion. He told the CO he would be officially relieved of his command as soon as the battle was over.

It was growing dark as E Company began closing in on the south-east corner of San Pietro. They bumped one enemy bunker so well camouflaged that, try as they might, they could not place its exact location. Finally

Captain Bergstrom ordered the company to by-pass it. By 2000 hours the company had reached some terraces directly beneath the village. They were ordered to stay put. At 2100 they were ordered to support an attack on the village by 141st Regiment. With the order came a remarkable grapevine account of the tank attack. 'Twelve have been hit by mines, four made it into town, three of them have been knocked out, and the fourth is running around loose in town.'

As soon as E Company began climbing the terraces the enemy opened up with Spandaus, but not mortars. This surprised Corporal Gallagher. He hoped they'd run out of shells. It was so dark that Captain Bergstrom ordered each man to hang on to the heel of the man in front of him. He also shifted the company's axis of advance, by-passing the Spandaus.

It became very quiet, too quiet for Corporal Gallagher's liking. 'The enemy knew roughly where we were but not exactly. As we climbed up one terrace we hit a double apron of barbed wire. We slipped under it, on our backs, holding the lower strand above us.' Beyond the wire Gallagher could just make out a road with a Sherman tank on it. 'The captain asked me and Sergeant Allen to check the tank. There might be some of our people inside it. We were then to remain in the area of the tank and kind of guard the Company's flank.' The party scrambled up to the tank and tapped on it. There was no reply. Gallagher was suddenly overwhelmed with a need to say his piece to Sergeant Allen. 'We've been in the line thirty days', he whispered. 'When the hell are we coming out of it?' Before Sergeant Allen could answer there was a loud explosion. Gallagher was badly hit in one leg and screamed with pain. 'Shut the hell up!' whispered Sergeant Allen. As Gallagher got a grip on himself he heard other men screaming and moaning. Wounded men were crawling downhill to the shelter of a small ravine behind the barbed wire. He followed them, pulling himself under the barbed wire. There were about a dozen men sheltering in it. One man was crying and saying it was all his fault. He'd noticed a cord attached to the barbed wire as he was climbing under it. Curious to see what it was he pulled it. Nothing happened. He pulled it harder and a booby-trap went off in his face. There is a 'curiosity killed the cat' man in every infantry platoon. Because they had no medics the wounded men bandaged each other. The number of wounded in the ravine grew to around twenty. Corporal Gallagher* and four other walking wounded were told to make their way back to the Battalion Aid Post and ask for medics to attend the company's seriously wounded. The party used the road to find their way. When they reached the Aid Post they were told medics were already on their way to E Company.

* Gallagher was operated on four days later and spent two months in hospital. He was back with his battalion at Anzio in March, 1944. 'It was nice to be home again'.

Before the medics arrived Captain Bergstrom led his thirty-strong company into an attack on the caves where Lieutenant Heinemann and other anti-tank gun crews were lying up. E Company lost nineteen men in the attack but they wiped out all the anti-tank gun crews. Lieutenant Heinemann was mortally injured by a grenade. An Italian lad of seventeen, making his way from the communal cave to the village fountain during a lull in the fighting, heard moans coming from one of the caves and found Lieutenant Heinemann lying in a pool of blood, his stomach ripped open. He muttered *'granat'* to the Italian, who took off his own shirt to bandage the wound. He then sat beside Lieutenant Heinemann, holding his hand. The officer kept on repeating the name 'Erika'. The Italian guessed it was his wife's name. He stayed with the officer until he died shortly after dawn.[7]

The 2nd Battalion, 141st Regiment, had been lying up on Monte Rotondo, a mile across the valley from San Pietro. Its companies' strength averaged 110 men. Their CO, Major Milton Landry, had been ordered to press home the attack 'until the last man'. It was timed to take place at 1155 hours. The Battalion would have to advance through a narrow defile at the base of Monte Rotondo and then fan out into the open. G and F Companies would lead the attack, with E Company and a platoon from H Company (Heavy Support) following up.

Minutes before the deadline an artillery support barrage opened up on San Pietro and the password for the attack, a splendidly defiant 'We're going into town to spend some money', passed round the companies. As the leading companies left the defile and took up open formation enemy artillery and Spandaus opened up on them. G Company's Commander, Captain Charles Hammer, was shot dead, and F Company's Commander, Lieutenant Charles Beauchamp and his executive Commander, Lieutenant Berry, seriously wounded. Sergeant Sammie Petty, 1st Platoon, F Company, lost all his squad killed or wounded within a couple of minutes.[8] F Company's acting commander ordered his platoon to return to the LOD to regroup. G Company kept going. It took them three hours to reach the shelter of a stone wall four hundred yards in front of San Pietro. At 1610 hours Lieutenant Berry sent a message by wire to Lt-Colonel Aaron Wyatt at Regimental HQ: 'Company moved through heavy gun fire and sniper fire. Pushed on to stone wall running east west outskirts San Pietro. I and Captain Beauchamp wounded. Lieutenant White in charge of company. Little or no mortar fire but till MG fire taken out it will be difficult to advance. Radios all knocked out'.[9] Shortly after Lieutenant Berry's report was received Lieutenant White was wounded and G Company were down to one officer and thirty-four men, 70% casualties in an afternoon. One of their platoons had strayed off the axis of advance to try and escape the enemy fire. They had gone left into the ravine where both Captain Meitzel and the San Pietrans had their headquarters. The enemy snipers had marked them down. Corporal Wells, who followed up the platoon with his water-cooled machine gun, was shaken by the number of dead T-patchers he passed. They had all been shot through the head. He and the survivors of the platoon huddled together behind some rocks in the middle of the ravine.[10] They would have been within pistol shot of Captain Meitzel's CP. As it grew dusk Corporal Well's party split up. While he climbed up and joined E and F Company in front of the village, the G Company men headed back towards the LOD. They'd had enough. The rest of the company had already withdrawn from the stone wall.

F and E Companies had found a fresh line of advance under cover of olive groves and at 1730 they advanced towards San Pietro under cover of a creeping artillery barrage. They reached the olive groves right below the village without further casualties. They only had eighty yards to go to its walls. Sergeant Petty and two other F Company sergeants tried to bomb their way up the terraces. They encountered trip wires, booby-traps, Spandaus and stick-bombs. One of the bombing sergeants had been a professional baseball player and could throw a grenade sixty yards. The enemy must have thought he was using a grenade launcher. It was a painfully slow business. Terrace by terrace, yard by yard, F and E Companies bombed their way forward. They were heartened by the arrival of Major Landry. E Company's commander had been seriously wounded and realizing he had no senior commanders left, Major Landry had come up to direct the assault on the village. The combined strength of E and F Companies totalled some 115 men. Lt-Colonel Wyatt had promised to reinforce the battalion with L Company, 3rd Battalion, 141st Regiment. Their Commander, Major Efferson, met Major Landry[11] beneath the walls of the San Pietro at around 2300 hours.

When Major Landry's Forward Observer was wounded Major Efferson took over his radio. Major Landry wanted the artillery to take out some Spandaus in a deep bunker. He passed on their location to Major Efferson. When the US artillery fired their shells landed on the other side of the village. An exasperated Major Landry ordered his men to work round the flanks of the bunker and kill the occupants with grenade or bayonet. This they did. By 0100 hours on 16 December all the Spandau posts protecting the southern walls of San Pietro had been eliminated.

The assault on the village went in at 0130 hours, men standing on each others shoulders to haul themselves through the partial breaches in the walls. Only about a dozen men made it into San Pietro. In the darkness they encountered an enemy who knew the ground. Most of the T-patchers were taken prisoner. A radio message sent to Major Landry to Regimental CP read: 'Part of E and F Companies got into village. Only Heavy Weapons platoon got out'.

By now the combined companies were down to about seventy men. As they took up positions close to the walls they came under fire from a Spandau in a farmhouse outside the village. As the bullets ricocheted off the walls Major Landry reflected on his orders to fight 'to the last man'. The way things were going it seemed quite possible he would obey that order to the letter. Then the enemy opened up with mortars, using phosphorous shells. One of them exploded close enough to Major Landry to burn his face. As he rubbed the wound he reflected that Regimental Intelligence had said that the enemy did not possess phosphorous shells. Technically this was correct. Only after the battle was over did Regimental Intelligence discover that the enemy possessed captured US 4.2″ mortars* as well as phosphorous shells.

A near miss from another bomb made Major Landry duck. His helmet scraped against the wall. There was a ringing sound of metal against metal. Curious to see what the other metal was, Major Landry took a close look at it. He could just make out that it was a US map grid marker. Before the attack Lt-Colonel Wyatt had told Major Landry that no large-scale maps of the area existed. 'Efferson was calling for another artillery barrage', Landry recalls. 'They socketed the shells so badly we asked them to try and hit the survey marker.'[12]

Lt-Colonel Wyatt got a message through to Major Landry, telling him to join L Company who had made their way to some terraces on the south-western approaches to the village. The remnants of E and F Company linked up with L Company at first light. Sergeant Petty was with a group of men sixty to seventy strong. 'There was only one terrace between us and the village. The orders were to rise above the terrace at 7 am and start firing into the village, which we did. But the enemy return fire forced the men back behind the terrace. Artillery and mortar shells came from all directions. The dead and wounded piled up. There was nothing we could do but lie there and take it. I heard someone shout, "Perhaps we should run up the white flag!" Somebody down the line shouted he'd shoot the first son of a bitch who raised a white flag.'[13].

At 0910 hours Lt-Colonel Wyatt sent a message to his executive officer: 'Company G stragglers coming back saying they are withdrawing. There are no orders for withdrawal. Company G is to go into reserve. Men are to be rested and reorganized. If they refuse they are to be shot.'[14] At 0940 Wyatt sent another message: 'Two companies of 2nd Battalion are disorganized. L

---

* They had been sent to the Russian front from the US, captured by the Germans, and re-directed to the Italian front.

Company pinned down. Orders have been issued to them to withdraw to reorganize.' The orders did not reach Major Landry's men until 1230 hours. By then the 2nd Battalion operations officer had been shot dead and eighty-four severely wounded men evacuated under heavy sniper fire. Although the medics wore red crosses on their helmets the enemy did not hesitate to shoot them.

Another entry in Lt-Colonel Wyatt's book reads: '1200 hours General Mark Clark visited regimental vicinity but did not visit command post.' From the 141st Regiment's point of view Clark had chosen an unfortunate time to visit their part of the front. But after talking with a second lieutenant who was now commanding a company Clark realized the 2nd Battalion had been in a fight. He walked round chatting with the men, telling them that Monte Lungo had fallen and that this meant the enemy would have to evacuate San Pietro.

142nd Regiment, whose attack on Monte Maggiore had been something of a sideshow, had scored a home run on Monte Lungo. It had attacked from the south at 1730 on 16 December. 2nd Battalion worked their way round to the western base of Pt 358, took an enemy platoon holding it by surprise, then assaulted the peak. A sharpshooter from G Company, Private First Class Gerald Wood, had the satisfaction of putting bullets into the muzzles of three Spandaus and seeing the guns and their crews destroyed in the ensuing explosions.

By dawn the Battalion had taken Pt 358 at small cost to themselves. 1st Battalion, attacking the saddle between Pts 352 and 343, ran into a minefield. Its leading company did not have the Battalion's pioneer platoon up front. Corporal John Waddell and Private First Class John Peralez cleared a way through the minefields themselves. In the process Pfc Peralez was mortally wounded. The rest of the company advanced through the gap in the minefield and, with snipers giving covering fire, took forty of the enemy holding the saddle prisoner.

The 1st Italian Motorized Brigade had the harder job of taking Pt 343, where Captain von Heyking had placed two out of his three companies. The Italian attack went in at 0915 on 17 December, with the reinforced 1st Battalion, 67th Regiment, once again in the lead. This time the weather was good. There was no mist. US artillery bombarded the summit of Pt 343, as well as providing a creeping barrage for the Italian infantry. Captain von Heyking phoned Colonel Ulich and told him the situation was critical. Colonel Ulich promised to send up 1 Battalion to reinforce 111 Battalion. At 1000 hours 1 Battalion raced up Highway 6 in tracked vehicles. US artillery destroyed eleven out of sixteen of them. The remaining five returned to base. Shortly before midday 1st Battalion, 67th Regiment closed with the enemy and after a sharp fight captured Pt 343. They lost one officer and nine other ranks killed, thirty wounded and eight missing. 142nd Regiment described their losses as 'light'. 111/15th Panzer Grenadier Regiment had lost around 200 men killed, wounded and captured. Clark and General Keyes both sent their congratulations to General Dapino on his brigade's achievement.[15]

Once Colonel Ulich knew that Monte Lungo had fallen he ordered Captain Meitzel to withdraw I Battalion from San Pietro at 1900 hours that evening and take up new positions at San Vittore. But as the Battalion was preparing to leave San Pietro it was once again attacked. Or so Captain Meitzel thought. He at once ordered it to stay put and defend itself. In fact the Battalion was not being attacked. It was being probed by a fighting patrol from 2nd Battalion. 143rd Regiment, game to the last. Captain Meitzel re-scheduled the withdrawal to San Vittore for 0200 hours on 17 December. One of his company commanders repaid 143rd Regiment in kind. He sent out a strong fighting patrol which located the 3rd Battalion, 143rd Regiment. They shot up I Company's outposts, penetrated the company's lines, killed one of the company's surviving officers and wounded the other, then moved on to K Company. Believing that they were being counter-attacked, the 3rd Battalion asked for close support DF.[16] The German patrol waited until the barrage was over, then probed K Company's defences again, killing and wounding a number of men, before finally withdrawing at 0100 hours. Once they had rejoined the rest of the Battalion it withdrew to San Vittore without losing a man.

On 17 December Colonel Martin led the 2nd and 3rd Battalions, 143rd Regiment, into San Pietro. The San Pietrans emerged from their cave and gave the troops a rapturous welcome, all their miseries forgotten in the joy of liberation. But of the 800 who had taken refuge in the cave 300 were dead or dying.* During the previous few days the elderly had had nothing to eat. Five figs a day had been given to each child. Colonel Martin arranged for all the villagers to be fed and contacted Brigadier Dapino. When Italian troops entered the cave and saw the condition of the sick and elderly they burst into tears. Later more Italian troops arrived to take the sick to hospital and bury the dead lying outside the cave. These included US troops from 2nd Battalion, 141st Regiment.[17]

The II/15th Panzer Grenadier Regiment was mentioned in the Wehrmacht's Order of the Day† for their defence of San Pietro, and Captain Meitzel was singled out by Kesselring in a 10th Army Order of the Day. The 2nd and 3rd Battalions, 143rd Regiment, received a 5th Army Commendation. The 2nd Battalion, 141st Regiment, which had come closest to

---

* A plaque commemorating the 500 who survived is fixed on a wall near the bottom of the old village.

† Communiqué issued by OKW.

taking San Pietro, received nothing at all, although Major Landry was awarded the Silver Star.*

II/15th Panzer Grenadier Regiment had suffered even less casualties in the second battle of San Pietro than they had in the first. The 2nd and 3rd Battalions, 143rd Regiment, had been reduced to much the same strength as the 1st Battalion, to less than one full-strength company. The daily battalion returns for 143rd Regiment have been lost for the period covering 1–20 December, so it is impossible to give an exact breakdown of killed, wounded and missing. But Colonel Martin's daily Regimental reports make it clear that it had lost 78% of its combat strength. (141st Regiment's monthly journal gives an exact breakdown of 2nd Battalion's casualties: thirty-five killed or died of wounds, 166 severely wounded and evacuated.) Lt-Colonel Denholm, whose battalion would lose a further 374 men at the Battle of the Rapido in January, 1944,† describes the fighting at San Pietro as 'by far the bloodiest, hardest fought battle of my experience or knowledge . . . When given orders to take San Pietro at all costs it did its best. (To me this was a difficult or impossible task, that is to breach a fortified position with only the equipment available in a normal infantry battalion.) When pulled out for rest and recreation afterwards, one company‡ was wiped out and the other two at one-third strength. The missing were killed or wounded not captured or unaccounted for. The junior officers fared as badly with a loss of three out of every four.'[18]

Major Landry describes his battalion's attack as 'a suicide job . . . the stupidest assignment the battalion ever received'.[19]

Corporal Gallagher writes: 'We did what was asked of us but perhaps it could have been done another way. I think now that the human waste in those stupid frontal attacks should be a lesson to our well paid professionals.'[20]

One at least of those well paid professionals showed deep concern about human waste. Recording his visit to a hospital after the battle General Walker wrote, 'Sergeant Hardway had lost both his legs . . . I felt like a cheapskate as I pinned a Silver Star on his pajamas shirt for there is nothing too good for such a soldier. The idea of trying to reward him for the loss of his legs by pinning a Silver Star on his shirt occurred to me as ridiculous. However, he seemed appreciative. When I think of the foolish orders of the higher command which cause those broken bodies and deaths unnecessarily, it makes me feel like crying HALT. Generally men who do the fighting and

---

* The British Army did not consider X Corps' part in the Battle of Mignano Gap worthy of a Battle Honour.

† Later that year he would be awarded the Distinguished Service Cross as well as the Distinguished Service Medal.

‡ E Company.

bear all the hardships are treated as so much hay or ammunition by the higher commanders and members of their staff.'[21]

But that came later. On 17 December Walker was as eager as Clark to exploit the breakthrough. He planned to use the 3rd Battalion, 143rd Regiment, supported by the 3rd Battalion, 141st Regiment, to break through enemy rearguards on the lower slopes of Monte Sammucro overlooking the area between San Pietro and San Vittore. The attack went in on the night of 19/20 December. It failed. The following night the 3rd Battalion, 141st Regiment, supported by the 2nd and 3rd Battalions 143rd Regiments – the combined strength of these battalions was about 120 men – tried a different route. This attack was also repulsed. Walker decided to change tactics – to tackle the rearguards on the western peaks of Monte Sammucro, in the hope that once these were overcome the rearguards on the lower slopes would withdraw. For his attack on the western peaks he obtained a regiment of the 1st SSF and 504th Parachute Regiment. The attack would be supported by heavy machine guns from 141st Regiment as well as by artillery. The attacks went in early on Christmas Day. The 2nd Battalion, 1st Regiment, First Special Service Force, moved down from Pt 1205 to attack Pt 730, while 504th Parachute Regiment tackled Pts 687 and 580. A heavy US artillery and mortar barrage was at once answered by a counter-barrage. Although the German gunners were firing blind, the accuracy of their fire completely disorganized the First Special Service Force's attack. Their CP was destroyed, the Battalion's Adjutant, Lieutenant Cotton, and a clerk killed, its CO, Lt-Colonel Akehurst badly wounded, and all communication with regimental HQ cut.

The Regimental Commander, Colonel Marshall, came up to lead the attack himself. It had to be postponed from 0200 hours to first light. As the two leading companies advanced on Pt 730 Spandaus opened up. There was very little cover and casualties mounted rapidly. Once the First Special Service Force came close to their objective – having been warned about the ravine, they were attacking Pt 730 over rising ground to the south – they saw the enemy were firing from two stone emplacements. They went on firing until the attacking troops were close enough to slip grenades through the bunkers' loopholes. 504th Parachute Regiment encountered the same last man resistance on Pts 687 and 580. The attack cost the First Special Service Force seventy-five casualties, including two officers killed. 504th Parachute Regiments casualties were equally heavy. Colonel Kruger's rearguards had been ordered to fight to the death. They had done so and taken many of their attackers with them.

On 26 December the 1st and 2nd Battalions, 141st Regiment, fought their way past the rearguards on the lower slopes of Monte Sammucro and took up positions overlooking San Vittore. The village appeared to be outflanked.

But Captain Meitzel had positioned most of his men on a hill overlooking the eastern approach to San Vittore. They covered the one company holding the village. San Vittore was not outflanked. A patrol from 142nd Regiment had entered the village on 19 December. They reported it unoccupied. But when B Company, 1st Battalion, 143rd Regiment, probed its defences on 26 December they encountered heavy automatic fire. The T-patchers, about thirty-five strong, managed to capture several houses before a heavy DF forced them out of the village.

It was the 36th Division's last shot in the battle for Mignano Gap. On 30 December they were relieved by the 34th Division. (On 31 December the 29th Panzer Grenadier Division was relieved by the Austrian 44th Infantry Division.) The 36th Division had spent forty-three days in the Line. Their battle casualties for November totalled 463, for December 1,772 – 2,235 in all. Their infantry companies were down to 33% strength. (The 143rd Regiment needed 1,100 replacements.) Their sick totalled only 2,186. It was a sign of a division who could look after themselves in appalling conditions with inadequate clothing and rations. Clark must have been reassured by such figures. But not for long.

John Huston's film *The Story of San Pietro*, was completed by the 143rd Regiment in January, 1944. The training shots, apart from two men charging up terraces, are not convincing. But the men taking part in the film certainly are. The easy confidence, youth and good looks of a platoon cleaning their weapons before an 'attack' is unforgettable. They had survived a terrible battle and knew they would soon be back on combat. You would never guess it from their faces. These likely lads are singularly relaxed, enjoying the novelty of acting in a movie. They survive a gung-ho script trumpeting about most of them being killed within minutes of beginning the 'attack', and the voices of the Mormon choir singing a lament for doomed youth. The shots of the tank attack were another matter. A more devastating picture of an armored cock-up could hardly be imagined. General Marshall's staff tried to suppress the whole film. General Marshall decided to cut out the cock-up, leaving a stately column of tanks going about their business.[22]

The 34th Division took San Vittore on 5th January, 1944. The Mignano Gap really was open. But progress towards Cassino was depressingly slow. Small towns like Cervaro and mountains like Monte Porchia held out for days. In their first battle in the Italian compaign an infantry regiment from the 1st US Armored Division, which attacked and held Monte Porchia, lost sixty-six men killed, 379 wounded, 516 hospitalized with exposure and trench foot, and an unknown number of men missing. X Corps were attacking on the Garigliano front and suffering equally heavy casualties.

It wasn't until 12 January, when the 34th Division took Cervaro and the

2nd Moroccan Division drove the enemy behind the Rapido, that Clark, who was planning the Anzio landings with Eisenhower and Alexander, had only one more river between him and Cassino. But by then the main defences of the town were almost complete, defences* that would 'break the Allies' teeth', just as Kesselring had intended.

A reinforced 36th Division, which now had more men from other states than from Texas, was called upon to cross the Rapido. The attack was a disaster. In forty-eight hours the Division lost 2,900 men. Another set of casualty figures would have concerned Clark even more. Battle casualties in the 5th Army between 15 December and 15 January totalled 15,930. Of these 7,046 were British, 8,884 American. During the same period US non-battle casualties totalled nearly 50,000.[23] No breakdown of these figures exist but by studying daily company casualty returns and battalion Medical Officers' reports it is possible to get an idea of the main causes of these casualties: respiratory diseases, exposure – US medical officers identified a separate illness: 'ground cold trauma', which caused acute rheumatism which sometimes resulted in a rheumatic heart condition – trench foot, battle fatigue – in some cases fatigue brought on by malnutrition as opposed to shell-shock – and jaundice. If the arctic combat suits and overshoes ordered by Eisenhower had arrived in October, instead of beginning to dribble in in mid-November many of these non-combat casualties could have been avoided. The US Chiefs of Staff policy of making the Pacific theatre of war their main priority, Operation Overlord their second, and the Mediterranean theatre a bad third proved devastating to the US 5th Army. The British 14th Army in Burma called themselves 'The Forgotten Army'. In the winter of 1943–44 the US 5th Army had good reason to call itself 'The Neglected Army'.

* At the end of nearly four months fighting that began on 24 January, the Germans still held Cassino and Monte Cassino. They only retreated because they had been outflanked by the Goums' breakthrough in the Aurunci mountains north-west of Cassino.

Postscript

After the fall of the Mignano Gap and the mopping up of the enemy strongholds in front of the Gustav Line the 5th Army regrouped. With Alexander's approval Clark planned two separate attacks – a frontal assault on the Gustav and an amphibious landing behind the 10th Army's lines at Anzio. The attack on the Gustav would take place shortly before the Anzio landings. Clark hoped that the enemy would commit the bulk of its reserves in the north of Italy to help the 10th Army defend the Gustav, so that the Allied Forces landing at Anzio would have a clear run to Rome.

On 11 January, 1944, the Free French Corps launched an attack on the Gustav in the mountains east of Cassino, denting the enemy positions. On 17 January the British 56th and 5th Division crossed the lower Garigliano, taking the enemy by surprise and capturing all their initial objectives. On 19 January the British 46th Division launched an attack across the upper Garigliano. The main object of the assault was to draw off enemy forces from the US 36th Division's front on the Rapido. Clark planned to use the Division to take Cassino. Its attack across the river was scheduled for 20 January. The British 46th Division's attack failed. The US 36th Division was now faced with attacking a well-dug-in enemy division across one of the most formidable river barriers in Italy. Clark realized that the attack was a forlorn hope but insisted it went ahead because the Anzio D-Day had been fixed for 24 January. The 36th Division's Corps Commander, General Keyes, compounded the Division's difficulties by refusing to allow its commander, General Walker, to choose his own crossing points. The two regiments of the Division that crossed the Rapido were beaten back. In forty-eight hours they suffered 1337 casualties. It was withdrawn from the line and replaced by US 34th Division. The Division's commander, General Ryder, was allowed to choose his own crossing points across the Rapido. On 24/25 January the Division crossed the river and advanced on Cassino and Monte Cassino. One of its regiments fought its way into the outskirts of Cassino. On Monte Cassino the Division forced the enemy back to their reserve positions. The enemy held on to them. The 34th Division was ground to pieces. When Clark authorized its withdrawal an entire company had to be carried down the mountain suffering from exposure.

On the 5th Army's left flank the British Divisions had come up against the enemy's second line of defences – the Aurunci muntains. Their commander, General McCreery, reported that only trained mountain troops could infiltrate through the enemy lines. On the Army's right flank the French attack had run out of steam. At Cassino and Monte Cassino the British 8th Army were confronted by impenetrable defences. Two frontal assaults ordered by Alexander were costly failures. In late April General Juin, commander of the French Corps, persuaded Alexander that the Corps' mountain troops could outflank the enemy in the Aurunci mountains. In May they did so. Only then did the enemy withdraw from their positions in Cassino and on Monte Cassino.

References

Chapter I

1. Kesselring, *The Memoirs of Field-Marshal Albert Kesselring*. Purnell Book Services by arrangement with William Kimber, London, 1974. Page 14.1
2. Martin Blumenson, *Salerno to Cassino, U.S. Army in World War II*, Office of the Chief of Military History, Washington D.C., 1970. Page 64.
3. *The Rommel Papers*, edited B.H. Liddell Hart. Collins, London, 1953. Page 430.
4. *Militarchiv Bundesarchiv*, Freiburg, Germany.
5. Colonel Ernst Baade's Messina diary. Imperial War Museum. See also Lt. General Frido von Senger und Etterlin, *Neither Hope nor Fear*, MacDonald, London, 1963. Pages 206–8.
6. The account of the evacuation is based on J.W. Roskill's *The War at Sea*, Vol III, Pt I H.M.S.O. London, 1960. Pages 144–151.
7. Von Vietinghoff MS. 'Italian Campaign' Chapter VI. National Archives. Washington D.C.
8. Major General Walter Fries, 29th Panzer Grenadier Division, 'The Battle for Sicily' MS T.2 Dept. of Defense Archives O.C.M.H.
9. Ronald Lewin, *Ultra goes to War*, Book Club Associates by arrangement with Hutchinson's. London, 1978. Page 281.
10. Sir Basil Liddell Hart, *History of the Second World War*, Pan, 1973. Page 465.
11. Fries op. cit.
12. Generale Pietro Badoglio, *Italia nella Secondo guerra Mondiale*, Mondadore, Milan, 1946. Page 103.
13. Badoglio op. cit. Pages 103–104.
14. Badoglio op. cit. Pages 104–106.
15. Kesselring op. cit. Page 177. See also Kesselring MS#C–013 'The day of Defection' N.A. Washington D.C.

16. Lt. General Siegfried Westphal, *The Italian Campaign*, Chapter VII (supplement to Chapter V) N.A. Washington, D.C.
17. *Le operazioni delle unità Italiane nel Settembre-Ottobre 1943: gli avvenimenti nell' isola di Cefalonia : 11th Armata*. Pages 488–490. Ministero della Defesa, Rome.
18. Kesselring op. cit. Page 105. See also MS#C–013.
19. Westphal op. cit.
20. Kesselring op. cit. Page 186.
21. Kesselring op. cit. Page 186.
22. Ralph S. Mavrogordato. 'Hitler's decisions on the defense of Italy' from *Command Decisions*, edited Kent Roberts Greenfield. O.C.M.H.
23. Details from Clark's autobiography, *Calculated Risk*, Harrap, London, 1951.
24. *The Eisenhower Papers: the War Years*, edited Alfred D. Chandler, John Hopkins Press, Baltimore, 1970. Page 1880, 1st edition. In later editions this entry has been suppressed.
25. Clark op. cit. Chapter heading.
26. Blumenson op. cit. page 140.
27. Brigadier C.J.C. Malony, *The Mediterranean and the Middle East*, Vol V.; *The Campaign in Sicily, 1943, and the Campaign in Italy Sept 3rd 1943 to 31st March 1944*, H.M.S.O. London, 1973. Pages 107–111.
28. Lt. General Lucian Truscott, *Command Missions*, Presidio Press, Novato, California, 1990. Pages 371–375.
29. Malony op. cit. Pages 332–333.
30. F.H. Hinsley, *British Intelligence in the Second World War*, Vol 3, Pt I. H.M.S.O. 1984: Page 197 footnote.
31. Von Vietinghoff op. cit.
32. Von Vietinghoff op. cit.
33. Ralph Mavrogordato translated 10th Army and O.K.W. documents for Martin Blumenson, compiling seven manuscripts which are held in the Dept. of Defense archives, O.C.M.H. All references to Mavrogordato refer to these manuscripts and not to the chapter in *Command Decision* op. cit.
34. Von Vietinghoff op. cit. See also Captain Alfred Steiger's translations of 10th Army documents. MS held Dept. of Defence, Ottawa, Canada.
35. Von Vietinghoff op. cit.
36. Major General Hans Bessell MS 'The Fortification of the Bernhardt'.

Chapter II

1. Clark op. cit. Pages 215–216.
2. Edwin Fisher. Background papers to his *Cassino to the Alps*, *U.S. Army*

33. U.S. 8″ gun. Monte Sammucro in background.

34. Out of it. Dead soldiers of the 143rd Regiment.

35. Out of it. Walking wounded of the 143rd Regiment.

36. San Pietro cave dwellers welcome the 143rd Regiment.

37. San Pietro. Colonel Martin gets a kiss.

38. San Pietro. Infantrymen from the 143rd Regiment leaving the village.

in World War II, Dept. of Defense archives. O.C.M.H. Box 6. Fisher made a detailed résumé of Clark's War Diary from 5 October to 31 December, 1943, and quotes from the diary.

3. Truscott op. cit. Page 266. The details of Operational Order and why the plan was changed and would certainly have been noted in Clark's diary. But after the War Clark presented it to the Citadel, a US Military school at Charlottesville, South Carolina, on condition that only US official historians would be allowed access to it. Clark clearly did not want anyone else to compare what he wrote in his diary with accounts of the same incident given in *Calculated Risk*. But Truscott's meticulous chapter-and-verse account of events and Fisher's background notes give the game away during the last three months of 1943.

4. Truscott op. cit. Page 266. See also General Lucas war diary 9 October. Lucas diary held at Carlisle Barracks, U.S. Army Military History Institute, Pennsylvania.

5. Lt.-Colonel Sir J.E.H. Neville, editor: *Oxfordshire and Buckinghamshire Light Infantry War Chronicle*, Vol 3, Gale and Polden, Aldershot, 1951.

6. Letter to the author from Sir Michael Howard, who served with 3rd Coldstream in Italy.

7. Truscott op. cit. Page 179.

8. Truscott op. cit. Page 235.

9. James Forsythe, *5th Army History, Part II. Across the Volturno to the Winter Line*, Annexe number one, Quartermaster supply. Page 71. 5th Army Historical section. Impronta Press, Florence, 1945.

10. Von Senger op. cit. Pages 132–141.

11. Vietinghoff op. cit. 5th Army prisoner interrogation reports. National Archives Administration, Suitland, Washington D.C. See also Von Senger op. cit.

12. Liddell Hart op. cit. Page 465.

13. Article by General McCreery that appeared in 12th Lancer's magazine, 1959.

14. Colonel William Darby and William Baumer, *We led the Way: Darby's Rangers*, Jove, New York, 1985.

15. Anders Arnbal, *The Barrel-Land Dance Hall Rangers*, Vantage, 1993. Page 118.

16. Colonel Robert McGraw, 2nd Battalion, 135th Regiment, U.S. 34th Division. One of 90 accounts and analyses of small-unit actions in the Italian Campaign made at The Infantry School, Fort Benning, Georgia 1946–1950. Carlisle Barracks.

17. 5th Army H.Q. House of Artillery report 6 November N.A.R.A.

18. From MS written by Lieutenant Michael Wheatley, 6th Grenadier Guards. Grenadier Archives. Wellington Barracks, London.

19. Clark op. cit. page 225.
20. Detail of reports quoted Blumenson op. cit. Page 213. Comments are the author's.
21. Truscott op. cit. Page 279.
22. CAB 121/128 NAF 486 24 October, 1943. Public Record Office, Kew, London.
23. Hinsley op. cit. All references to Ultra decrypts in this and following chapters are taken from Chapter 34.
24. Vietinghoff op. cit. Mavrogordato op. cit.
25. MS Lucian Hechler O.K.W. diary entry 6 November, 1943. MS Westphal. Dept. of Defense archives.
26. Fisher op. cit.
27. Report by Brigadier Oliver. Its CO was sent home.
28. Truscott op. cit. Page 547.
29. Von Senger op. cit.
30. Von Senger War Diary October, 1943 – January, 1944. The diary is in narrative form, few dates are mentioned. It can also be found in Chapter 5 of *Neither Hope nor Fear*.
31. Steiger op. cit.
32. Field Studies number 4. XIV Panzer Korps. 1st Battle for the Bernhardt Line. One of 17 translations of 10th Army documents made for Maloney by Mrs N.B. Taylor. Public Record Office, Kew, London. CAB 146/141.
33. Mavrogordato op. cit.
34. Taylor op. cit.
35. Mavrogordato op. cit.
36. 4th Rangers After Action report by Major Roy Murray. N.A.R.A.
37. Von Senger War diary.
38. Lucas diary entry 4/11/43.
39. Truscott op. cit. Page 284.

Chapter III

1. Lieutenant Michael Wheatley part MS 6th Grenadier Guards action on Monte Camino. Grenadier Guards Archives, Wellington Barracks, London.
2. Part MS written for the author by Len Sarginson.
3. Michael Howard and John Sparrow, *The Coldstream Guards 1920–1946*, O.U.P. 1951.
4. From F Company, Scots Guards, After Action report Monte Camino written by Captain Richard Coke M.C. Scots Guards Archives, Wellington Barracks, London.

5. F Company After Action report.
6. F Company After Action report.
7. Information given to Mike Sterling, Gordon Beale's nephew, by Guardsman Hollis.
8. Letter from Major Richard Coke, DSO, MC, Ret, to the author.
9. Letter from Major Richard Coke to the author.
10. 15th Panzer Grenadier Divisional reports issued in XIV Panzer Korps Daily and Interim reports. November 1943. Militarchiv, Bundesarchiv, Freiburg, Germany.
11. David Erskine, *The Scots Guards 1919–1955*, William Clowes Ltd, London. Pages 193–186.
12. Letter from Major Richard Coke to the author.
13. Neville op. cit.
14. 15th Panzer Grenadier Division's monthly report. Militarchiv.
15. Donald G. Taggart, ed: *History of U.S. 3rd Infantry Division*, Infantry Journal Press, Center of Military History. Pages 99–102.
16. After Action report 2nd Battalion 180th Regiment. N.A.R.A.
17. Mavrogordato op. cit.
18. Joachim Lemelsen, *Das Buch der Falke Division: 29. Division*, Podzun Verlag Bad Nauheim, Germany. Page 333.
19. Steiger op. cit.
20. Letter to author from Colonel Helmut Meitzel, Knight's Cross.
21. Conversation between Colonel Nye and author.
22. 4th Rangers After Action report. Major Roy Murray. N.A.R.A.
23. Captain Ernest Davis. Fort Benning report. Carlisle Barracks.
24. 5th Army Operations report. N.A.R.A.
25. XIV Panzer Korps diary. Militarchiv.
26. 5th Army G.2 report. N.A.R.A.

Chapter IV

1. Malony op. cit. Page 479.
2. Details Cassino defences Malony op. cit. Chapter XIV and Lemelsen op. cit. Pages 333–335. The *Times* correspondent William Buckley visited the underground bunkers after the final battle and found them intact.
3. Antonio Zambardi, son of the village grocer, in conversation with author (see Preface).
4. Letter to the author from Colonel Helmut Meitzel. All Colonel Meitzel's comments on the battles for San Pietro are made in other letters to the author.
5. Lemelsen op. cit. Page 339.

6. From MS written for the author by Lee Fletcher.
7. 141st Regiment's journal, December, 1943.
8. From MS written for the author by William Gallagher.
9. Extracts from General Walker's original war diary September, 1943–February, 1944. Held Carlisle Barracks. The diary was later expanded and published as *From Texas to Rome, a general's journal*, Fred L. Walker, Dallas, Texas, Taylor Publishing Co, 1969.
10. Letters to the author from Notar Jurgen Wöbbekin and James Skinner, formerly captain US 36th Divisional Artillery.
11. Truscott op. cit. Page 277.
12. Details *Militarchiv* and from Colonel Gerhard Muhm, who served with the 71st Panzer Grenadier Regiment in the Italian Campaign, and who now lectures at the Italian War School at Civitavecchia near Rome.
13. The account of 1st and 4th Rangers action on Monte Corno is based on Colonel Darby's After Action report, N.A.R.A. and *We Led the Way* op. cit.
14. Gallagher op. cit.
15. Fisher op. cit.
16. From MS sent to author by Lt. Colonel Fred Young, Sen.
17. Letter to author Ray Wells.
18. Hinsley op. cit.
19. Letter to author from Notar Wöbbeking.
20. Fisher op. cit.
21. Meteorological Report. Appendix S.2. 1st Special Service order. N.A.R.A.
22. Part tape made for author by Bob Davis.
23. Origins of the 1st S.S.F. taken from *The First Special Service Force* by Lt-Colonel Robert D. Burhams, Lee Publishing Co, Dalton, Georgia, 1985.
24. Steiger op. cit.
25. Captain P.N. Tregoning, MC, *History of 2/5 Queen's*, Gale and Polden, Aldershot, 1947.
26. From an unpublished MS sent to author by Brigadier Edward Thomas.
27. Details concerning Monte Camino bombardment taken from Malony op. cit. and *History of 113 Field Regiment, R.A. 1939–45* by Allen Matthews, privately printed. Problems at Conca part of tape made for author by Major-General John Douglas-Withers, CBE, MC, who in November, 1943, was a Forward Observer with 113 Field Regiment.

Chapter V

1. Burhans op. cit. Page 98.
2. From MS written for author by Donald Mackinnon.

3. Conversation between Brigadier Thomas and author.
4. Brigadier Thomas op. cit.
5. Letter to author from Brigadier Thomas.
6. Bob Davis op. cit.
7. Von Senger War Diary.
8. Bob Davis op. cit.
9. Letter to author from Brigadier Thomas.
10. Letter to author from Bill Story.
11. MS Private Herbert Forester.
12. Mackinnon op. cit.
13. Letter to author from Lt-Colonel Robert Moore.
14. Letter to author from Brigadier Thomas.
15. *History of the Queen's Royal Regiment* Vol VIII, Colonel John Davis. Gale and Polden, Aldershot, 1953.
16. Conversations with Colonel Toby Sewell, 2/6th Queen's.
17. Letter to author from C.F. Cranville.
18. From MS written for author by Colonel Toby Sewell.
19. Letter to author from Major Alan Sanders, DSO.
20. Article written by David Story and sent to author.
21. Letter to author from David Story.
22. Letter to author from Brigadier Thomas.
23. Burhans op. cit. Page 118.
24. Michael Howard and John Sparrow op. cit.
25. *The D.L.I. at War, 1939–45.* David Rissik, Durham Light Infantry Depot, Durham Castle, 1970. Pages 148–150.
26. 15th Panzer Grenadier Division Daily Report. XIV Panzer Korps Dairy.
27. Nigel Nicholson and Patrick Forbes, *The Grenadier Guards in the War of 1939–45*, Vol II. Gale and Polden, Aldershot, 1960.
28. From MS History of X Corps. Imperial War Museum, London.
29. Part MS written by Colonel Larkin and sent to author.
30. Letter to author from Carl Lehmann.
31. 3rd Rangers After Action report by Lt. Colonel Dammer N.A.R.A.
32. Letter to author from Carl Lehmann.
33. Major John Moore, 1st Battalion, 168th Infantry, U.S. 34th Division. Fort Benning report. Carlisle Barracks.
34. Letter to author from Major General Charles Denholm, DSC, DSM.
35. 143rd Regiments daily Unit Reports December, 1943, N.A.R.A. Suitland, and letter to author from Major General Charles Denholm.
36. Part Lt-Colonel Young's MS.
37. Letter to author from Joe Gallagher.
38. Larkin op. cit.
39. Letter to author from Carl Lehmann.

40. Article by Jack Clover in *The Fighting 36th*, historical quarterly.
41. Letter to author from Colonel Harold Owens.
42. Letter to author from Nick Bozic.
43. Letter to author from James Skinner.
44. Letter to author from Major General Wendell Phillipi, National Guard.
45. Lemelsen op. cit. Pages 346–347.
46. Letter to author from Major General Denholm.
47. *Il Primo Raggruppamento Motorizzato italiono. Stato Maggiore dell'Escercito. Ministero della Defesa*. Pages 57–63. Rome.
48. Lemelsen op. cit. Page 339.
49. Blumenson op. cit. See also 1st R.M.I. op. cit.
50. Lemelsen op. cit. Pages 341–343.
51. Letter to author from Donald McCollum.
52. 'Fifth Army at the Winter Line'. American Forces in Action series. War Dept. Military Intelligence. Washington D.C.
53. Letter to author from Bill Ebberle.
54. Letters to author from Leonard Rice.
55. Letter to author from Joe Gallagher.
56. Pyle, Ernie, *Brave Men*, Holt, New York, 1944.
57. Quoted Robert L. Wagner, *The Texas Army*, published privately 1972.
58. James Forsythe op. cit. Page 69.
59. Letter to Brigadier Burrage to Leonard Rice.
60. Letter from Richard Stealey.
61. Letter to author from Anders Arnbal.
62. Anders Arnbal op. cit. Page 194.
63. Anders Arnbal op. cit. Page 199.
64. Kesselring op. cit. Pages 191–2.

Chapter VI

1. Letter to author from Colonel Fred Walker, Jun.
2. Letter to author from Colonel Fred Walker, Jun.
3. Letter to author from Colonel Fred Walker, Jun.
4. Letter to author from Colonel Landry.
5. Letter to author from James Skinner.
6. Letter to author from Colonel George Fowler.
   The description of the rest of the tank attack is based on Major Fowler's After Action report. N.A.R.A.
7. Antonio Zambardi.
8. From MS written for author by Sammie Petty.
9. 141st Regiment's Journal. December, 1943.
10. From MS written for author by Ray Wells.

11. Letter to author from Colonel Landry.
12. Letter to author from Colonel Landry.
13. Sammie Petty op. cit.
14. 141st Regiment's Journal. December, 1943.
15. 5th Army at the Winter Line. Pages 62–64. See also Lemelsen op. cit. and *Il Primo Raggrupamento Motorizzato Italiano*.
16. 143rd Regiment's After Action report. December, 1943. N.A.R.A.
17. Antonio Zambardi.
18. Letter to author from Major-General Charles Denholm.
19. Letter to author from Colonel Landry.
20. Gallagher MS.
21. General Walker MS diary entry 26 March 1944.
22. Copy of film held N.A. Films section. Captain Joel Westbrook, 143rd Regiment, acted as John Huston's technical adviser, and wrote to author about the film.
23. *Fifth Army at the Winter Line*, op. cit. Page 114.

Sources and Bibliography

Archival Sources

National Archives Records Administration
Suitland, Washington. D.C.

5th Army Operations. October 1943–January 1944

5th Army Operations Instructions. October 1943–January 1944

5th Army G.2 Reports. October 15th–November 16th

5th Army House of Artillery Report. Nov 6th 1943

5th Army Interrogation Reports. October 1943.

5th Army incoming messages Dec 5th–26th, 1943.

1st Special Service Force Operations Memorandum Monte La Difensa. November, 1943

U.S. 3rd Infantry Division G.2 Periodic Reports. October–November 1943

15th Regiment, U.S. 3rd Infantry Division Operations Report November 1943

30th Regiment, U.S. 3rd Infantry Division Operations Report November 1943

7th Regiment, U.S. 3rd Infantry Division After Action Report Monte La Difensa

36th U.S. Infantry Division. 143rd Regiment's Operations Report December 1943

36th U.S. Infantry Division. 143rd Regiment's Daily Unit Reports December 1943

U.S. 36th Infantry Division. 141st Regiment's Journal

1st, 3rd, 4th Rangers After Action Reports. November–December 1943

U.S. 45th Infantry Division, 2 Battalion, 180th Regiment's After Action Report. Monte Corno. November 1943.

National Archives, Washington, D.C.

Von Vietinghoff Chapter VI. The Campaign in Italy: Salerno to Cassino
G.266677/EFE/6/50/35

Westphal Chapter VII. The Campaign in Italy:

The Army's Groups Version G.274342/EJW/8.50.35

Von Senger. War Diary MS# C095.B.

Bessel. The Fortifications of the Bernhardt Line MS# D.013

The manuscripts were written under the auspices of the Office of the Chief
of Military History, Washington D.C. between 1947 and 1951. Von Vietinghoff's MS was translated by the British Air Ministry, the rest by M.
Bauer.

Military History Institute of the Army, Carlisle Barracks, Pennsylvania

MS. Walker diary
MS. Lucas diary
Fort Benning studies

Department of Defense Archives, O.C.M.H.

Ralph S. Mavrogordato's translation of O.K.W. and 10th Army documents
made for Martin Blumenson R88–R123.

Edwin Fisher. Background papers to *Cassino to the Alps*, Box 6.

Major General Walter Fries, Commanding Officer 29th Panzer Grenadier
Division. 'The Campaign in Sicily' MS T-2 series translated M. Bauer.

XII Air Support Command. Undated paper on tactical bombing of bridges
and viaducts.

MS. Lucian Hechler. O.K.W. entry Nov 6th 1943, translated Westphal.

Department of Defence. Ottowa. Canada

MS. Captain Alfred Steiger's translations of 10th Army Documents.

Public Record Office, Kew, London

Mrs N.B. Taylor's Field Study number 4 'XIV Panzer Korps. 1st Battle for
the Bernhardt Line' translated for Malony CAB 146/141.

Alexander's signal to Eisenhower re number of divisions required in Italy

CAB 121/128, NAF 486 of 24 October, 1943.

X Corps Diary
X Corps Intelligence reports } October–December 1943
56th Division's Intelligence reports

Imperial War Museum

Colonel (Lt. General) Ernst Baade's Messina War Diary.

Ministero della Defesa, Roma

Il Raggrupamento Motorizzato Italiano. 1943–1944 Stato Maggiore dell'Escercito.

Le opperazioni della unità Italiane Settembre–Ottobre, 1943: gli avvenimenti nell isola di Cefalonia – Il Armata. Stato Maggiore dell'Escercito.

Bundesarchiv, Militarchiv, Freiburg

10th Army Diary.
XIV Panzer Korps Diary.
XIV Panzer Korps Daily Reports. } October 1943
XIV Panzer Korps Interim Reports. –
XIV Panzer Korps Occasional Reports. } January 1944
XIV Panzer Korps Casualty Returns.

15th Panzer Grenadier Division Monthly Reports, November and December 1943.

Herman Göring Panzer Division Monthly Reports, November and December 1943.

British Regimental Archives

6th Grenadier Guards After Action report Monte Camino. Captain Ralph Howard's account of earlier part of action. Lt. Michael Wheatley MS of the whole action, and another MS. by him describing those leading up to it. Grenadier Guards Archives. Wellington Barracks, Birdcage Walk, London. 2nd Scots Guards After Action report Monte Camino by Captain (Major) Coke, MC (DSO). Scots Guards' Archives. Wellington Barracks, Birdcage Walk, London.

Bibliography

Badoglio, Generale Pietro, *Italia nella Seconda Guerra Mondiale*, Mandadore, Milan, 1946.

Blumenson, Martin, *Salerno to Cassino*, U.S. Army in World War II. Office of the Chief of Military History. Washington D.C. 1967.

Buckley, Christopher, *Road to Rome*, Hodder & Stoughton, London, 1945.

Clark, Mark Wayne, *Calculated Risk*, Harrap, London, 1951.

Clark, Alan, *Barbarossa*, Hutchinson, London, 1965.

The Eisenhower Papers: the War Years, edited Alfred D. Chandler, John Hopkins Press, Baltimore, 1970.

Forsythe, James. *5th Army History, Part II*, 5th Army Historical Section. Impronta Press, Florence, 1945.

Garland, Albert N. and Smith, Howard, *Sicily and the Surrender in Italy*, Washington D.C., 1965.

Guderian, General Heinz, *Panzer Leader*, Michael Joseph, London, 1952.

Sir Basil Liddell Hart, *History of the Second World War*, Pan, 1973.

B.H. Liddell Hart, *The Other Side of the Hill*, Cassell, 1951.

Haupt, Werner, *Kriegschauplatz Italien 1943–1945*, Motorbuch Verlag, Stuttgart, 1977.

Hickey, D. and Smith, G., *Operation Avalanche*, Heinemann, London, 1983.

Hinsley, F.H., *British Intelligence in the Second World War*, Vol III. Pt. I. H.M.S.O. London, 1984.

Jackson, W.G.F., *The Battle for Italy*, Batsford, London, 1967.

Kesselring, Albert, *The Memoirs of Field Marshal Albert Kesselring*, Purnell (Kimber), London, 1974.

Lewin, Ronald, *Ultra goes to War*, Book Club – Hutchinson, London, 1978.

Linklater, Eric, *The Campaign in Italy*, H.M.S.O. London, 1950.

Malony, Brigadier C.J.C., *The Mediterranean and the Middle East. Vol 5. The History of the Second World War*, H.M.S.O. London, 1970.

Mavrogordato, Ralph S., 'Hitler's decisions on the defense of Italy' from *Command Decisions*, edited R. Greenfield O.C.M.H. 1960.

Plehnf, Friederich-Karl von, *Reiter, Streiter und Rebel, Eine Biographie von Lt. General Ernst Baade*, Schauble Verlag, Rheinfelden, 1960.

Pond, Hugh, *Salerno!* Kimber, London, 1962.

Pyle, Ernie, *Brave Men*, Holt, New York, 1944.

The Rommel Papers, edited B.H. Liddell Hart. Collins, London, 1963.

Roskill, J.W., *The War at Sea*, Vol III, Pt I. H.M.S.O., 1960.

Von Senger und Etterlin, Frido, *Neither Hope nor Fear*, MacDonald, London, 1963.

Truscott, Lucian K., *Command Missions*, Presidio, Novata, California, 1990.
Westphal, Siegfried, *The German Army in the West*, Cassell, London, 1951.

Unit and Formation Histories

Adleman B.H. and Walton G., *The Devil's Brigade*, Chilton, Philadelphia 1966.

Arnbal, Anders K., *The Barrel-land Dance Hall Rangers*, Vantage, 1993.

Altieri, James, *The Spearheaders*, Bobbs Merrill, New York, 1960.

Burhans, Lt. Colonel Robert D., *The First Special Service Force*, Lee. Dalton, Georgia 1947.

Howard, Michael and Sparrow John, *The Coldstream Guards, 1920–1946*, O.U.P., 1951.

Davis, Colonel John, *History of the Queen's Royal Regiment Vol VIII*, Gale and Polden. Aldershot, 1953.

Erskine, David, *The Scots Guards 1919–1955*, Clowes, London.

Lemelsen, Joachim, *Das Buch der Falke Division: 29 Division*, Podsun-Verlag. Bad Nauheim 1960.

Matthews, Alan. *History of 113 Field Regiment, R.A. 1939–1945.*

Neville, Col Sir J.E.H., *War Chronicle. Oxfordshire and Buckinghamshire Light Infantry. Vol III*, Gale and Polden. Aldershot, 1954.

Nicholson, Nigel and Forbes Michael, *The Grenadier Guards in the War of 1939–45. Vol II*, Gale and Polden. Aldershot, 1960.

Peak, Clifford, editor, *5 years, 5 countries, 5 campaigns*, History of 141st Regiment, U.S. 36 Infantry Division. Bruckman. Munich, 1946.

Rissik, David, *The D.L.I. at War 1939–45*, Durham Light Infantry Depot. Branchpeth Castle, 1953.

Taggart, G. *History of the U.S. 3rd Division*, Infantry Journal Press. Washington D.C., 1947.

Tregonin, Captain P.N., MC, *History of the 2/5th Queen's*, Gale and Polden, Aldershot, 1960.

Wagner, Robert L., *The Texas Army*, Wagner, Austin, Texas, 1972.

Williams, David, *Black Cats at War, History of the 56th Division* MS. Imperial War Museum.

Anon. History of U.S. 504 Parachute Regiment. O.C.M.H.

Anon. History of U.S. 509 Parachute Regiment. O.C.M.H.

Anon. History of British X Corps MS. Imperial War Museum, London.

1. From the Volturno to the Winter Line.

2. 5th Army at the Winter Line
   American Forces in Action series. Military Intelligence. War Department. Washington D.C.

Eyewitness sources 1
Unpublished manuscripts sent to the author

Colonel James T. Larkin   3rd Rangers operations December, 1943
Brigadier Edward Thomas   Approach march to Monte La Difensa
     December, 1943.
Lt-Colonel Fred Young Sen.   History of 1st Battalion
     143 Infantry Regiment
     MS held by 36th Division's Archives,
     Austin, Texas

Eyewitness sources 2
Manuscripts specially written for the author

Robert Davis (tape), 2nd Regiment, 1st SSF Monte La Difensa.
Lee Fletcher, 3/143rd Regiment, US 36 Infantry Division. San Pietro.
William Gallagher, 2/143rd Regiment, US 36th Infantry Division. San Pietro.
Donald R. Mackinnon, 2nd Regiment, 1st SSF Monte La Difensa.
Samuel H. Petty, 2/141st Regiment, US 36th Division. San Pietro.
Len Sarginson, 6th Grenadier Guards, 201 (Guards) Brigade, British 56th Division. Monte Camino.
Colonel Toby Sewell, 2/6th Queen 169 (Queen's) Brigade, British 56th Division. Monte Camino.
Ray Wells, 2/141st Regiment, US 36th Division. San Pietro.
Major General John Douglas-Withers (tape), 113 Field Regiment, RA, British gunners and Forward Observers at Monte Camino.

Appendix A

'The German command in Italy always regarded with envy the clear-cut chain of command of the Allied Forces. The enemy had *one* Commander-in-Chief to whom all the services were subordinate. The German Supreme Commander of the Theatre of War was such in name only. In Italy there were 8 co-ordinated organizations of equal status. These were: The Army Group, the Luftflotte, the German Naval Command, the G.O.C. German armed forces, the senior officers of the S.S. and police, and the commissars of the "Alpenoorland" Operational Zone and Istria. The Commander of the Army Group in his capacity of Supreme Commander of the Italian Theatre of War could issue orders to the other organizations named only in the event of a large-scale landing on or in circumstances of the greatest danger. Otherwise he was to all intents and purposes no more than first amongst equals.'

Von Vietinghoff. Chapter VI

The Campaign in Italy, written O.C.M.H. December, 1947.
Translated British Air Ministry, 1950.

Appendix B

The German Schmeisser was a much more reliable sub-machine gun than the Allied Tommy gun, which tended to jam. (British troops in the 5th Army were issued with Tommy guns because the British equivalent, the Sten gun, sometimes broke when dropped.) Up to early 1943 the Schmeisser was hand-finished. The World War I Lüger remained the best pistol available and was much sought after by Allied officers (and Rangers).

Appendix C

APPENDIX 'B' TO
FIFTH ARMY INTELLIGENCE SUMMARY NO. 42

PW INTERROGATION REPORT NUMBER 24

NAME AND RANK: Kanonier Herbert Heide (radio & telephone operator)

CAPTURED AT: RUVIANO by 135th Inf Regt at approx 1300 hrs 15 Oct 43.

PW'S UNIT: 21st Btry, 56 Pz Werfer Regt. (rocket Regt.)
APO NO.: 58594.

PERSONAL HISTORY:

On morning of 12 Oct at 0900 hrs PW was near a farm approximately 2 kms of RUVIANO when our artillery started firing and wounded him. He went to the town of RUVIANO and stayed with Italians who betrayed his presence to the Americans when they arrived.

HISTORY AND LOCATION OF UNIT:

Battery was trained as a separate unit both at Cella and Belzen-Bergen. PW trained from 5th May to 1 Aug 43. Everything connected with this weapon is very secret. Batteries are separate units and not organized into regiments except for organizational reasons. Each battery is independent. Battery was attached to 29 PGR on 10 Oct. On 12 Oct, retreated approximately 4 kms behind RUVIANO.

21ST BATTERY: a. Organization:

8 Werfer (rocket) 150mm. S.P.

8 Munition trucks (40 shots in each truck)

3 Volkswagen – for personnel

5 LKW (light ½ tracks) to haul range finders etc.

2 Tank trucks – ½ tracked LKW carrying 300 cannisters, each holding 20 liters of petrol.

8 LMG's

b. Strength:

100 men; no casualties.

c. Equipment:

1. Each Pz Werfer (rocket gun) has ten barrels.

2. Range – 3500 to 5000 yards approximately.

3. Rate of fire: in 3–4 seconds, all 8 guns together can fire 80 rounds. Usually are fired singly.

4. Types of shells:

(a) Fragmentation type similar to artillery shell. Range of fragmentation – radius of 200–300 metres.

(b) Gas shells.

(c) Bacteria shells – no one knows much about this.

(d) 'Kaltegeschese (liquid air shell). This is supposed to freeze the body and is effective for about one minute.

(e) Compressed air shell: PW believes this shell is just a fantasy.

NOTE: This battery, the only one in Italy, has only shells of the fragmentation type. Firing orders come from Battery C.O. who stayed at Regimental C.P of 29 PGR

d. Radio Equipment:

1. 30-watt sender (sends and receives, range 60 kms short wave)

2. Dora Gerät (range 5–20 kms)

3. Berthe Gerät (range 5–20 kms)

4. Gustav Gerät (range 5–20 kms) (sends and receives.)

5. Friedrich Gerät (range 5–20 kms)

e. Personalities:

Battery 6.0 – Lt Witt

Observer   – Lt Papke

            – Lt Von Geier

NOTES FOR FUTURE OPERATIONS;
1. There are 3 types of Pz Werfer (rocket guns) 15, 21, and 28 mm.
2. Training camps for Werfer Units are located at Cella and Belzen-Bergen in Germany.
3. Tactical Signs:
4. Every precaution is being taken to keep information concerning this weapon from Allied hands. For this reason, guns seldom remain in one position longer than one hour unless no activity is nearby.

LKW (light ½ track)
Speed – 60 km per hour.
Max speed – 80 km per hour.

(Source: 34th Div)

Appendix D

Hube, promoted Captain-General, commanded the 2nd Panzer Army during the Russian counter-offensive in February, 1944. His was the only German army to hold its ground. But von Manstein, C-in-C of all German armies in Russia, realized that the 2nd Army would be caught in a pocket and ordered Hube to retreat. Hube, who believed that, once the advancing Russian armies were well to his rear, their supply lines would be at his mercy, refused to retreat. Von Manstein was on the point of relieving Hube of his command when Hitler relieved von Manstein. Hube's army wrecked the Russian supply lines so effectively that their advance was halted. With the aid of another Panzer army Hube fought his way back to the new German front. On 4 April – Hitler's birthday – Hitler summoned Hube to his headquarters at Obersalzburg, promoted him to Colonel-General, and awarded him the Knight's Cross with diamonds.* The next day Hube flew back to Berlin on leave. He chose a route out of bounds to all German transport planes because it was under surveillance by Russian fighters. One of them shot his plane down and he was killed in the crash.

* The Wehrmacht's highest award.

Appendix E

In 1945 the mayor of San Pietro asked the provincial capital of Caserta for funds to rebuild the village. The authorities in Caserta said that they would only provide them if San Pietro was rebuilt on its original 10th century site at the bottom of Monte Sammucro. The rebuilding went ahead and the mayor decided to leave the old village exactly as it was, as a war memorial. (Two acres of the Cassino battlefield were left untouched from May, 1944, to 1969. This patch of bomb-craters, burnt-out tanks, and a church tower that seemed to be about to fall to the ground at any moment was the most moving war memorial the author has ever seen.)

Only San Pietro's church was partially restored. Italian tourists have scribbled obscenities on its inner walls. They match the obscenities that took place in San Pietro in 1943.

The Medaglio d'Oro, Italy's highest award for gallantry, is given to towns as well as individuals. Cassino was awarded the Medaglio d'Oro. So was Mignano, which had 124 of its inhabitants killed by Allied shelling and bombing. But San Pietro did not receive the Medaglio d'Oro. Its present mayor is still trying to persuade the authorities in Rome to award it the medal.

Index

Wilson, Sgt, US 143rd Regt, 137
Winter Line *see* Bernhardt Line
Wöbbeking, Maj Jürgen, German
  29th Div Artillery, 88, 90–91,
  149
Wood, Pte Gerald, US 142nd Regt,
  169
Wright, Capt J.P.P., Ox & Bucks,
  71
Wright, CSM P., 3rd Coldm Gds (VC),
  25

Wyatt, Lt-Col, US 141st Regt, 167,
  168–69
Wyld, Lt P.H., 3rd Coldm Gds, 59

Y Force, British signals unit, 41, 57
Young, Lt Fred, US 143rd Regt, 95,
  134, 136–38 and n, 139
Young, Sgt, 6th Gren Gds, 61

Zielberg, Maj-Gen von, German 65th
  Division, 100